The Play's the Thing!

This book is part of the Peter Lang Humanities list.
Every volume is peer reviewed and meets
the highest quality standards for content and production.

PETER LANG
New York • Bern • Berlin
Brussels • Vienna • Oxford • Warsaw

The Play's the Thing!

Selections from Playing Shakespeare's Characters, Vols. 1–4

Edited by
Louis Fantasia

PETER LANG
New York • Bern • Berlin
Brussels • Vienna • Oxford • Warsaw

Library of Congress Control Number: 2022008160

Bibliographic information published by **Die Deutsche Nationalbibliothek**.
Die Deutsche Nationalbibliothek lists this publication in the "Deutsche
Nationalbibliografie"; detailed bibliographic data are available
on the Internet at http://dnb.d-nb.de/.

ISBN 978-1-4331-9554-9 (paperback)
ISBN 978-1-4331-9555-6 (ebook pdf)
ISBN 978-1-4331-9556-3 (epub)
DOI 10.3726/b19462

Peter Lang Publishing, Inc., New York
80 Broad Street, 5th floor, New York, NY 10004
www.peterlang.com

For Mrs. Fantasia

"Suit the action to the word, the word to the action, with this special observance: that you o'erstep not the modesty of nature. For anything so o'erdone is from the purpose of playing, whose end, both at the first and now, was and is to hold, as 'twere, the mirror up to nature …"

(*Hamlet*, Act 3, scene 2)

Table of Contents

Contributors

Olivia Buntaine is an Intimacy Director for theater based in Los Angeles and Boston, and an apprentice with Intimacy Directors International. She specializes in choreographing unconventional and creative intimacy scenes through a pedagogical lens of intersectionality, trauma-informed care, and the investigation of power and privilege. She has worked extensively as an assistant to Jessica Steinrock, Lead Instructor for Intimacy Directors International. Buntaine is also the artistic director of Project Nongenue, a Los Angeles-based theater company which centralizes the voices of women and marginalized populations in classical theater and mythology.

Charles Duff is an actor, teacher, theater director critic and writer. A graduate of the Bristol Old Vic Theater School, he has taught and directed at the Mountview Theater School, Trinity College of Music, and at the London Theater School, where he was Vice Principal and Director of Productions. He became involved with the rebuilding Shakespeare's Globe Theater in 1985 and taught for Globe Education from the outset. He was on the faculty of Notre Dame University and Roger Williams University, Rhode Island London Campuses for many years, teaching Shakespeare and theater history. He has acted and directed in London and in regional theaters in the U.S. and U.K. His opera productions have been seen both in Britain and Spain. His book, *The Lost Summer, the Heyday of the West End Theater* (Heinemann/Nick Hern Books, 1995) was called by Sheridan Morley in *The Sunday Times* "the best theatrical history I have come across in years." His memoir, *Charley's Woods* (Zuleika, 2017) was a Spectator Book of the Year. His latest book *The Best of the West End 1930–2000*, was published by Zuleika in January, 2022.

Louis Fantasia (Series Editor) is Artistic Associate at the Shakespeare Center of Los Angeles. He has served as Dean of the Faculty of the New York Film Academy and President of Deep Springs College. His books include *Instant Shakespeare* (published by Ivan R. Dee), *Tragedy in the Age of Oprah*, (Scarecrow Press), and *Talking Shakespeare: Notes from a Journey* (Peter Lang Publishers). In 2003, the Council of Europe named the theater collection at its library in the European Parliament in honor of Louis Fantasia, who holds both U.S. and European Union passports. In 2016 he was awarded the Officer's Cross of the Order of Merit of the Federal Republic of Germany (*Verdienstorden der Bundesrepublik Deutschland*) for his contributions to German culture and theater.

Timothy Harris has lived in Japan for 46 years. His translations and essays on poetry, drama, music and art have appeared in *PN Review* (Manchester), *Agenda* (London), *SNOW* (Lewes), *Quadrant* (Melbourne), *Plays International* (London), *Art International* (Lugano), the Asian edition of *The Financial Times*, and *The Chicago Review*; he also contributed to *The Oxford Companion to Twentieth-Century Poetry in English* (Oxford University Press). He acts and directs, lectures on British and Irish literature, and works as a diction coach for (English) opera, oratorio and song, at the New National Theater, Tokyo, and elsewhere.

Baron Kelly, Ph.D., is a critic, historian, practitioner, and scholar. In addition to his long list of acting and directing credits on and off Broadway, he is a four-time Fulbright Scholar. Formerly Professor and Head of the Graduate Acting Program at the University of Louisville, he is Vilas Distinguished Professor of Theater and Drama at the University of Wisconsin-Madison.

Brian Lohmann is currently on the faculty at Pepperdine University, and teaches Shakespeare through Improvisation for the Shakespeare Center of Los Angeles. Brian also directs, acts and teaches for Impro Theater, Los Angeles. Stage credits include A.C.T., The Old Globe, Shakespeare Santa Cruz, Laguna Playhouse and The Magic Theater. He has received Garland, Drama-Logue, and StageScene LA Awards. Brian was core faculty for the American Conservatory Theater's MFA program, and has been a guest instructor at Stanford, The Guthrie Theater, The Public Theater's Shakespeare Lab, The Old Globe/USD, Oregon Shakespeare Festival.

Jessie Lee Mills (Associate Editor) is an Assistant Professor of Theater at Pomona College and a professional director. She directs, adapts, and devises theater, opera, musicals, films, and new works in venues throughout the United States and abroad. She received her M.F.A. in Directing from Carnegie Mellon University and is a John Wells Fellow. Her scholarship centers on ensemble-theater, empathy, and comedy-as-community.

Dr. Janna Segal is an Assistant Professor of Theater Arts at the University of Louisville. Prior to U of L, she was an Assistant Professor of Theater and Shakespeare and Performance at Mary Baldwin University, and an IHUM Postdoctoral Fellow at Stanford University. She received her Ph.D. in Drama and Theater from the UC Irvine/UC San Diego joint doctoral program, her MA in Theater from CSUN, and her BA in Theater Arts from UC Santa Cruz. She has published single- and co-authored works on *Romeo and Juliet, As You Like It, Othello, Midsummer, The Roaring Girl,* and Fo and Rame's *Elisabetta.* Dr. Segal is also a freelance dramaturg and the Resident Dramaturg for the Comparative Drama Conference's Staged Reading Series.

Armin Shimerman is mostly known to the public as a television actor with over eighty major television roles, notably Quark on *Star Trek* and Principal Snyder on *Buffy, the Vampire Slayer.* With an English degree from UCLA, his primary focus has always been on Shakespeare and Elizabethan studies. He is a sought-after Shakespeare coach for actors and is a current associate professor at the University of Southern California. He is the author of the Science fiction trilogy, "The Merchant Prince", with its Tudor mathematician hero, Dr. John Dee. On stage, he has acted in over a third of the Bard's canon, appeared several times on Broadway as well as major regional theater stages. He helps run a small theater in Glendale, the Antaeus Company, and has directed several Shakespeare productions. He lives with his wife, Kitty Swink, in Los Angeles.

Dr. Elaine Turner (B.A., Brandeis University; Ph.D., University of Warwick): after working as stage manager and director on the London stage, Dr. Turner became a lecturer at several universities including University of Warwick, Brunel University, Central School of Speech and Drama, and Queen Mary and Westfield University. She created and taught both BA and MA Distance Learning degrees at Rose Bruford College and Central. Dr. Turner was a founding and long term member of the Shakespeare studies teaching team at the International Shakespeare Globe Centre. Script reader and assessor at the Royal National Theater and Channel 4, her publications include: "War Plays by Women" in *Continuum Encyclopedia of British*

Theater, Routledge, 1999; and "Practical Theater" in *St. James Compendium of Playwrights and Plays*, Stanley Thornes, 1997.

Susan Gayle Todd, Ph.D., was the Producing Artistic Director of Austin (TX) Scottish Rite Theater and co-founder/director of The Weird Sisters Women's Theater Collective. Since 2003, she has taught Shakespeare Through Performance pedagogy in various settings, including the Huntington Library and The University of Texas at Austin.

Edit Villarreal's play *The Language of Flowers*, a contemporary Chicano adaptation of Shakespeare's *Romeo and Juliet*, received its equity premiere at A Contemporary Theater ACT in Seattle. Other plays include *Marriage is Forever*, and *My Visits With MGM (My Grandmother Marta)*. For television, she co-wrote three scripts for the award winning series, "Foto-Novelas" produced by PBS. Other PBS credits include "La Carpa", a one hour drama about Chicano vaudevillians in the 1930's.. She is one of only two Latino playwrights to be included in the *Encyclopedia of Latinos and Latinas in the United States*, Oxford University Press. A graduate of the Yale School of Drama, she is Vice-Chair Graduate Studies and Professor in Playwriting at the UCLA School of Theater, Film and Television.

Introduction: The Play's the Thing!

LOUIS FANTASIA

This omnibus edition presents selections from the four previous anthologies in Peter Lang's *Playing Shakespeare's Characters* series: *Playing Shakespeare's Lovers*, *Playing Shakespeare's Villains*, *Playing Shakespeare's Monarchs and Madmen*, and *Playing Shakespeare's Rebels and Tyrants*. I have been lucky enough to have been the editor of this series since its inception.

"Lucky" is not an adjective most academic press editors would apply to themselves or their role, given the current challenges in both academia and the publishing industry. But I have been very lucky in that my supervising editors have allowed me the opportunity to bring a wide spectrum of voices to these anthologies. In each volume I have tried to include not only Shakespeare critics and scholars, but also working actors and directors, educators (including high school teachers) and commentators from outside the usual theatrical or Shakespearean field. I have been lucky not only to have had the support of my editors and publisher, but also, crucially, to also have the outstanding contributions of the wide variety of the thinkers and practitioners noted above.

The "unlucky" aspect of all of this is the fact that not all of these contributors could be selected for this volume. What I have tried to do instead is to go back and pull those essays that most directly relate to the problems of acting and directing Shakespeare today: Olivia Buntaine on intimacy direction; Brian Lohmann and Armin Schimmerman on playing Shakespeare's villains; Jana Segal on cross-gender casting; Baron Kelly on performing *Othello* in an era of Black Lives Matter; Timothy Harris on *Hamlet*; Charles Duff on *King Lear*; Jessie Lee Mills on the casting options for the Fool and Cordelia in *Lear*; Elaine Turner on the problematic *Measure for Measure*; Susan Todd on the sexual dynamics of *The Tempest*; Edit Villarreal on role of foils and servants in Shakespeare; and my own essay on those angry young men who wreak so much havoc and destruction in Shakespeare's world, and our own.

This means, unfortunately, that more than one brilliant, insightful, pointed, intelligent and useful essay has had to be passed over, and for that I offer their authors my apologies. This is not a "best of" volume. Some of the series' best writing remains in its original volumes, and I encourage you to discover it. This is a curated volume, that is, as I said above, focused on essays for the actor, director, producer or designer of Shakespeare in production. With that in mind, what follows here are brief synopses of the Introductions to each of the four volumes - *Lovers, Villains, Monarchs,* and *Rebels* - in the order in which they were published:

I. *Playing Shakespeare's Lovers: "I know thou wilt say 'aye'"* (R&J, 2.2.95)

Is there a Shakespeare play that doesn't have a brace of lovers in it? ... To begin with, let's consider two things: first, Shakespeare's lovers never exist in the singular. It's always Romeo *and* Juliet, Antony *and* Cleopatra, Beatrice *and* Benedick. Even in the single-named tragedies (*Hamlet, Lear, Othello,* etc.) the lovers are paired: Hamlet/Ophelia, Othello/Desdemona, and, in my opinion, Lear/Cordelia. Shakespeare, unlike the early classic Greeks and Romans, and later French neo-classicists, never sets up the single lover, such as Phaedre, Berenice, or Medea who longs or lusts for some unobtainable love object, suffers, and dies (often by his or her own hand).

Shakespeare's romantic duopolies exist because love in Shakespeare is always framed, shaped, contained, and probably managed by the outside world. Romeo and Juliet, Hamlet and Ophelia, Beatrice and Benedick, etc., live and behave within the rules of Verona, Denmark, or Messina. If their love is successful, they live happily ever after (in comedies, mostly), even if they have to run into the forest (of Arden, outside Athens, Windsor, etc.) to burn off a little steam. If it is not ultimately successful, they die (in tragedy, usually). In either case, tragedy or comedy, the world around them continues. Montagues and Capulets join hands, the state of Venice reverts back to normal, and so on. The lovers in Shakespeare's world are part of a complex society which has a lot on its plate. Which leads me to my second point.

Shakespeare's lovers may die tragically, but they do not – with the exception of Othello/Desdemona (and possibly Antony and Cleopatra) kill each other. Look at the playwrights just before Shakespeare, such as Kidd, Turner, or even Shakespeare's contemporary John Webster. Plays like *The White Devil, The Duchess of Malfi, The Revenger's Tragedy* and *The Spanish Tragedy* run on

Senecan revenge and Machiavellian duplicity, where poisons, stabbings, and lustful forced beddings occur within castle walls at the whim of a degenerate duke or rejected suitor, whispering darkly to his evil servant ...

[M]ost of Shakespeare's lovers exist in a real, modern world where there are laws, contracts, and consequences. Tragedy does not take place in the vacuum of some dank, musty castle ... Imagine a rewrite of *Romeo and Juliet* by Turneur or Webster. Rosaline (remember her?) would poison Juliet as soon as she heard Romeo was interested in a rival. Old Capulet might have incestuous longings for his daughter *a la* Count Cenci. Romeo would sneak back from banishment, disguised as a servant, and stab the Prince in his sleep, and so on. The possibilities [in these plays] are endless because there are no rules governing the amorphous, immoral worlds of those plays. But Shakespeare's lovers are *constrained*, limited by the practicalities of the modern real world, even when they are disguised and living in a forest. Rosalind and Viola may put on pants and play on the gender fluidity of girls playing boys (or boys playing girls playing boys) in *As You Like It* or *Twelfth Night*, in what Jan Kott called "Shakespeare's bitter Arcadia," but eventually everybody has to go home, usually paired off in marriage. Society is stabilized (in the comedies at least), perhaps stretched a bit, but –what you will! - nothing that we can't all live with. For Shakespeare, love is an illness, which while pleasant when indulged, ultimately has to be cured if one is to survive ...

The Elizabethans believed love literally entered the body through the eye, like some sort of germ, passing down into the bloodstream, affecting the body's balance of its four humors. The obvious example is Romeo falling for Juliet. Even long-time "friends" such as Beatrice and Benedick, must have a moment of "unmasking" before they can "see" each other, suddenly and anew, as lovers. To her detriment, Desdemona claims that she saw Othello's visage only "in his mind," ignoring the racial differences between them that everyone else, especially Iago, focuses on. This sight/fever imagery ranges through all of Shakespeare's lovers from Titania falling for Bottom, to King Lear finally being able to "see" his daughter Cordelia. Another image popular with Shakespeare, and worthy of the pun, is hunting the "hart." Shakespeare's lovers love to go on a heart-hunt: Helen after Bertram, the four young lovers in *Midsummer*, even *Antony & Cleopatra* can be seen as one long chase, half-way around the world. And again, once the chase is over, what happens? Usually it is to die in each others arms (tragedy!) or marry (comedy!) – neither of which seems half as much fun as the chase itself.

Playing Shakespeare's characters means showing how character is formed through *action*, through the process of making choices, often when neither choice is particularly good. Juliet not only knows Romeo will say "aye" to her, but in doing so, encourages him (as it were) to have the *courage* to speak up! We, the audience, leave the theater, hoping that we, too, might have the courage speak our love (or our politics, or our morals) whether it comes to love, politics or living a "good" life … For Shakespeare, this was "the purpose of playing" as Hamlet put it. Holding up the mirror to nature shows us both who we are and who we aspire to be. Showing the "form and pressure" of the times, be they "out of joint" or not, should give us, like the characters we see on stage, hope that life moves forward, even in the darkest times. That is why theater, indeed all good art, is so dangerous. It inspires us to hope in a better future. Love is the greatest expression of that hope that we have. Shakespeare shows that others have been there and loved, even if they were not always immediately victorious …. The purpose of playing Shakespeare's lovers is to remind us how to be human. Is there any better art than that?

II. *Playing Shakespeare's Villains*

> *On my wall hangs a Japanese carving,*
> *The mask of an evil demon, decorated with gold lacquer.*
> *Sympathetically I observe*
> *The swollen veins of the forehead, indicating*
> *What a strain it is to be evil.*

> "The Mask of Evil" - Bertolt Brecht[1]

Unlike Brecht's evil demon in the poem above, Shakespeare's villains rarely strain to be evil. They are smooth, unctuous, without a conscience, and surprisingly successful. Richard and Claudius become kings. Edmund almost does. In a zero-sum game, Iago wins and Othello loses. Don John escapes at the end of *Much Ado*, and the shipwrecked villains in *The Tempest* are forgiven … Crime may not pay, but in Shakespeare's world it doesn't cost very much. This may be, perhaps, because Shakespeare does not see the world in a Manichean good/evil dichotomy. Rather … it seems to me that Shakespeare has a sliding scale or "great chain of badness" (apologies to E.M. Tillyard) that goes from a kind of amoral expediency to villainy and finally to evil. There are villains in Shakespeare who are mischievous (Don John, and Iachimo perhaps); characters who are amoral but not evil (mostly in the histories, but also Juliet's Nurse, and, perhaps Claudius, if we are feeling sympathetic); and characters who become (and this may be the key) truly evil only in the course of their actions. These would include Richard III, Macbeth, Edmund, and possibly Angelo. They reach a point where their "badness" is irreversible and possibly irredeemable.

Shakespeare lays out for us a panoply of evil, villainy and amorality – of characters doing bad things for good reasons, bad things for bad reasons, and bad things for no reasons at all. What are we to make of this world view where some villains get their "come-uppance" and others seem to be rewarded; where mischievousness can quickly turn violent (think of the lads in *Romeo and Juliet*); and where an entire world can be brought down by someone's willful insistence on having his or her own way (Iago? Shylock?) . . .

Shakespeare left us not mustache-twirling caricatures, but "real," "flesh and blood" exemplars of cruelty and evil, I think, as warnings. The villainy in the world is not the work of the Devil or Queen Mab, but of other human beings, just like ourselves. We are capable of being both victim and torturer. The choice is up to us. As we watch a Richard or Claudius or Lady Macbeth in action, we see that nothing is inevitable. They make their own choices every inch of the way. And so do we. The examples are here. The choice is ours. Nothing is written. The readiness is all.

III. *Playing Shakespeare's Monarchs and Madmen: A Mad World, My Masters!*

Americans have mixed feelings about monarchs and monarchies. We revolted against one, yet, in our periodic yearnings for the trappings of the occasional "imperial presidency" we sometimes wish we had a king. We embrace, unknowingly perhaps, the medieval concept of "the king's two bodies," often equating the health and stability of the man (almost always men in Shakespeare) who rules, with the "body politic" of the country itself, whether it is the *Life* magazine-style glamour of Kennedy's "Camelot" or the Twitter-fed tribalism of Trump's "American carnage."

Americans, speaking very broadly again, tend to view Shakespeare's histories through the first of these two bodies. We look to the plays for a study of the man, not the monarchy: Hal's growing up, Hamlet's angst, Richard III's seductive villainy, Lear's madness, etc. Then we pause and look kindly, if not condescendingly, on the political bits, cutting them where we can ("maybe the Brits get this stuff, I don't") or trying to make them relevant (setting the Henriads in the American Civil War, for example). All of which tends to imbue the plays with an over-coating of rugged American individualism that I am not sure Shakespeare had in mind (as if one could ever know) . . .

Jan Kott, in his seminal study "The Kings," wrote of history as a "Grand Mechanism," a staircase or a great wheel, on which a Henry or Richard is always rising or climbing to the top while another of the same name is tumbling down. History is a ruthless machine, implacable and impersonal. There was no Lord's anointed in Shakespeare's view of history, Kott argued, only a lust for power that drove monarchs to chop off heads, build or break alliances, and "busy giddy minds / With foreign quarrels" (*2HIV*, 4.1.372–30). But when Henry V reads out the list of English dead after the battle of Agincourt, those mentioned are nobility, like himself, the one per-center "band of brothers." Of those of no "name" but "five and twenty" who died (*HV*, 4.8.110), both Hal and Kott seem to have forgotten the likes of Mouldy, Shadow, Wart, Feeble, Fang, Bullcalf, Snare and Davy, who Shakespeare and Falstaff use for cannon fodder in *Henry IV, Part 2*. To the one percent they are indeed of no name.

Shakespeare takes an uncommon interest in these common men and women. They are the Citizens in *Richard III*, who remain mute as "breathing stones" when Buckingham tries to get them to shout "God save Richard. England's royal king!" (*RIII*, 3.7.20–25). They are Grooms and Gardeners in *Richard II*, the Quicklys and Tearsheets in *Henry IV*, the poor Bardolfs hanged in *Henry V*, the Pompeys and Overdones of *Measure for Measure*, the Servants in *Lear* who go to Gloucester's aid, and the Soldier who somehow manages to find his way into Cleopatra's bedroom to boldly beg Antony not to "fight by sea" (*Ant.* 3.7.77) on the morning of battle.

It is through these men and women that we know something is rotten in Denmark. Note that Shakespeare is careful to have the foot-soldier, Marcellus, tell us that something is "rotten in the *state* of Denmark" (*Hamlet*, 1.4.100)—we already know the old king's physical body has been poisoned. It is the body politic that is rotting now. Marcellus, a commoner, speaks truth to power about the corruption of the state. He is part of the body politic, erupting like a blister or abscess, who must be attended to but is often ignored. These nameless subject-citizens know when the country bleeds. They suffer most when Kott's "Grand Mechanism" begins to turn ... Does it matter to those of no name which Richard it was or what Edward or Gloucester or Northumberland? No matter the name, it will not to turn out well for those at the bottom. At best you might get a Richmond, Malcolm or an Edgar/Albany (depending which ending of *Lear* you prefer). At worst, you get a Fortinbras, or the post-assassination civil war of *Julius Caesar*. It is always the body politic that pays for the madness of the body private ...

[I]t is in the Histories where the collision of monarchs and madmen does the most damage, because the monarch is more often than not his (or her) own madman. Rash actions, such as Richard's banishment of Bolingbroke, bring equally rash reactions (rebellion and regicide), which, in turn move the Grand Mechanism to its next phase. In this context, Henry's son Hal is less the foundational national hero of a St. Crispian's Day emerald isle than a pause in a long and inevitably downward turn of the wheel towards Richard III (which then turns upward in Richmond and the establishment of the Tudor line, and so on). The "band of brothers" of *Henry V* is the same set of nobles who carve up Henry VI's kingdom like hyenas, leading to the assent of a madman for a monarch in *Richard III...*

We live in an era where the institutions of democracy and a civil society, such as free speech, a free press, and an educated electorate, seem to be at risk, not from some outside alien battering at our gates, but from within. We are in danger of letting the body politic rot, like the state of Denmark, because of the madmen we let rule. The times, indeed, are out of joint, and only we, in the lists of battle with no name, can set it right ... We are the madmen if we let our monarchs take this future from us. Resist!

IV: *Playing Shakespeare's Rebels and Tyrants: "'Tis time to fear when tyrants seem to kiss." (Pericles, 1.2.24)*

A surprising number of Shakespeare's characters are both rebels *and* tyrants. The operative word here is the "and," [as above with *Lovers*] which Merriam-Webster's dictionary defines (in part) as a "function word used to indicate connection or addition."[2] How is this connection and addition possible? And what is that "connection"? Leaving aside the History plays for the moment (and only a moment) let us look at some of Shakespeare's characters who seem to fill these seemingly contradictory roles simultaneously or sequentially.

To name a few: Petruchio is obviously a rebel against the norms of Italian (male) society, *and* a tyrant to his bride. Shylock is a tyrant to his daughter, *and* rebels against the Venetian state in demanding his "bond." Similarly, Lord Capulet tyrannizes his daughter, and probably his wife, *and* is a rebellious subject and enemy to the peace of Verona. Macbeth, having put down one rebellion, rebels against Duncan *and* goes on to be Scotland's greatest tyrant. Hamlet rebels against his uncle *and* proceeds to tyrannize (and/or kill) nearly everyone around him. Edmund, Gloucester's rebellious bastard son in *King Lear*, while not given the chance to rule, shows his tyrannical instincts soon enough. And, for a final example, Coriolanus seems to be schizophrenically rebellious *and* tyrannical with every breath he takes.

This personal rebelliousness in Shakespeare's characters seems to come from a sense of grievance, which resonates with our own cultural and political moment. Edmund, Coriolanus, Capulet, etc., insist on their right to do whatever they want, whenever they want, even if it upsets everyone else's apple cart. Shakespeare's women are no less rebellious: Juliet, Cordelia, Desdemona, Kate, among others, demand their moment of full personhood, usually against tyrannical, or at least obtuse, fathers. The problem is that the women die or are married off before they can get the opportunity to show whether their "rule" would be equally tyrannous or not. (If the examples of Cleopatra, Queen Margaret, and Coriolanus' mother, Valeria, are any indication, I am not overly optimistic.)

This sense of grievance (the word has been unfortunately hijacked in the U.S. at the moment by debates about "white grievance"[3]) is a powerful motivator. Shakespeare's rebels feel that they have a right to what they think they lack—the throne, love, money, lands—and will take the steps necessary to achieve their goals. Part of this is the *zeitgeist* of England in the era of early modern capitalism. The feudal "great chain of being," to use E.M. Tillyard's well-worn phrase, was slowly being eroded by individualists like Edmund or Juliet, let alone a Richard or Henry, who believed they knew what was in their own best interests, and took the actions needed to reach their aims. This breath-taking seizing of the moment and risking all is thrilling and exciting when it comes to young love, less so when heads are rolling or stuck on pikes over London Bridge. Of course, the problem is that one person's act of rebellion is another's declaration of independence.

It is this shifting point that makes the term "rebel" so problematic: do we approve or not approve of the rebellion? Whose side are we on? Federation rebels against Darth Vader and the Deathstar? Okay, I can cheer them on. Confederate rebels defending a supremacist way of American life? Definitely not—at least for this editor . . .

Shakespeare uses the word "tyrant" seventy times in his complete works, not counting uses of "tyrannical" and "tyrannous," etc. (https://www.opensourceshakespeare.org), and the word is evenly divided between politics and love. Olivia is a "marble-breasted tyrant" (*TN*, 5.1.126); Leontes a "jealous" one (*WT*, 3.2.142). Cressida fears Troilus will play the tyrant, now that he knows how much she loves him (*Tro.* 3.2.119). Time is love's "bloody tyrant" in several *Sonnets* (5, 16, 120, 149). Bottom, lest we forget, wasn't sure, when given the role, if Pyramus was a lover or a tyrant. He could play either, the tyrant being more "lofty," the lover more "condoling." (*MSND*, 1.2. 38–9). And, to come full circle, to Peter Quince's way of thinking, Bottom is definitely a disruptive rebel in rehearsals.

In the comedic world of forests of Arden and Athens, and seacoasts in Illyria or Bohemia, Shakespeare's rebels and tyrants joust over love and, frankly, sex, escaping, or at least subverting, the tyrannies of convention and the established order by cross-dressing, gender fluidity, flashes of wit, mistaken identities, and the occasional poem stuck on a tree trunk. These are the weapons of choice in this sort of lusty rebellion. In the politic world of

Shakespeare's kings and queens, heads roll, daggers come out at night, and something is rotten in more places than just Denmark. No man, woman or child is safe. Even the king has nightmares. Uneasy, indeed, "lies the head that wears a crown" (*2HIV*, 3.1.31) . . .

There is one curious exception to this: the rebellion of Jack Cade in 1450 that Shakespeare takes up in the second part of *Henry VI*. The *dramatis personae* list to *Henry VI, part 2* describes Cade, as a "rebel" (or in some editions as "leader of the Kentish rebellion"), but Shakespeare loses no time in painting Cade as a clown. His pompous entrance with Dick the Butcher, Smith the Weaver, and "infinite numbers" of rebels in Act IV, scene 2, sets the tone, as the rebels start sniggering under their breaths about Cade's ancestry and his leadership skills . . . Shakespeare then goes on for the bulk of Act 4 to turn Cade and his Kentish comrades into riff-raff led by a man who would be king, who seems equal parts Falstaff, Bottom and Iago . . .

After a surprisingly successful start to [his] rebellion, Cade, both on stage and in real life, ruins it all by looting wealthy Londoners' homes, summarily executing nobles and followers alike, and dashing off, when defeated, with a treasure trove of "booty." While much of the Kentish army (numbering as many as 40,000 at one time) was pardoned, eight of Cade's accomplices were executed, and Cade himself was caught and killed by the newly-appointed Sheriff of Kent, Alexander Iden. Cade's corpse was dragged to London, beheaded and his dead body quartered, with the four parts sent to Blackheath, Salisbury, Gloucester and Norwich as a reminder to the locals of what happens to rebels. With that, Cade is dispatched and Shakespeare returns to his main story, with the Duke of York returning from Ireland, "to claim his right / And pluck the crown from feeble Henry's head." (*2HVI*, 5.1.1–2).

Yet, I can't stop thinking of Jack Cade and his rebels as insurrectionists[4] who would have felt right at home at the January 6, 2021 attack on the U.S. Capitol. Perhaps Jacob Anthony Chansley (a.k.a. Jake Angeli), the QAnon "shaman" dressed in "horns, a bearskin headdress, red, white and blue face paint, shirtless, and tan pants," carrying "a spear, approximately 6 feet in length, with an American flag tied just below the blade,"[5] could be convinced to play the role of Cade. The Capitol rebels believed, as did the Kentish ones, that their liberties were at risk, that noble elites were destroying the country they had fought for and defended, and that the true monarch, be it the Duke of York or Donald Trump, should be restored to the throne. Moreover, these rebels found themselves (or their supporters in office) equally adept at being tyrants, as does the disgruntled Trump base, pushing for voter suppression laws across the country. Though both rebellions were quickly brought to heel and the rebels arrested,[6] the immediate consequence in England was to give rise to the rapacious Richard III. We can only hope America continues to avoid such a fate ...

I shall be very lucky indeed to have the opportunity to edit four more such volumes, and, in time, another omnibus edition. "The play's the thing" through which Shakespeare reflects the challenges of our own time, and through which we find our way to our own solutions. I hope you will find this volume - and this series - a helpful, thoughtful and inspiring companion in that search; one that, with luck, encourages you to think afresh about your own approach to playing Shakespeare's characters today!

Notes

1 Brecht, Bertolt. "The Mask of Evil." *Poems 1913–1956*. Edited by John Willett and Ralph Manheim, with the cooperation of Erich Fried. Eyre Metheun, 1976. p. 383.
2 https://www.merriam-webster.com/dictionary/and
3 Corn, David. "Post-Trump, the GOP Continues to be the Party of (White) Grievance." *Mother Jones*, March 24, 2021.
4 There is a legal distinction between rebellion and insurrection, and between both and sedition: rebellion and insurrection (in U.S. law at least) refer to acts of violence against the state and its officers, while sedition is the organized incitement to rebellion. See Teka, Maddy, Esq. https://www.findlaw.com/criminal/criminal-charges/rebellion-or-insurrection.html).
5 Albert, Victoria & McNamara, Audrey. "Jake Angeli, Arizona QAnon supporter, taken into custody over assault on the U.S. Capitol." *CBS News* Jan. 10, 2021/7:36 AM. https://www.cbsnews.com/news/jake-angeli-qanon-shaman-jacob-chansley-arrested-capitol-riot/.
6 Rubin, Olivia. "Number of Capitol riot arrests of military, law enforcement and government personnel rises to 52." ABC News April 23, 2021/1:14 AM. https://abcnews.go.com/US/number-capitol-riot-arrests-military-law-enforcement-government/story?id=77246717.

Works Cited

All textual citations refer to: Folger Shakespeare Library. Folger Digital Texts. Ed. Barbara Mowat, Paul Werstine, Michael Poston, and Rebecca Niles. Folger Shakespeare Library, 11 April, 2017. www.folgerdigitaltexts.org.

Kaufman, Alexander L. *The Jack Cade Rebellion: A Sourcebook*. Lexington Books, 2020.

Kott, Jan. *Shakespeare, Our Contemporary*. W.W. Norton & Co., 1974.

Norwich, John Julius. *Shakespeare's Kings*. Scribner, 1999.

Tillyard, E. M. W.. The *Elizabethan World Picture*. Vintage, 1994.

1. The Story of Cressida's Body: The Rebellion of Survivorship in Troilus and Cressida (and Our Responsibility in Storytelling)

OLIVIA BUNTAINE

Within a society that ignores, suppresses and doubts the existence of sexual violence, survivors are inherently rebellious agents. Survivor-narratives are largely societally defined by the skepticism and denial with which they are most often greeted. Those narratives and their ensuing public reactions have been seen on our world's stages with increasing frequency, from Hollywood, to the Supreme Court, to the Oval Office. The politics of believing survivors is relevant to an anthology on Shakespeare's rebels because the issue of whose rebellious narrative is centered and validated in society trickles down into the ways we produce, direct, and act in the theater. I posit here that we are just beginning to develop the political and practical storytelling tools to center the theatrical exploration of survivor-narratives in Shakespeare's canon.

With the emergence of the #MeToo movement, increased visibility of survivors in media, and the new field of Intimacy Direction, theater artists have an opportunity to unearth new and dynamic aspects of these classic stories. We are developing the tools to explore the often unaddressed or poorly handled themes of sexual violence laden in Shakespeare's work. In a case study of the "Kissing Scene" (4.5) in Shakespeare's *Troilus and Cressida*, I shall outline a jumping off point for consent-focused and trauma-informed textual analysis, as well as possibilities for staging using the frameworks and pedagogy of Intimacy Direction, the burgeoning field dedicated to safely choreographing moments of sex and intimacy on stage.

Cressida's status as a survivor-rebel can be easily attested to by taking a cursory glance at a vast majority of Shakespeare scholarship's villainization of her actions. Interpretations of Cressida as the unfaithful villain dominate the twentieth century's body of dramatic and scholarly interpretations of this play. To this point, scholar James O'Rourke wrote in a footnote that "Cressida's detractors are too numerous to cite" (O'Rourke 139), citing even the liberal thinker and author Joyce Carol Oates among them.

In her essay, "The Tragedy of Existence: Shakespeare's *Troilus and Cressida*," Oates falls back on the antiquated language of "purity" to signal and confirm Cressida's promiscuity: "She [Cressida] is content to think of herself as a 'thing' that is prized more before it is won (1. 2.313), and how else can one explain her behavior with Diomedes unless it is assumed that she is 'impure' before becoming Troilus' mistress?" (Oates 1976), while describing her additionally as "evil" and "villainous." Even in more moderate analyses of Cressida, her actions are only forgiven (if forgiven is the word) because of the play's overall tone of immorality and vice. In his analysis, Harold Bloom posits that, " if Troilus is no Romeo but only a witless version of Mercutio, then what should Cressida be except the Trojan strumpet ... this is a play in which the women are whores, and the men are too" (Bloom 1999). From numerous angles, Cressida, her body, and what happens to it, receive decisively damning judgments.

We see these themes of Cressida's careless infidelity carrying over even to contemporary platforms as benign as "Shakespeare made easy" websites such as *Shmoop*, the homework help-and-study-guide website aimed at teenagers. Focusing on the infamous "Kissing Scene" —the cheeky but accessible *Shmoop* has this to say about her:

> Set against the backdrop of the Trojan War, *Troilus and Cressida* is the story of how two people fall in love (okay, lust) and promise to be true forever and ever, only to have their romance completely destroyed about 2 seconds later when the following two things happen: [One,] Our lust birds are separated by the politics of warfare. [Two,] Someone decides to cheat. (Ahem. Cressida, we're talking about you here).

Rarely is there an earnest attempt to explore the intent behind Cressida's actions. In Charles Boyce's *Shakespeare A to Z*, he describes Cressida as "a frankly sensual woman, as has been evident from her affair with Troilus, and now, alone in a new world ... she succumbs to her nature" (Boyce 1991). By painting Cressida as sexual "by nature" we deny the theatrical and intellectual possibility of Cressida and her body being *sexualized*—to put it more plainly, what if the sexualization of Cressida results from how she is treated, not from an inherent sinful disposition? With further analysis of this scene, and a political positioning of Cressida as a survivor of sexual assault, the story becomes richer, more complex, and more realistic.

The night before Cressida is removed, without her consent, from the Trojan to the Greek camp, Trojans Cressida and Troilus swear their undying love to each other. Upon waking, the pair realize that Cressida's father, a Trojan defector to the Greeks, has arranged for the bodily transaction of Cressida to the Greeks (in exchange for his ransom), and there is "no remedy" (4.4.55). Cressida experiences extreme grief being torn away from her new lover and leaving for a hostile enemy camp—a reaction which her uncle, Pandarus, entreats her to moderate. "Why tell you me of moderation?" she says, "The grief is fine, full perfect, that I taste / And violenteth in a sense as strong / as that which causeth it. How can I moderate it?" (4.4.2–5). Despite Cressida's depth of grief, she is quickly sent to the Grecian Camp, escorted by the Grecian officer, Diomedes.

The following scene, 4.5, takes place in the Greek camp. Known as the "Kissing Scene," we see Cressida passed around to various Greek soldiers, receiving kisses from several men as a form of greeting. Of the forty-three lines of text between Cressida's entrance and exit, only six of those lines are her dialogue. The kissing scene is almost universally seen as evidence of Cressida's infidelity—even the Royal Shakespeare Company describes Cressida as "almost immediately betray[ing] Troilus" ("The Plot"). If further evidence is needed as to the necessity of a new perspective on this scene, the stage directions read *"he kisses her"* four times in a row, the fifth being *"he kisses her again."* Little attention seems to be paid as to how a captive woman, in an enemy camp, with no secured allies, surrounded by men, may be trying to navigate this situation. Her dialogue in response to the men, often interpreted as flirtatious, succeeds in effectively ending the kissing portion of the scene and distracts the men from further touching her.

A trauma-informed and survivor-narrative focused textual analysis of the "Kissing Scene" creates deep theatrical nuance and potential. I posit we do the play an injustice by not taking advantage of it. Although this analysis refers to a later part in the play (Cressida's scene alone with Diomedes (5.2)), Laurie Maguire, in *Performing Anger: The Anatomy of Abuse(s) in "Troilus and Cressida,"* provides an astute framework for what could be seen as Cressida's passivity in 4.5: "Cressida gives in verbally to pacify Diomedes' verbal violence, and she submits sexually to prevent his physical violence" (Maguire 2002). This textual analysis highlights the stakes of Cressida's situation: that love is a luxury that cannot always be afforded while under the threat of sexual violence. If we realistically imagine Cressida firmly and assertively pushing away these advances, in the culture of a Greco-Roman soldier's camp, in an overall plot anchored in a war over a woman's body, it is no wild conclusion that she would be greeted with violence, rape, or death.

My argument is that Cressida only accepts these kisses as a way to avoid worse. She is accepting them out of coercion, which we know is not consent. Under this lens, these kisses are assaults. There is opportunity for directorial choice and character-building among the "kissers," —Agamemnon, Nestor, Achilles, Patroclus—depending on whether these characters engage in group assault with eagerness or with ambivalence—but the end result of a nonconsensual interaction remains the same.

Unearthing the survivor-narrative of this scene reveals an abundance of staging opportunities, particularly when approached with an eye for intimacy direction. Under traditional understandings of Cressida, this scene is staged centering flirtatious physicality on her part, perhaps with her initiating some of the kissing (even in contradiction to the text's stage directions). We can imagine Cressida's body as infused with coyness, flexibility, looseness: opening enough to draw us in and then closing enough to leave the men—and the audience—wanting more. In the soldier's bodies, we see an easy aggression, we see angular lines, we see taught muscles around the softness of Cressida. As an intimacy director, I see two alternatives to this interpretation in the physicality of Cressida and the soldiers which would support a trauma-informed survivor-narrative.

A first possibility includes using the story of Cressida's body to create self-aware physical flirtation as a tactic of self protection, as in Maguire's analysis, using coquettishness to avoid further harm. This could look like Cressida's dodging of some kisses and quick acceptance of others—in character, this could be read as coyness, but also could physically indicate a calculated plan to be touched as little as possible. Within the field of intimacy direction, no gesture is too small to indicate the story of a physical interaction: a sharp inhale from Cressida upon a soldier grabbing her arm can indicate an awareness of danger in contrast to a slower exhale upon wiggling out of his grasp. Cressida could move a soldier's hand placed on her waist and place it, still in hers, on the soldier's heart. This physical change could be believed by the soldiers as an act of flirtation, but for Cressida, she gains more physical control and less physical contact. What do we, as the audience, see of Cressida's body's story that the soldiers miss? Do we watch her soften into relief at not being touched in the moments she is not? Do we watch her eyes look for exits, as she distracts them from touching and observing her thoughts by moving her hair to reveal the nape of her neck? Intimacy can be used as a tool of power, and in no way does the existence of intimate touch immediately indicate consent. The presence of consent is indicated by the physical story we tell, or the one we do not.

Another way of centering Cressida as a survivor, and of looking at the "Kissing Scene" as the real time unfolding of an assault, could potentially depict Cressida's physical state as totally disassociated, or in a state of "freeze," using the trauma-informed language that describes four different types of reaction to abuse or assault: fight, flight, freeze or fawn.[1] This concept might translate physically to complete tenseness in Cressida's body, unlike the first example, we would see no softness or melting in her limbs, but "freezing," an inability to escape complete stiffness, creating a physical tension for the soldiers who are, on some level, looking for physical affection in return. This approach is not in contradiction to the text. Cressida's lines can still be seen as a way to create a sense of normalcy to prevent something worse from happening to her. The motivations of her brief dialogue can be seen as an attempt to verbally soften where she physically cannot. Bodily rigidity might appear to the soldiers as antagonistic, and the creation of conflict as a hostage is something to avoid.

There are many other choreographic paths beyond the above. Perhaps we see Cressida's physicality begin with confident and limber ease, but over time it becomes more rigid and closed as she feels more in danger. Directorially, this could be viewed as a motivation for her later alliance with Diomedes as a form of protection. Or maybe Cressida is choreographed as "grinning and bearing it," flinging herself wildly and passionately onto the soldiers (fawning), only to directorially surprise the audience later with a moment alone, in deep grief or fear or hopelessness. There is no "right" interpretation, but I argue that whatever interpretation of the sexual violence which occurs should be intentional—and intimacy direction provides a comprehensive set of tools to allow us to tell that story.

The above textual analysis and suggestions for intimacy staging in *Troilus and Cressida* are undoubtedly political, but so is theater. As we, as a society, reckon with the history of Shakespeare being traditionally interpreted and produced in exclusionary and oppressive ways, we must open our minds to the possibility that just because a play, scene, or character has always been seen one way, that does not mean we cannot see them differently now. I have often noticed, as a director of Shakespeare and an intimacy director, that we avoid intentionally addressing sexual violence in his plays, dismissing those moments as "products of their time" or unfortunate plot devices. The impulse to look the other way from how Cressida is treated, or the violence Kate experiences in *The Taming of the Shrew*, or the often comically played infringements on Imogen's bodily autonomy in *Cymbeline*, is a professional impulse we must learn to resist, as it mirrors our resistance to acknowledge and address sexual violence in our off-stage society. There are rich and dynamic story-telling moments in the incidents of sexual violence in Shakespeare's canon, and ignoring them is not only an unethical way of making theater, but a less interesting and compelling path as well. The burgeoning field of intimacy direction, as well as an increasingly diverse and political generation of theater-makers, gives us the tools to tackle these issues.

To briefly engage in situating this essay within a larger philosophical question of the purpose of theater, I find myself turning to Hamlet's speech in Act 3, Scene 2: "the purpose of playing, whose end, both at the first and now, was and is, to hold, as 'twere, the mirror up to nature" (*Hamlet*, 3.2.21–24). If we accept Hamlet's position on theater for the purpose of this article (especially as it is included as prefatory material in this anthology), it behooves us to consider the impact that half-hearted or poorly analyzed depictions of sexual violence can have on the audience. Succinctly put by Perac and Şerban in *Women Under Siege. The Shakespearean Ethics of Violence*, "A major aspect of such plays ... is the theater's potential to reflect violence. They prove that tragedy not only represents an assault on the body but is also violent in its effect on the spectator" (98). We owe Cressida, Sylvia, Lavinia, Isabella, and many others a very thoughtful and intentional analysis and staging of their experiences, not just for the sake of their stories, but for the way our artistic work can affirm or disrupt social norms and the lives of women, survivors of sexual assault, and society as a whole.

Cressida is a rebel merely by existing. I see her as surviving and fighting for control of her bodily autonomy in a contextual world obsessed with male ownership of the female body. We have a choice, as art makers, as to whether we enact unexamined violence on our audiences and our characters, or encourage rebelliousness against the unjust. For those attempting the latter, the story of Cressida's body can light the beginning of our path.

Note

1 See: Gaba, Sherry. "Understanding Fight, Flight, Freeze and the Fawn Response." *Psychology Today*, Sussex Publishers, 22 Aug. 2020, www.psychologytoday.com/us/blog/addiction-and-recovery/202008/understanding-fight-flight-freeze-and-the-fawn-response.

Works Cited

Bloom, Harold. *Shakespeare: The Invention of the Human*. Riverhead Books, 1999.
Boyce, Charles. *Shakespeare A to Z: The Essential Reference to His Plays, His Poems, His Life and Times, and More*. Round Table Press, 1991.Maguire, L. "Performing

Anger: The Anatomy of Abuse(s) in 'Troilus and Cressida.'" *Renaissance Drama* 31 (2002): 153–83.

Oates, J. C. *The Edge of Impossibility: Tragic Forms in Literature*. New York: Vanguard, 1976.

O'Rourke, J. "Rule in Unity" and Otherwise: Love and Sex in "Troilus and Cressida." *Shakespeare Quarterly* 43. 2 (1992): 139. https://doi.org/10.2307/2870878

Percec, D., and Şerban, A. "Women Under Siege. The Shakespearean Ethics of Violence". *Gender Studies* 11. 1 (2012): 98.

Shakespeare, William. *Troilus and Cressida* from The Folger Shakespeare. Ed. Barbara Mowat, Paul Werstine, Michael Poston, and Rebecca Niles. Folger Shakespeare Library, April 11, 2021. https://shakespeare.folger.edu/shakespeares-works/troilus-and-cressida/

"The Plot: Troilus and Cressida: Royal Shakespeare Company." Royal Shakespeare Company, www.rsc.org.uk/troilus-and-cressida/the-plot. 31 January 2021.

"Troilus and Cressida Introduction." *Shmoop*, Shmoop University, www.shmoop.com/. 31 January 2021.

2. Smiling, Damned, Villains: The Pleasure of Not Caring

BRIAN LOHMANN

When you meet Shakespeare's villains, what is it that makes your blood run cold? Is it that Richard of Gloucester has locked his nephews in the Tower of London to be murdered? That he drowned his brother in a cask of wine? Or is it that he is unaffected by their deaths? Is it that Iago overthrows Othello's "noble mind," warping it until his general murders Desdemona? Or is it that Iago appears to coldly take it all in stride? Is it that Lady Macbeth's ambition feasts on King Duncan's life? Or is it that she first feeds her ambition with the sacrifice of her maternal instincts?

We will examine these three Shakespearean villains and ask what they uncouple in their psyches in order to do the things they do. Does Shakespeare relegate to the lower circles of Hell those without compassion, those who appear incapable of empathy? The lack of empathy has been included in the modern definition of the sociopath, those who seem to take pleasure in not caring.[1]

We shudder at the contemporary monsters who commit atrocities, and then shrug them off. Judges look for remorse before passing sentences because they want the convicted criminal to take on the emotional weight of their victims' experience, something that stretches past an intellectual understanding of the consequences of their crimes. Empathy in leaders can be a stirring, and very quotable, quality, as demonstrated by Bill Clinton's "I feel your pain," or JFK's "Ich bin ein Berliner." "I feel you" has replaced "I understand you" in contemporary slang. Perhaps because more and more of our time is spent interacting with devices, empathy is more important than ever to us. But what about those who don't have it? What does this missing element of compassion tell us about them? Shakespeare has given us three very revealing examples to examine.

As we investigate the actions of Richard III, Iago, and Lady Macbeth some questions arise. Do these three understand what impact their actions will have on others? Do they care? Do they enjoy the havoc they create? Is it possible that Shakespeare had an early read on what not only makes a human being, but also what, when missing, unmakes one? These characters provide cautionary examples, warning us what might happen if we discover their ilk in others or ourselves.

"I am determined to prove a villain." (Richard III, *1.1.30*)

We meet Richard of Gloucester on the day of his brother's imprisonment. We learn that he has orchestrated that imprisonment and laid plots, "by drunken prophecies, libels and dreams" (*RIII*, 1.1.33). He fascinates us. This fiend does things we could never do because of our sense of guilt or shame or evil. But Richard's cold-blooded audacity ensnares us as accomplices. As we hang on his every word, his speeches make us complicit in each atrocity he commits. We sit mute while he brags about his wooing of Lady Anne ("I'll have her, but I will not keep long" (1.2.249)). He's determined to prove a villain, determined to drag us along as witnesses. If he can get us to enjoy being wicked along with him, so much the better. We may cringe at his violence, but if we gasp with admiration at his cool, steady resolve, we are no better than he is. We may be slowly, subconsciously aligning ourselves with someone whose ambition has devoured his decency. Fourteen lines into the play, Richard tells us why: he lacks beauty. Since he himself has been rudely stamped, why should he not stamp rudely on the lives of others? Do we not wonder if his unfinished outside also houses an incomplete soul:

> RICHARD. But I, that am not shaped for sportive tricks,
> Nor made to court an amorous looking glass;
> I, that am rudely stamp'd and want love's majesty
> To strut before a wanton ambling nymph;
> I, that am curtailed of this fair proportion,
> Cheated of feature by dissembling nature,
> Deformed, unfinished, sent before my time
> Into this breathing world scarce half made up,
> And that so lamely and unfashionable
> That dogs bark at me as I halt by them – (*RIII*, 1.1.14-23)

Shakespeare, expecting we might question whether Richard has a soul at all, answers us in the last line Richard has alone in this part of the scene.

"Dive, thoughts, down to my soul. Here Clarence comes" (1.1.41). Richard tells us exactly what he plans to do to get the crown:

> RICHARD. And, if I fail not in my deep intent,
> Clarence hath not another day to live;
> Which done, God take King Edward to His mercy,
> And leave the world for me to bustle in.
> For then I'll marry Warwick's youngest daughter.
> What though I killed her husband and her father?
> The readiest way to make the wench amends
> Is to become her husband and her father; (*R III*, 1.1. 153-60)

Henry VI's widow, Lady Anne, knows Richard killed her husband and hates him for it. Richard is unmoved by that hatred. Stopping her funeral procession, Richard stands over Henry's body, wooing her while Henry's wounds bleed "afresh" as testimony to Richard's guilt. With an astonishing lack of compassion, he accepts her, her spittle and her rage in his monomaniacal pursuit of her. She indicts his lack of empathy, but his focus is so absolute, unwavering and magnetic that, in spite of her better judgment, she becomes his wife.

It is not until much later in the play, when the ghosts of those Richard has murdered come to him in his tent to curse him, that Richard confesses his doubts and confusion. But does he really understand what carnage he has left in his wake when he says, "O coward conscience, how thou dost afflict me!" (5.3.191). Richard sees his conscience as something outside himself, a vestigial fragment he wishes he could shed. Perhaps his body and spirit are warring with themselves after preying so long on others.

What fate awaits a character whose conscience is outside their being? The answer might come from Queen Margaret when she tells Richard, "Hie thee to hell for shame, and leave this world, / Thou cacodemon! There thy kingdom is" (1.3.147-48). Richard is condemned to hell by those for whom he has made a hell of earth; a hell where your good intentions are present, but beyond your reach.

"What do I fear? Myself? There's none else by." (Richard III, 5.3.194)

Richard's hell is also the psychological drawing and quartering of aspects of his personality. He pulls himself apart. His disintegration is a sentence of schizophrenia after the fact. The late, unexpected remorse, haunts him and drives him to fracture himself. But Richard does not regret what he has done as much as fear its reckoning.

> RICHARD. Cold fearful drops stand on my trembling flesh.
> What do I fear? Myself? There's none else by.
> Richard loves Richard, that is I am I.
> Is there a murderer here? No. Yes, I am.
> Then fly! What, from myself? Great reason why:
> Lest I revenge. What myself, upon myself?
> Alack, I love myself. (*R III*, 5.3. 193-9)

He is not lying. Richard's great love is Richard. He is so impressed with himself that he needs to refer to himself in the third person. But Richard loves Richard in no small part because no one else loves Richard, and, because Richard is unlovable to all else, Richard hates Richard. This contradiction blossoms as the speech continues:

> RICHARD. O, no. Alas, I rather hate myself
> For hateful deeds committed by myself.
> I am a villain. Yet I lie; I am not.
> Fool, of thyself speak well. Fool, do not flatter.
> My conscience hath a thousand several tongues,
> And every tongue brings in a several tale,
> And every tale condemns me for a villain. (*R III*, 5.3. 201-7)

His crimes, which he delights to list throughout the play, now return as a list read by his conscience. The fractured Richard speaks in a thousand tongues and each tongue is a piece of himself.

We live in an era where armies kill by remote control. Drones are sent from command centers far distant from the sometime civilian victims they kill as collateral damage. It is an extreme example of how modern technology has the capacity to neutralize empathy. What would Richard's hired killers feel if the Duke of Clarence and the princes in the Tower were blips on screens that could be terminated with a touch of a button? The question of what toll the unempathetic act takes on the psyches of contemporary soldiers is still under study. This dissociative aspect to PTSD resonates with the fracturing of Richard III.[2]

Perhaps Richard and Iago are examples of what happens when this combination of inurement to violence and the righteous, selfish impulse are taken to extremes. Richard sees his family as a series of obstacles to power. He does not mourn their deaths, he celebrates them. For Richard, like Iago in *Othello*, people in his way are not humans, just problems to be dealt with.

"What's he, then, that says I play the villain." (Othello, 2.3.356)

Iago's systematic destruction of Othello may be motivated by envy, jealousy, racism, or all three. Iago has been passed over for a promotion and that honor given to Michael Cassio. There is an unproven rumor abroad, too, about Othello cuckolding Iago:

> IAGO.   And it is thought abroad that twixt my sheets
> 'Has done my office. I know not if 't be true,
> But I, for mere suspicion in that kind,
> Will do as if for surety. (*Oth.* 1.3.430-33)

Why is Iago so intent on ruining the happiness Othello has found with Desdemona? Shakespeare (who often supports his character's claims by having them list examples to bolster those opinions) gives Iago no factual supporting evidence for his hatred, but shows him plotting sadistic acts against the innocent for "mere suspicion" as in the quote above. Is it because he craves recognition? An official title? In order for Iago to feel empathy, does he first need to be acknowledged and deemed worthy? Unlikely, since Iago does nothing to create the world of justice, recognition and fairness this would imply. He destroys Michael Cassio and Roderigo, but not for any injury they have done him. Iago's plot is hatched for the pleasure of the act, rather than what results the act might bring. Iago's discontent comes not from Othello himself, but from a hatred and envy of Othello's happiness. Othello is honored by the world, while Iago feels his own achievements are underappreciated. To our sensibilities, Iago may be a sociopath acting out of petty jealousy, but Shakespeare labels him as something more unholy, a "Divinity of hell!" (2.3.370).

Does Iago see himself as damned or as a devil? Like Richard III he references his soul, but does so casually, as if it were an accessory, again like Richard, something that exists outside himself. This casual relationship to the soul is a one way Shakespeare indicates that Iago simply cannot care about what happens to other people; cannot "feel their pain." Iago feels neither dread nor fear nor shame. But because Desdemona, Cassio and Othello all act as caring, feeling individuals, Iago is able to take their innocent compassion and turn it against them, as he does here with Desdemona:

IAGO.   So I will turn her virtue into pitch
         And out of her own goodness make the net
         That shall enmesh them all. (*Oth.* 2.3.380-3)

Earlier in the same speech, Iago famously challenges us, daring us to
speak against him:

IAGO.   And what's he, then, that says I play the villain,
         When this advice I give is free and honest,
         Probal to thinking, and indeed the course
         To win the Moor again? For tis most easy
         Th' inclining Desdemona to subdue
         In any honest suit. (*Oth.* 2.3.356-361)

Desdemona's compassion for Michael Cassio becomes the weapon that
destroys her. When she pleads Cassio's case to Othello, she only succeeds in
fueling her husband's jealous rage. Michael Cassio's respect for Othello, cou-
pled with his own lost reputation, gives Iago the leverage he needs to undo
them all. Iago sees the endgame clearly and maps out the moves to his goal.
If we look at his chess game through a racial lens, then Iago is white with the
advantage of moving first. Does Iago hate Othello because of his skin color?
Iago rouses Desdemona's father with images of dark overcoming light: "an
old black ram is tupping your white ewe" (1.1.97), and, "you'll have your
daughter covered with a Barbary horse?" (1.1.125). Iago knows what triggers
will prod action and he makes his moves like a grand master.
    It is love, even more than racial enmity, that Iago uses for his purposes.
Iago uses false claims of love to mislead others. "I do love Cassio well and
would do much / To cure him of this evil" (2.2.150-1); or, "I protest in the
sincerity of love and honest kindness" (2.3.347); and "My lord, you know
I love you" (3.3.134). That he only speaks of his love when he is lying is a
strong indicator of Iago's total lack of empathy. Iago lives in a world where
love and honesty are interwoven. Othello demands that Iago, if he loves him,
be honest with him. "Speak. Who began this? On thy love I charge thee"
(2.3.189). But if Iago sees love alive in others, he speaks of his own love as a
corrupted counterfeit, an alloy of revenge and lust:

IAGO.   That Cassio loves her, I do well believe't.
         That she loves him, 'tis apt and of great credit.
         The Moor, howbeit that I endure him not,
         Is of a constant, loving, noble nature,
         And I dare think he'll prove to Desdemona

A most dear husband. Now I do love her too,
Not out of absolute lust, (though peradventure
I stand accountant for as great a sin)
But partly led to diet my revenge, (*Oth.* 2.1.308-16)

Iago is uncoupled from compassion. To him, lovemaking is an act of lust or revenge – "making the beast with two backs" (1.1. 130). Iago can find no tenderness within himself. He puts his energies into manufacturing so great a false version of himself that any light he might have once had inside himself is overcome by his own darkness.

How to play the villain.

Shakespeare writes Iago and Richard III as though they were tour guides through a nightmare. They make us sit up and pay attention, confronting us with examples of what human beings are capable of at their worst. Richard III talks to his audience as if we enjoy his villainy as much as he does. Iago speaks to us with bravado, daring us to stop him from inflicting pain on others. But at the end of the plays we are faced with confronting the truth of what they did.

Actors playing these roles need to be deft and precise about when the mask of evil is on and when it is off. We need to see the multiple layers of truth and falsehood. Performers have to make us want to descend deeper into the hell Richard III and Iago create. They have to make us want to come back after intermission. Performers of these roles must be personable, charming, witty, emotionally present and available, as well as inwardly mercurial within their outward steadfastness. Most of all, these villains must appear honest and credible. These are the nuances necessary to avoid the clichéd pitfalls of a wicked super-villain.

The actors in these roles must make it clear that the characters they play are damned, in part, because they smile so convincingly. They must use their skill as actors to portray characters who use their acting skills to spread destruction. The layered contradiction of "don't believe this character who is acting, but believe me, the actor, playing this character," is a tricky feat to pull off. "When devils will the blackest sins put on, they do suggest at first with heavenly shows, as I do now" (*Oth.* 2.3.356).

What is Shakespeare saying about acting? Perhaps he is proposing that there is a role the ordinary citizen, the average audience member, can play. Perhaps we must question our own initial impressions and judgments of these villains, and not uncritically leave all interrogation to others. As Bertolt Brecht said, we must not hang up our heads with our hats when we go to theater.[3]

Brecht and Shakespeare ask us to scrutinize the world around us and make informed judgments rather than take surface appearances as true. There are multiple examples in Shakespeare's plays of unscrupulous rulers (the Queen in *Cymbeline*, for example), or secret plotters scheming to stage a coup (Scroop, Cambridge and Grey in *Henry V*). The fear in Shakespeare's day was that one rebel could bring down a nation. This makes these individual portraits even more powerful. Given that the political realities of Shakespeare's time informed the creation of his characters, perhaps we should look to the headlines of our own era for examples that resonate with contemporary audiences. What nuances of deception and ambition abound today that could be woven into a modern actor's interpretation of Iago or Richard?

These roles require high levels of intensity and a sense of unstoppable momentum. The words are the fuel for the performance's propulsion. Look at Lady Macbeth's language when she calls on "murdering ministers," "thick night" and the "dunnest smoke in hell," so that heaven will not "peep through the blanket of the dark to cry, 'Hold! Hold!'" (*Mac.* 1.5. 55-61). Actors who invest in the text as if it were a musical score of operatic power will discover rhythms and sounds that unlock performances filled with dynamic momentum, without caricature or cliché.

The disintegration of Lady Macbeth: "The torture of the mind to lie in restless ecstasy." (Macbeth, 3.2.23)

Our final character to consider is Lady Macbeth. She is not a tour guide and never addresses the audience. Unlike Richard and Iago, she is not a soldier and has not killed before. In order to rise, she sheds her better self before our eyes. She mutates into a distortion of herself. Once she heads down the path of "What's done cannot be undone" (5.1.71), her choices are irrevocable.

When Lady Macbeth makes her plea to the "spirits that tend on mortal thoughts" (1.4.46) she is asking them to divorce her from her own humanity. In only 125 lines, she sheds first womanhood, then motherhood all in the service of ambition. She betrays Duncan by first betraying her own body. Her treason is not only political but biological. Hers is a personal, intimate descent into darkness, one that we witness as secret voyeurs rather than as accomplices. She peels away woman, mother, loyal subject until all that remains is a wife urging her husband to fulfill his destiny and hers. She is un-tethered from all her human roles.

It is Lady Macbeth who goes back to smear the grooms with blood. Her husband still is "too full o' th' milk of human kindness" (*Mac.* 1.5.17). She also rejects more of her body when she sheds her diurnal nature and becomes a nocturnal, vampire-like creature, one that is obsessed with blood, walking at night and asking to keep the light of day at bay. It is interesting that Shakespeare gives her no first name. She is Lady Macbeth, or simply the "Lady" in stage directions. Her role as partner to Macbeth submerges her and conscripts her to the service of securing the crown.

The action of empathetic uncoupling continues throughout the play. Macbeth steps back from the reality he shares with his wife when he alone sees Banquo's ghost. Macbeth spirals away as the other guests look on, unsettled and confused. He inhabits a sinister separate reality:

> MACBETH. Stones have been known to move and trees to speak.
> Augurs and understood relations have
> By maggot-pies and choughs and rooks brought forth
> The secret'st man of blood. What is the night?" (*Mac.* 3.4.152-5)

The Lady will uncouple herself from the narrative throughout Act IV, and when we finally see her again in Act V, she has separated herself from her sleep and her sanity. Her last line in Act III to her husband, "You lack the season of all natures, sleep" (3.6.173), is a prophetic statement about her own future. By the end of the play she is caught in an infinity loop, trying to separate herself from Duncan's blood by washing her hands again and again in a dream world. The actor who takes on this role takes on the task of peeling her persona back like an onion, down to a center that is raw, disintegrating into chaos. Once there is nothing left but chaos, Lady Macbeth disappears for good, imploding in her offstage suicide, leaving the black hole of her ambition to pull her husband down towards his doom. "I am not what I am." (*Othello*, 1.1.44)

Lady Macbeth, Iago and Richard III follow no code of loyalty other than one of self-interest, the creed of personal gain above all else. They are egoists in the service of themselves. We the audience are their witnesses, sometimes their confidants, and through our silence, complicit partners in their deeds. We wonder at the atrocities they are capable of. Richard poses as a holy man deep in prayer. Iago pretends to be a simple soldier concerned about his general. Lady Macbeth greets Duncan as a loyal and gracious hostess. "I am not what I am" (*Oth.* 1.1.44), says Iago after he has made clear why he needs to keep his true nature hidden:

IAGO.   Others there are
Who keep their hearts attending on themselves,
And throwing but shows of service on their lords
Do well thrive by them, and, when they have lined their coats
Do themselves homage. (*Oth.* 1.1.51-57)

Anything can be justified. Actors playing these roles investigate how to take their character's side, to see the world through their eyes and align themselves with their characters' motivations.

Leaders of Indonesian death squads were asked to play themselves in the 2012 film *The Act of Killing* (http://theactofkilling.com). Watch them disassociate themselves from their actions, and you will realize that Iago, Richard and Lady M are not 400 year-old fantasies. They are examples of sociopathic self-interest that has mowed down opposition throughout history. These personalities are single-minded in their pursuit of power, and unrepentant in their ambition. Like the mass murderers in the film, Shakespeare's villains speak openly about their crimes, to us as either tour guides or as co-conspirators. These characters not only make their victims suffer but torture us, the audience, as witnesses to the unfolding tragedy. The public commitment of the characters to fulfill their plans keeps the stakes high and feeds the tension of the drama. The momentum of the storyline is fed by the actions of the victims - those characters who fail to see these villains for what they are.

We also identify with those victims. Like the audience at a horror film, we want to shout out the equivalent of "Don't go into the basement," each time we see one of them make an unwitting choice. Duncan chooses to spend the night in Macbeth's castle ("Don't go in!). Emelia gives the incriminating handkerchief to Iago (Don't give it to him!). Richard makes the most of Lady Anne's grief. (Don't marry him!). Human nature has not changed much since Shakespeare. There are leaders today who exhibit a shocking lack of empathy, modern examples for actors to draw inspiration from as they play these villains.

Actors, watch the world as you create your Richard, Iago or Lady Macbeth. As for the rest of us, stay alert, know whose castle you are invited into! If someone wants a handkerchief really badly, ask "why?" Do not hang up your head with your hat! If their nose isn't running, maybe you should be.

Notes

1 Thomas, M.E. "How to Spot a Sociopath." www.psychologytoday.com/us/articles/201305/how-spot-sociopath
2 Lanius, Ruth. www.thetraumatherapistproject.com/podcast/ruth-lanius-phd/

3 "Epic Theater and Brecht." www.bbc.com/bitesize/guides/zwmvd2p/revision/2

Works Cited

All textual citations refer to: Folger Shakespeare Library. *Shakespeare's Plays* from Folger Digital Texts. Ed. Barbara Mowat, Paul Werstine, Michael Poston, and Rebecca Niles. Folger Shakespeare Library, 15 January, 2019. www.folgerdigitaltexts.org.

3. Re-"Claiming from the Female": Shakespeare's Henry V

JANNA SEGAL

Battle lines between scholars and among practitioners have been drawn over the political agenda of *Henry V*, Shakespeare's third and final play depicting the transformation of England's prodigal Prince Hal into a king "full of grace and fair regard" (*HV*, 1.1.24). Some poststructuralist critics, like Greenblatt and Tennenhouse, have positioned the play as state-solidifying stagecraft in service to the Elizabethan court.[1] Others, such as Dollimore and Sinfield and Hedrick and Reynolds, have situated the play as inadvertently or otherwise undermining its seemingly state-consolidating function.[2] Between these two factions are critics like Rabkin and Gurr who declare the play indecisive about the English monarchy's martial impulses and the titular character who embodies them.[3] Modern to postmodern stage and screen productions have tended to be divided into comparable camps that either celebrate, denounce, or ambivalently represent the historical monarch's military conquests. For instance, Sir Laurence Olivier's World War II-era film idealized the exploits of "the warlike Harry" (1.P.5). Unlike Olivier's jingoistic depiction, Michael Kahn's Vietnam War-era production for the American Shakespeare Festival at Stratford, Connecticut, denounced the horrors of warfare.[4] Produced two years after Trump's triumph over the Oval Office, Robert O'Hara's 2018 production for the New York Public Theater's Mobile Unit landed in between these politically-pendulum swinging wartime renditions. According to *New York Times* reviewer Alexis Soloski, O'Hara's production was most notable for its indecisiveness: "it doesn't seem to know which story it's telling. This version isn't an unthinking endorsement of rah-rah patriotism, but it's not really an attack on nation-building either."

Despite their differing positions on the ideological imperatives of the play's representation of Henry V, the scholarly factions share some common ground. These contrasting critical camps implicitly agree that Shakespeare's version of this chapter of the Hundred Years War is largely concerned with the martial (and concluding marital) exploits of a male monarch in a male-dominated dramatic landscape. While some critics, like McEachern, Hedrick and Reynolds, and Newman, attend to the play's representation of Princess Katherine of France,[5] the tendency among critics of even the most polarized positions has been to follow the male characters' voices and deeds. This is unsurprising given that among the play's over 45 discrete characters written to be played by the Lord Chamberlain's Men, there are a mere four female-identified figures: Hostess Quickly; Katherine; Alice, Katherine's gentlewoman; and the Queen of France. With the exception of the Act Three scene between Katherine and Alice, these four only appear on stage with male characters. Moreover, these women are all directly or indirectly associated with France, and therefore among those vanquished by the invading Englishmen at the center of the action. Even the lone English woman among the cast, Hostess Quickly, is among the Frenchified enemy: a source of contention between the English soldiers Nym and Pistol, her final line in the play is the French salutation "Adieu" (2.3.62), and Pistol reveals in the final act that she has died "of a malady of France" (5.2.85–86). The text also linguistically defaults to a male subject position; indeed, according to the Oxford Shakespeare concordance for *Henry V*, the word "man" appears fifty-one (198–99) and "men" forty-six times in the dialogue (204–05), while "woman" is stated twice and "women" is uttered six times (350).

Not unlike the common ground covered by those on the frontlines of criticism on the play, the British and American boards upon which *Henry V* has historically tread have primarily prioritized the play's male-laden landscape. However, some more recent productions have used casting to pressurize assumptions, including those circulating in the play, regarding gender and power. Robert Hastie's 2016 production at the Open Air theater in Regent's Park featured Michelle Terry as the King, a choice Dominic Cavendish of *The Telegraph* declared "the biggest cross-gender shock to the Shakespearean system this year." According to Cavendish, Terry's "neutral stance, neither overtly a woman in a man's world, nor attempting male impersonation," effectively encouraged "perceptions to shift" and threw "the gauntlet down to any prejudices." *The Guardian*'s Michael Billington similarly praised Terry's "astonishing" performance, and found the casting of a woman in a role written for and traditionally played by a man especially "appropriate" at this "time of heightened awareness of gender equality." While not as critically well-received as Hastie's version, O'Hara's 2018 production also cross-gender cast the lead role: Zenzi Williams, an African American female performer, played the English King. In her *New York Times* review, Soloski praised O'Hara for this "canny move that makes us ask some useful questions about whom we expect to see leading an army and rocking a crown." Unlike Cavendish's praise for Terry's gendered "neutral stance" as a female cast as a Henry operating within "a man's world," Soloski found O'Hara's production's indeterminacy regarding Henry's place within a gender binary problematic: "It's unclear whether she's playing the part as male or female. It's extraneous, too. Gender doesn't seem to matter to this production."

Given *Henry V*'s concentration on male characters' exploits and its linguistically male preferences, it is hard to imagine a production in which "Gender doesn't seem to matter." The fact that the play's central conflict is ignited in response to the imposition of a patriarchal law and after a lengthy discussion of gender-based entitlements further evinces the importance of gender to Shakespeare's rendition of England's conquest of France. As the Bishop of Canterbury tells the King in Act One, Scene Two, in order to deny Henry V's claim to the French throne, the French court has invoked the Salic law that declares, "No woman shall succeed in Salic land" (1.2.43). Canterbury first argues that this law has been arbitrarily applied to Henry: previous French kings "all appear / To hold in right and title of the female. / So do the kings of France unto this day, / Howbeit they would hold up this Salic law / To bar your Highness claiming from the female" (1.2.93–97). The Bishop's exposure of the current French rulers' hypocrisy is not what convinces the English King to take action. Henry's immediate response to the Bishop, "May I with right and conscience make this claim?" (1.2.101), indicates he needs further justification than the arguably unjust application of a secular law to a non-French king to validate his "claiming from the female" a prerogative of power over France. Canterbury's response to the King's query further emphasizes the import of gender to the play's central conflict. The Bishop invokes non-secular law to provide Henry with the "right" he seeks: "For in the Book of Numbers is it writ / 'When the man dies [and hath no son], let the inheritance / Descend unto the daughter'" (1.2.103–05).[6] The biblical positioning of "the daughter" as a conduit of her father's property if there is no son provides Henry with the religious "right" he needs. The Bishop then invokes Henry's male lineage to provide the King with the "conscience" he desires to "make this claim": "Look back into your mighty ancestors. / Go, my dread lord, to your great-grandsire's tomb, / From whom you claim; invoke his warlike spirit, / And your great-uncle's" (1.2.107–10). Canterbury's recourse to the King's "great-grandsire" and "great-uncle" for validation is reiterated by the Bishop of Ely, who impresses upon the King that his claim to the French crown is warranted by his patrilineal inheritance of traits imagined as naturally male: "You are their heir, you sit upon their throne, / The blood and courage that renownèd them, / Runs in your veins" (1.2.122–24). The King's uncle Exeter reiterates the Bishop's "blood"-based point: "Your brother kings and monarch of the Earth / Do all expect that you should rouse yourself / As did the former lions of your blood" (1.2.127–29). According to the bishops and the King's uncle, "courage" and a "war-like spirit" are fundamental characteristics passed through and among men. A "daughter" may be the channel for "the inheritance" of "the man" left without a male heir, and thereby provide Henry with a "right" to land originally belonging to a "man," but, the imagined as innately masculine "conscience" Henry seeks to legitimize his authority over France is to be found in the "blood" that runs through the "veins" of his "brother kings" and other male relations. It is only after hearing the claims concerning his inherited patrilineal privileges that Henry becomes "well resolved" that "France" is "ours" to "bend" to "our awe / Or break" (1.2.230–33). In this opening scene, the play establishes that while Henry may have a biblically defensible "right" to breach the Salic law that would bar him from "claiming from the female," it is more important that he is the "heir" of men. This exposition scene's discussion of matrilineal claims to property and patrilineal claims to manly power confirms that gender is a determining factor in the play's dramatic conflict. Thus, even if Soloski correctly identifies O'Hara's production as striving to make gender "seem" irrelevant, it remains at the root of the "matter" of the play.

The role of gender in *Henry V* was forefront on my mind when I was invited in November 2018 by director Jennifer Pennington to serve as dramaturg for an all-female production of the play for the Spring 2019 Young American Shakespeare Festival at the Commonwealth Theater Center (CTC) in Louisville, Kentucky. Pennington's initial impetus for an all-female *Henry V* was a desire to offer more Shakespearean performance opportunities for her female-identifying Conservatory students at the CTC. Founded in 2015 as a merger of Walden Theater (established 1976) and the Blue Apple Players (established 1976), the TCG-affiliated CTC annually provides practical training, performance opportunities, and productions for roughly 50,000 youth and 5,000 adults. Operating under the umbrella of the CTC, the Walden Theater Conservatory trains emerging theater artists through classes and productions of classic and contemporary plays. The CTC's Young American Shakespeare Festival, which is the nation's longest-running Shakespeare festival for youth, is fundamental to the Conservatory students' training. Cast in one of three Shakespeare productions or adaptations that run for two weeks in May, the Festival annually provides Conservatory students with

Shakespearean production experience. The CTC routinely practices cross-gender casting in order to afford more female students parts in plays initially written for Shakespeare's all-male company; however, the CTC had not yet attempted to produce an all-female *Henry V.* Artistic Director Charlie Sexton enthusiastically embraced Pennington's casting proposal as an exciting challenge for the company and an innovative approach to the play.[7]

In our pre-production meetings, Pennington and I discussed a number of questions raised by her proposed casting of twenty young women in a play dominated by male characters. For instance, why should Shakespeare's rendition of Henry V's story, which is populated with men fighting a war over prerogatives then forbidden to women, be told through the voices of female-identifying performers to our American target audience? How might an Elizabethan drama depicting an English medieval king "claiming from the female" (1.2.97) a right to land initially held by a man and characterizing power as a male birthright be reclaimed to champion women's rights in this #MeToo moment, when women are hash-tagging out sexual harassment while having their right to choose stripped away? How might the performers' legibly female forms inform the patriarchal conceptions of gender circulated in the text and in our dominant culture? How might a play written for an all-male company that has a male protagonist, no lead female role among its over 45 individualized parts, and a scant four supporting female characters be performed by a company of twenty young women? Our answers to these questions led to production choices that punctuated the ways in which socially-prescribed gender designations regulate the characters' lives, as well as Americans' daily lives. Primary among these was a bookended, multimedia framing device and a cross-gender and multi-cast Henry. The following description of these choices is offered not as a prescription for future productions seeking to resolve the play's patriarchal imperatives, which may be irresolvable and more productively engaged with dialectically. Rather, these strategies are discussed to open pathways for scholars and practitioners interested in pursuing the dramaturgically important matter of the female gender to the world of *Henry V.*

"Chorus to This History" (Henry V, *1.P.33*)

During our first conversation about the production, Pennington and I probed the possible resonance of war for our young actors. Born after 9/11, our cast had not experienced life untouched by the threat of terroristic attacks or encountered a world inaccessible over the internet. The omnipresence of iPhones ensured that our actors were routinely inundated with images of violence enacted at home and abroad. We wondered how these young women respond to the constant projection on small screens of video and still images of women under siege overseas and on our shores. This conversation ultimately led to what became the production's framing device, with which we opened and closed our staging of Shakespeare's rendition of a received history. The play's first Chorus and concluding Epilogue uses direct address to bridge the space between the audience and "this unworthy scaffold" (1.P.11), and the time between the spectators' lives and those of these "two mighty monarchies" (1.P.21). Similarly, our bookended frame was delivered to the audience in order to contextualize "this history" (1.P.33) and "work" upon the spectators' "imaginary forces" (1.P.21). While layered on top of and in keeping with the meta-theatrics of the play's Chorus, our frame departed from Shakespeare's text in significant ways: it provided a contemporary context; it was in multiple visual and aural mediums; and it was performed by a large, multi-generational group of female-identifying performers.

Performed on a bare, thrust stage equipped with two platforms and a scrim backdrop, this *Henry V* started with the entrance from offstage right of a single young woman (Beatrice Friesen) dressed in the typical teenage uniform of jeans, a khaki green T-shirt and sneakers. She entered engaged in an activity ubiquitous among her generation walking while staring at a cell phone screen. The audio-visual material emanating from her device was projected onto the scrim and played over the theater's speakers, situating the audience within her subjectivity. The actor and spectators were exposed to an image of women and children in a prison camp accompanied by the sounds of machine gun fire and a news report about the war in Afghanistan.[8] As the performer dropped to her knees center stage, similarly dressed young women engaged in the same activity entered the space from the wings and the house, first two at a time, then three, and so on. Linked by their casual attire and cellphone use, but oblivious to each other or the audience, the actors stood or sat around the playing area, absorbed by the images and sounds springing from their handheld devices. Dispersed around the bare set, they stayed disconnected from each other while sharing the same space and induced by the same media. The scrim behind the performers displayed the montage of photographs flickering before the actors' eyes on their cell phone screens, and the rapidly overlapping audio clips arising from their phones rang throughout the theater. Like the performers, the spectators were inundated with such images as women and children fleeing violence in modern-day Syria; female soldiers in South Vietnam; Japanese rape victims in a World War II camp; and present-day migrants seeking refuge at the Greek-Macedonia border. The sounds cascading around actors and spectators alike included archival reportage from the Vietnam War, current reportage on the Syrian War, and the pro-life sound bites of prominent Republican politicians

As Dan Rather's commentary on President Trump's response to a chemical attack in Syria played over-head, the actors looked up from their miniature screens and took a collective, audible breath in. Still oblivious to anyone else and still either seated or standing, they turned their backs to the audience and faced the scrim, which now featured a photograph of protesters at a #MeToo rally holding signs pronouncing the legitimacy of female voices. The sounds swirled as the flashing stills landed on that of an African American woman at a Black Lives Matter rally with white tape across her mouth, upon which was written Eric Garner's final words, "I can't breathe!" The first actor to enter the space, who had remained on her knees center stage, faced front, dropped her head backwards and, invoking Helene Weigel's iconic silent scream from Brecht's production of *Mother Courage and Her Children*,[9] issued forth a voiceless cry. Recognizing this noiseless burst of anguish, the ensemble immediately became aware of the silent screamer and each other (Fig. 1). Theatricalizing the lifting up of women's voices, those standing extended a hand to help raise those still seated on the stage floor. The now uplifted group faced each other to collectively sing the Wyrd Sisters' folk ballad, "Warrior" (1996).[10]

The Wyrd Sisters' "Warrior" song was chosen and arranged by Sarah Hoeppner, Artistic Director of Nevertheless Arts Ensemble, a Louisville-based, all-female arts collective with whom we partnered to create the framing device.[11] Lyrically, the "Warrior" song traces a journey from youthful apathy to adult acceptance of responsibility; thus, it has parallels to the protagonist's journey from the rambunctious Prince Hal to the conquering King Henry V. The song's protagonist, though, is neither male nor an invader; rather, it is an older woman reflecting upon the "shy and lonely girl" and the "lost and angry youth" she once was. The singing subject reflects on her younger iterations' failure to act in response to "the echoes of her cries." The song initially equates inaction with the female gender: "I cannot fight / I cannot a warrior be / It's not my nature nor my teaching / It is the womanhood in me." Towards the song's conclusion, the "now" "older woman" vows she will "a fierce warrior be / 'til not another woman dies." Correcting the characterization of passivity as an essential trait of "womanhood," the song attributes the newfound realization that "I can and will fight" to "nature," "duty," "womanhood," and "sisterhood." Embodying the "shy and lonely girl" of the song's first stanza, our young female company sang facing each other until the first chorus's line, "I cannot fight," at which point the actors shame-facedly turned towards the audience, inviting them to correct the lyrical attribution

Fig. 1: A silent scream heard by the ensemble in the Commonwealth Theater Center's production of *Henry V* (courtesy of Commonwealth Theater Center, by Crystal Ludwick Photography)

of inaction to an imagined-as-innate "womanhood in me." As they sang the next verse from the perspective of the "lost and angry youth," Nevertheless Arts Ensemble members appeared on stage in long, colorful skirts and tops (Fig. 2). The Nevertheless collective vocally joined in with the more casually-clad younger performers as the song shifted perspective to that of the "older woman now." The two groups were visually distinguishable, with the jeans and khaki tees of the teenage CTC cast in stark contrast to the flowing skirts and blouses of the adult Nevertheless singers. Their harmonic vocalization of the song's coming-of-age and coming-to-resistance story connected the cross-generational groups. Fulfilling the lyrics' promise that in time a "young girl" "can and will a warrior be," the harmony situated the older singers as projections of what the younger performers could become. At the song's conclusion, the Nevertheless ensemble left the stage and the CTC cast launched into the first act Chorus of the play. Starting the dramatic narrative at the Nevertheless singers' exit suggested that the anticipated maturation process would begin with the young women collectively re "claiming from the female" (1.1.97) the identity of "warrior" repeatedly denied to women and assigned to men in such canonized texts as Shakespeare's *Henry V.*

Fig. 2: The Commonwealth Theater Center actors performing with the Nevertheless Arts Ensemble (courtesy of Commonwealth Theater Center, by Crystal Ludwick Photography)

Forsaking the Epilogue, and along with it a concluding focus on the male "author" (5.E.2) and the succeeding Henry VI, our staging of Shakespeare's play ended with an emphasis on two marginalized female characters: the Queen of France, who only appears in the final scene; and her daughter Katherine, who at the conclusion is the "first" "article" "granted" by the French King to the newly-minted "Henry Le Roi" (5.2.344–45; 351). At the end of Act Five, Scene Two, the male characters filed out through the house in preparation for the royal wedding, leaving behind Katherine and her mother to create a tableau that pronounced the agency denied to the Princess in the matrimonial negotiations. Seated diagonally and facing upstage right, Katherine (Lilly Stanley) looked anxiously at the standing Queen (Ruby Osborne) facing her. The Queen tentatively offered a hand, echoing the lifting gesture extended to the seated CTC cast members in the opening sequence. Despite the urge to assist her daughter, the Queen withdrew her outstretched hand, motioned with her head for her daughter to follow, and left the stage to join the male characters. Only Katherine remained on stage, muted by her assigned role in the historical record, but not yet ready to cross over the threshold of an arranged marriage necessary to unite "the contending kingdoms" (5.2.361).

The abandoned Katherine stayed diagonally seated at this crossroad as the CTC and the Nevertheless ensembles slowly re-entered from the wings and house and sat or stood facing the Princess. Transitioning away from Shakespeare's script and back to the contemporary frame, the young performer playing Katherine dropped her royal role and returned to her offstage persona. She began to tell the onstage, all-female audience facing her about a #MeToo moment she had at age thirteen. Other performers in the united ensembles began sharing similar experiences, creating a cacophony akin to the barrage of violent sounds and images with which the show opened. The vivid accounts reverberated off each other, and the resounding effect recalled the "echo of her cries" refrain from the opening sequence's rendition of "Warrior." The swirling stories gave way to their collective recitation, now for the offstage audience, of Teresa Willis's poem "Unbreakable Heart." The poem then bled into an acoustic performance of Catherine Dalton's Celtic-flavored song, "She Rises" (2012).[12] Willis's poem's insistence that "our voices rise" was complemented by Dalton's lyrical assertion that "She rises up" and "she'll rise again." The theater went dark after the unified, multi-generational company sang Dalton's final line announcing that she "lights the fire within." Thus, when the lights came back up for the CTC cast and Nevertheless singers' shared bow, it seemed as if they were lit by the performers' "fire."

This bookended, multi-modal framing device drew an analogy between the play's depiction of the Hundred Years War and the military and cultural battles fought today. In an interview with local NPR reporter Ashlie Stevens, Pennington pronounced the parallels drawn between the battles fought in *Henry V* and those invoked in the frame: "There's a lot of war against women right now, okay? Literally and figuratively and metaphorically [. . .]. And this play, *Henry V*, is very masculine, like hyper-masculine, ultra-theatrical telling of a story of war. And specifically men at war." By the end of their staging of the play, the CTC company had collectively appropriated Shakespeare's "hyper-masculine, ultra-theatrical telling" of Henry's successes in France. Opening and closing this chapter of history with the cast confronting today's struggles re-impressed the relevance of Shakespeare's text to our present moment, when there is, among other conflicts, wars being waged here and abroad against women.

The framing device's emphasis on the use of an all-female cast furthered the deconstructive pressure effected by their performance of roles Shakespeare conceived of as male and wrote for the Lord Chamberlain's Men. The twenty female-identifying CTC performers' occupation of these "hyper-masculine" parts revealed that "masculine," like feminine, is "theatrical." It is a construct reliant upon the repeated performance of gendered actions and the circulation of narratives that, like *Henry V,* essentialize a patriarchal binary.[13] Challenging the play's claim that the King's "warlike spirit" is an innate male trait that only courses through the "veins" of men (1.2.107; .124), the legibly female actors played the male characters without adopting stereotypical "masculine" postures or lowered voices. They played the Shakespearean text and the contemporary text within the bookended frame in their socially-assigned roles as young women, which they play daily. In their designated-female forms, they embodied Shakespeare's "hyper-masculine" history, re- "claiming from the female" (1.2.97) the privileges, characteristics, leading parts, and heroic narratives often imagined as only available to men. Performed by an all-female cast within a frame addressing modern-day issues, *Henry V* was situated as a Shakespearean-play-within-a-play, with the early modern historical drama serving not as an endorsement or critique of an idealized monarch or as an ambivalent representation of war. Instead, *Henry V* was an onstage rehearsal for the warrior that the signifiably female performers, and members of all genders, are equally capable of becoming.

"She Is So Idly Kinged" (Henry V, 2.4.27)

The frame established that this production of Shakespeare's *Henry V* would be collectively devised by a group, lending a collaborative spirit to the proceedings. This communal storytelling suffused each of the play's five Prologues, which were delivered by the ensemble in unison and with assigned lines. All of the casting choices were likewise informed by this collaborative approach, as was most evident by the use of five different performers (Cicely Warren, Lilly Stanley, Zoë Peterson, Brooklyn Durs, and Shannon Austin-Goodin) to represent the King, with one actor playing Henry for the entirety of each act. The ensemble-based Prologues were staged such that it seemed as if the company elected a Henry per act by selecting their leader from within. Each Prologue's first reference to Henry became an opportunity for either the company to elect a ruler, or for the current actor playing the King to put forward a potential successor whose title might then be vocally conferred by the Chorus. Once confirmed as the monarch, the selected cast member received a red armband with gold stripes to indicate their new title. For instance, when the Act One Chorus says, "Then should the warlike Harry" (1.P.5), the ensemble repeated, "Harry?" three times before the group thrust forward its collectively agreed upon ruler (Cicely Warren). After this chosen Harry eagerly took the proffered red-and-gold armband, the Chorus repeated the phrase, "Then should the warlike Harry" to cement her occupation of the role. The selection of successive Harrys emphasized the import of collective action in the fight for women's rights in our historical moment. Pennington pointed towards this goal in the program's director's note, which informed the audience that, "instead of having a typical hero," the all-female cast would be "holding each other up" and would "lead together."

Pronouncing the selection of a ruler per act and spreading the King's complicated political machinations among the cast also countered the play's naturalization of power as a patrilineal birthright handed down through "blood" and God from one male "heir" to another (1.2.122–24). The swapping out of kings each act required other court and non-court roles to likewise be traded among multiple actors; thus, in this staging, leadership was granted by a populace of all social ranks that then shared in the responsibilities of governance. The cast distinguished through performance the various characters they played and, when necessary to clarify a character's identity, we added an appellation to the text; however, no attempt was made to disguise the fact that the same character was played by different actors. The resulting casting tracks created dialectical exchanges between roles. For instance, the Act Two Henry (Lilly Stanley) also played an English soldier in Act Four and Katherine in Act Five, which added weight to Katherine's silence after she is betrothed in Shakespeare's play's conclusion. The performer playing Katherine at the finale had experienced the throes of power in Act Two, during which King Henry condemns to death the Earl of Cambridge, Lord Scroop, and Sir Thomas Grey for their "conspiracy" with France (2.P.27); and she had fought alongside Henry in Act Four. Thus, this French Princess knew what it was to hold the English seat of power, and what it meant to be beholden to it.

The passing of power between performers in the Prologue to each act also allowed for critical commentary on war and provoked questions concerning complicity. A reluctant Henry was selected in Act Three when a performer (Zoë Peterson) begrudging took the proffered armband tossed to her after no one responded to the Chorus's call for a King with the repeated phrase, "Tells Harry" (3.1.31). The actor's reticence was rooted in the violence exerted in Act Three, the first scene of which finds King Henry leading his soldiers "Once more unto the breach" (3.1.1). Cruelty hovers in the air in the Act's post-battle scenes, as when Henry threatens the Governor of Harfleur to surrender, lest Henry give "the fleshed soldier" "liberty" to "range / With conscience wide as hell, mowing like grass/Your fresh virgins and your flow'ring infants" (3.11–14). After conquering Harfleur and condemning the English soldier Bardolph to death, the performer playing King Henry was eager to relinquish the throne. During the Act Four Chorus, the third Act Henry handed off the part on the line, "O now, who will behold / The royal captain of this ruined band" (4.P.29–30). The "royal captain" Henry role was then given to a performer (Brooklyn Durs) strewn on the stage among the "poor condemnèd English soldiers" referenced in the Prologue (4.P.23). In this exchange of authority, the former Henry gently bent the chosen soldier's forehead to her own in a gesture of anointment and of contrition for all the slain, including Bardolph (Fig. 3). That the crown was now taken up by an actor formerly playing a soldier added another layer to the Act Four King's disguise as "Harry le Roy" (4.1.50). This was especially pronounced when, in a debate with the weary combatants in camp, the once soldier, now-monarch-disguised-as-a-soldier abdicated responsibility for the lives lost in war: "The King is not bound to answer the particular endings of his soldiers" (4.1.161). The fact that the actor playing this King was moments earlier laying among the "poor condemnèd English soldiers," and could be returned to that status in the next Act, suggested that a ruler may be "bound" to the "endings" met by those under their command.

Fig. 3: An exchange of authority between two actors (Brooklyn Durs and Zoë Peterson) playing King Henry in the Commonwealth Theater Center's production (courtesy of Commonwealth Theater Center, by Crystal Ludwick Photography)

The presence of legibly-female figures in the role of King Henry V heightened the play's patriarchal imperatives, and at times created a dissonance that troubled gendered terms in the dialogue resonant today. We made no effort to soften the play's more patriarchal rhetoric since, as Pennington explained to Ashlie Stevens, there was a "punch" created by "hearing some of these lines that are so awful, some of them, so misogynistic . . . hearing them come out of the mouths of these young ladies." Such blows were felt when the Act Five Henry (Shannon Austin-Goodin) objectified Katherine by calling her "our capital demand" (5.6.98). Hearing the actress refer to Katherine as a thing to be "demand[ed]" in an exchange of "capital" suggested how women can participate in the commodification of women. In other instances, the visibility of a woman as the monarch pronounced the ways in which the play presumes power and daring are innately male. For example, the effeminizing tennis balls sent by the Dauphin in Act One, Scene One were gifted to a visibly female King Henry (Cicely Warren). The performers' gender returned the gambit's volley by revealing that bravery is not determined by the possession of balls. Having a legibly-female performer deliver lines positioning "man" as a universal subject had a distancing effect, as when the Act Four Henry-as-Harry le Roy (Brooklyn Durs) told the soldiers, "I think the King is but a man as I am" (4.1.105–06). In this moment, the performer's legible gender rubbed against the line's assumption that "man" signifies all "humans."

While the "multiple roles" the King performs may be "commonplace" among criticism on the play (Hedrick and Reynolds 171), it is uncommon for a production of *Henry V* to showcase such multiplicity by having even more than one actor represent Henry. Casting five different performers in the role pointed towards what some critics have identified as the text's interest in the performative qualities of an authoritative figure, whose control is consolidated through the repeated display of power for viewers, and thus reliant upon audiences to be maintained.[14] Having five members of an all-female cast enact the role of Henry V pronounced the import of gender to this play's representation of monarchical power, and problematized its patriarchal preconceptions. The presence of multiple female-identifying performers in a title role written for a member of the Lord Chamberlain's Men yielded a canonized Shakespearean part traditionally restricted to men to new voices. The young women's reclamation of a dramatic narrative whose conflict is launched by the denial of a leader's legitimacy because of a decree that "no female / Should" rule (1.2.55–56) created a multiplicity of meanings that challenged gender constructions circulating in the text and reverberating in our post-2016 political climate.

"Our Bending Author Hath Pursued the Story" (Henry V, 5.E.2)

Our production's frame and casting intended to pressurize the gender politics of Shakespeare's play and of our historical moment. In our efforts to interrogate the role of gender in *Henry V*, we made choices one might consider radical departures from Shakespeare's text. One could argue, however, that our use of gender-specific casting and a framing device to impress the import of the play to a target audience was in keeping with the conditions in which *Henry V* was initially produced by the Lord Chamberlain's Men. We cannot know for certain how the gendered identities of the all-male company impacted the text's conceptions of masculinity. Likewise, we cannot determine how the Elizabethan audience would have responded to the Chorus's comparison of Henry to the Earl of Essex, "the general of our gracious empress" (5.P.31), who in 1599 was commanding English troops in Ireland (Gurr 1; Taylor 4). Nevertheless, the first quarto (1600) title-page's pronouncement that the play was performed by the Lord Chamberlain's Men suggests that the company's socially-prescribed identities as a collection of male servants of a court figure had the potential to legitimize the text's historical narrative.[15] Similarly, the Chorus's reference to Essex's anticipated return "from Ireland" (5.P.32) indicates an awareness of the offstage conflicts on the minds of the Elizabethan spectators, and an interest in drawing parallels between their historical moment and that which was unfolding on stage. We, too, had a cast whose socially-assigned identities helped legitimize the story we sought to tell, and who told that story partly by making direct references to offstage struggles identifiable to their immediate audience.

The story our *Henry V* production sought to tell through its multi-media frame and cross-gender, multi-casting was shaped by the cultural moment in which it was produced. Similarly, Shakespeare's chronicle of King Henry's conquest of France was informed by its time and place. Offstage cultural shifts are among the contingencies of live performance that impact onstage meaning. When we started rehearsal, in Spring 2019, we could not have foreseen that the run of our all-female *Henry V* (May 10–19, 2019) would coincide with Georgia Governor Brian Kemp's passage of a "fetal heartbeat" law restricting a woman's right to choose (May 7, 2019), and with Alabama Governor Kay Ivey's passage of a law banning most abortions (May 15, 2019).[16] These legislative acts enhanced the production's parallels between the play's war in France and that waging against women on our shores. The links audiences drew between these offstage battles and those on stage were evidenced by *Arts-Louisville* reviewer Keith Waits' comment that the production's framing of the play's "war as a metaphor for the War on Women many claim to be happening in the United States right now [. . .]. is a difficult point to argue against, especially on the day that Alabama's Governor signed the most restrictive anti-abortion legislation ever written."

In Waits' estimation, the CTC production's "radical" casting, opening establishment of "a community of women telling the story," and "stunning, evocative ending" was exemplary of how innovative approaches to Shakespeare can have "the power to enlighten." The production sought to stage Shakespeare's early modern English chronicle of Henry V's conquest of medieval France for a postmodern American stage grappling with, among other issues, gender inequality. With an overt political agenda, we "pursued the story" of Shakespeare's King Henry (5.E.2). This pursuit demonstrated that Shakespeare works are not static. As the Epilogue states, they were penned by a "bending author" (5.E.2). The flexible play has withstood a myriad of scholarly and artistic interpretations, some of which have sought to prove the text's state-solidifying function, some its subversive potential, and some its ambiguity. The CTC production joined these ranks, but with important exceptions. It illustrated a way one might reclaim for women their pivotal role in the dramaturgy of Shakespeare's *Henry V*; claim for them the right to a historical narrative that has been traditionally restricted to men; and encourage them to retell the "bending author['s]" history in a way that chronicles the times in which they live.

Notes

1 While the first quarto was published in 1600, scholars generally agree that the play was composed for the Lord Chamberlain's Men in 1599, towards the end of Elizabeth I's reign. In their respective introductions to the play, Andrew Gurr (1) and Gary Taylor (4) both refer to the fifth Act Chorus's reference to the Essex campaign in Ireland to fix the composition date to the summer of 1599. In "Invisible bullets: Renaissance authority and its subversion, *Henry IV* and *Henry V*," Stephen Greenblatt compares the overt theatricality of *Henry V* to that employed by Elizabeth I to consolidate her power (44–45). Like the play's audience, Elizabethan subjects were "powerfully engaged" by the Queen's "visible presence while at the same time held at a certain respectful distance from it" so as to occlude their role in conferring power onto the monarch (44). Leonard Tennenhouse likewise argues that *Henry V* serves to consolidate the authority of the Elizabethan state in "Strategies of State and political plays: *A Midsummer Night's Dream*, *Henry IV*, *Henry V*, and *Henry VIII*." Tennenhouse asserts that Henry V's use of "strategies of disguise and inversion to occupy a range of positions" centralizes the authority of the monarch, who is represented as "virtually everywhere" (122). In Tennenhouse's estimation, Henry's ability to occupy so many localities within the body politic is a form of containment: the King strips the social identities he embodies of their "autonomy but he

gives them their ideal identity. In other words, he instates a political hierarchy by practicing forms of inversion" (123).

2 Jonathon Dollimore and Alan Sinfield's "History and ideology: the instance of *Henry V*" uses the example of Shakespeare's text to disclose how Elizabethan state institutions did not necessarily achieve ideological coherency. They write, "even in this play, which is often assumed to be the one where Shakespeare is closest to state propaganda, the construction of ideology is complex—even as it consolidates, it betrays inherent instability" (211). Donald Hedrick and Bryan Reynolds suggest in "'A Little Touch of Harry in the Night': Translucency and Projective Transversality in the Sexual and National Politics of *Henry V*" that the play has an overtly subversive effect. Analyzing the play's employment of what they term the "principle of translucency," which they define as "a mechanism [. . .] by which one signifier or identity is incompletely concealed within another, a disguise apparently flawed or inadequate, producing a particular kind of mixed coding for audiences or spectators" (171), they come to the conclusion that Henry's occupation of multiple subject positions serves to rupture the ideological parameters consolidating Elizabethan subjectivity.

3 Norman Rabkin proposed in "Either/Or: Responding to *Henry V*" that the "ultimate power" of *Henry V* is its ambiguous representation of the titular character, which provokes opposing interpretations of the King as either an exemplary or a cynically Machiavellian monarch (35–36). In his Preface to his edition of *Henry V*, Gurr attributes the play's "ambivalence" about the King to "the ideology of its day" (xi). Claire McEachern identifies the "ambivalent practice and effect" of *Henry V* as "critical commonplace" (292) in "*Henry V* and the Paradox of the Body Politic." Rather than locate this indecisiveness in the protagonist's personality, McEachern focuses on the play's participation in "a particular Elizabethan political affect—that of corporate identity" (293). McEachern concludes that the uncertainty "is an ambivalence fundamental not to his personality but to a fantasy of social union which employs the tropes of personhood as a means to its realization" (314).

4 Emma Smith's Introduction to *Henry V* praises Olivier's 1944 film "as the most remembered and probably the most influential single production of the play" (50). Smith also lauds Kahn's 1969 production as "The most important American production" of *Henry V* (64). In his 1969 *New York Times* review, Mel Gussow offered less effusive praise for Kahn's production. Declaring *Henry V* "a patriotic hymn to Great Britain" whose nationalism accounted for the "timeless but also timely" success of Olivier's film, Gussow found Kahn's "antiwar" staging "heretical, but also tantalizing" (43). In addition to Smith's Introduction, a stage and screen production history of *Henry V* can be found in Gurr's Introduction to the play (37–55); and John Russell Brown's "'*Henry V*' on *Stage and Screen*."

5 Both McEachern and Hedrick and Reynolds find subversive potential in their respective readings of Katherine. Focusing on the Katherine and Alice French scene, McEachern notes that the Princess's "titillating recitation is indeed a male-authored ventriloquist fantasy of female eroticism, but she also performs what patriarchy most fears" (313). Hedrick and Reynolds argue that the "linguistic instability" produced by Katherine's "bad English" and Henry's "bad French" undermines the coercive possibilities of language (179). Unlike these critics, Karen Newman concludes in *Fashioning Femininity and English Renaissance Drama* that these two scenes re-solidify a patriarchal structure and an English national identity. Newman argues that

the bawdy scene with Alice, which "powerfully represents Katherine's linguistic dis-
advantage" (101), also serves to subscribe "women discursively to the sexual sphere"
(102). Newman determines that in the wooing scene, which she locates within "a
long tradition [...] that conflates courtship and pedagogy" (103), Henry schools
Katherine so as to erase her cultural difference, thereby "refashioning the other as
the same" (104).

6 As Taylor (104) and Gurr (80) note in their respective editorial note accompanying
the Bishop's line, the cited passage specifies that "the daughter" inherits if the man
is without a son. Q1 (1600) replaces "the man" with "the son" to clarify the point.

7 Further information about the Commonwealth Theatre Center can be found at
www.commonwealththeatre.org.

8 Our designers were crucial to the production's success. The set and projections
were designed by Gerald Kean. Jacob Richie constructed the set and designed the
lights. Sound design was by Kathy Preher-Reynolds. Lindsay Chamberlain and Jill
Schierbaum created the ensemble's red (English) and blue (French) armbands and
uniform of jeans, sneakers, and khaki t-shirts.

9 Weigel's silent scream was likewise a response to a still image of a women during wartime. In "The Mother Courage Model," Brecht attributes the inspiration for Weigel's
"unscreaming open mouth and backward-bent head" to "a press photograph"
Weigel encountered "years before" his production that featured "an Indian woman
crouched over the body of her dead son during the shelling of Singapore" (113).

10 "Warrior" is on the Canadian trio's *Inside the Dreaming* album (1995). A 1997 live
recording can be found at www.youtube.com/watch?v=OvvVAzyH6o8.

11 Established in 2018, the Nevertheless Arts Ensemble is dedicated to creating a more
inclusive artistic canon by focusing on works by women. Further information about
the organization can be found at www.neverthelessarts.com.

12 Willis's unpublished poem was written for this production. The lyrics to Dalton's
"She Rises" (2012) can be found on her website, www.catherinedalton.net/works/
she-rises.

13 For a discussion of gender as performance, see, among other works, Judith Butler's
Gender Trouble: Feminism and the Subversion of Identity.

14 See footnotes 2 and 3.

15 The Q1 title page asserts that *Henry V* was "sundry times playd by the Right honorable the Lord Chamberlaine his Servants." A digital version of the title page can be
found at https://shakespearedocumented.folger.edu/exhibition/document/henry-
v-first-edition.

16 *The New York Times*'s coverage of Georgia's bill is available at www.nytimes.com/
2019/05/07/us/heartbeat-bill-georgia.html. Coverage of Alabama's law is available
at www.nytimes.com/2019/05/15/us/alabama-abortion-facts-law-bill.html.

Works Cited

All textual citations refer to: Folger Shakespeare Library. *Shakespeare's Plays* from Folger
Digital Texts. Edited by Barbara Mowat, Paul Werstine, Michael Poston, and
Rebecca Niles. Folger Shakespeare Library, 15 January, 2019. www.folgerdigitalte
xts.org.

Billington, Michael. "Henry V Review—Astonishing Gender-Switched Reinvigoration." Review of *Henry V*, directed by Robert Hastie. *The Guardian*, 23 Jun. 2016, www.theguardian.com/stage/2016/jun/23/henry-v-review-open-air-theater-regents-park. Accessed 20 July 2019.

Blinder, Alan. "Alabama Governor Signs Abortion Bill. Here's What Comes Next." *The New York Times*, 15 May 2019, www.nytimes.com/2019/05/15/us/alabama-abort ion-facts-law-bill.html. Accessed 29 July 2019.

Brecht, Bertolt. "The Mother Courage Model." *Mother Courage and Her Children*, edited by John Willett and Ralph Manheim, translated by John Willett, Penguin, 2007, pp. 91–135.

Brown, John Russell. " 'Henry V' on Stage and Screen." *The Life of Henry V*, edited by John Russell Brown, Signet, 1988, pp. 249–66.

Butler, Judith. *Gender Trouble: Feminism and the Subversion of Identity*. Routledge, 1990.

Cavendish, Dominic. "This Female Henry V Cuts to the Heart of Warfare's Horror—Review." Review of *Henry V*, directed by Robert Hastie. *The Telegraph*, 23 June 2016, www.telegraph.co.uk/theater/what-to-see/this-female-henry-v-cuts-to-the-heart-of-warfares-horror---revie/. Accessed 20 July 2019.

Commonwealth Theater Center. 2017, www.commonwealththeater.org. Accessed 21 July 2019.

Dalton, Catherine. "She Rises." *Catherine Dalton*, 2015, http://www.catherinedalton. net/works/she-rises. Accessed 26 July 2019.

Dollimore, Jonathon, and Alan Sinfield. "History and Ideology: The Instance of *Henry V*." *Alternative Shakespeares*, edited by John Drakakis, Routledge, 1985, pp. 206–27.

Greenblatt, Stephen. "Invisible Bullets: Renaissance Authority and Its Subversion, *Henry IV* and *Henry V*." *Political Shakespeare: New Essays in Cultural Materialism*, edited by Jonathon Dollimore and Alan Sinfield, Cornell UP, 1985, pp. 18–47.

Gurr, Andrew, editor. *King Henry V*. Cambridge UP, 1992.

———. "Introduction." *King Henry V*, edited by Andrew Gurr, Cambridge UP, 1992, pp. 1–64.

———. "Preface." *King Henry V*, edited by Andrew Gurr, Cambridge UP, 1992, pp. x–xi.

Gussow, Mel. "Stage: Antiwar 'Henry V'." Review of *Henry V*, directed by Michael Kahn. *The New York Times*, 11 Nov. 1969, L 43, www.nytimes.com/1969/11/11/ archives/stage-antiwar-henry-v-michael-kahn-directs-brechtian-production.html. Accessed 20 July 2019.

Hedrick, Donald, and Bryan Reynolds. " 'A Little Touch of Harry in the Night': Translucency and Projective Transversality in the Sexual and National Politics of *Henry V*." *Performing Transversally: Reimagining Shakespeare and the Critical Future*, edited by Bryan Reynolds, Palgrave Macmillan, 2003, pp. 171–88.

Henry V: A Concordance to the Text of the First Folio. Oxford UP, 1971. Oxford Shakespeare Concordances. edited by T.H. Howard-Hill.

"Henry V, first edition." *Shakespeare Documented*, Folger Shakespeare Library, https:// shakespearedocumented.folger.edu/exhibition/document/henry-v-first-edition. Accessed July 29, 2019.

Mazzei, Patricia, and Alan Blinder. "Georgia Governor Signs 'Fetal Heartbeat' Abortion Law." *The New York Times*, 7 May 2019, www.nytimes.com/2019/05/07/us/heartbeat-bill-georgia.html. Accessed 29 July 2019.

McEachern, Claire. "*Henry V* and the Paradox of the Body Politic." *Materialist Shakespeare: A History*, edited by Ivo Kamps, Verso, 1995, pp. 292–319.

Nevertheless Arts Ensemble, www.neverthelessarts.com. Accessed 26 July 2019. Sarah Hoeppner Tonini, Artistic Director.

Newman, Karen. *Fashioning Femininity and English Renaissance Drama*. University of Chicago Press, 1991.

Pennington, Jennifer. "Notes on the Productions: *Henry V.*" *Commonwealth Theater Center's Young American Shakespeare Festival Program*, CTC, 2019.

———. director. *Henry V.* Commonwealth Theater Center, 10–19 May 2019, Louisville, KY. Performance.

Rabkin, Norman. "Either/Or: Responding to *Henry V.*" *William Shakespeare's Henry V*, edited by Harold Bloom, Chelsea, 1988, pp. 35–59. Modern Critical Interpretations.

Smith, Emma. Introduction. *King Henry V*, edited by Emma Smith, Cambridge UP, 2002, pp. 1–79. Shakespeare in Production.

Soloski, Alexis. "Review: Does Power Corrupt in 'Henry V'? Absolutely." Review of *Henry V*, directed by Robert O'Hara. *The New York Times*, 13 May 2018

Stevens, Ashlie. "Commonwealth Theater Reinterprets 'Henry V' With All-Female Cast." *89.3 WFPL*, 8 May 2019, https://wfpl.org/commonwealth-theater-reinterprets-henry-v-with-all-female-cast/. Accessed 26 July 2019.

Taylor, Gary, editor. *Henry V.* Oxford UP, 1982.

———. Introduction. *Henry V*, edited by Gary Taylor, Oxford UP, 1982, pp. 1–74.

Tennenhouse, Leonard. "Strategies of State and political plays: *A Midsummer Night's Dream*, *Henry IV*, *Henry V*, and *Henry VIII*." *Political Shakespeare: New Essays in Cultural Materialism*, edited by Jonathon Dollimore and Alan Sinfield, Cornell UP, 1985, pp. 109–28.

Waits, Keith. "We Band of Sisters." *Arts-Louisville.Com*, 16 May 2019, http://arts-louisville.com/2019/05/16/we-band-of-sisters/. Accessed 29 July 2019.

Willis, Teresa. "Unbreakable Heart." Unpublished, 2019.

"The Wyrd Sisters—Warrior (live)." *YouTube*, 9 May 2013, Red River Relief Concert, Winnipeg, 1997, www.youtube.com/watch?v=OvvVAzyH6o8. Accessed 25 July 2019. The Wyrd Sisters.

4. Othello: *In the Age of Black Lives Matter and DACA*

BARON KELLY

In the age of Black Lives Matter, when unarmed Black and Brown boys and men in America are being senselessly killed by law enforcement, when the racist divisions in our country are becoming more overt, what are the different ways Shakespeare's *Othello* can resist any attempt to endorse what are labeled racist assumptions? Shakespeare wrote about characters who are socially excluded, discriminated against, alien: Caliban, Shylock, Othello, Sycorax, the witches of *Macbeth*. Also, the association of Blackness with both innate evil and natural servitude is exemplified in Aaron, the demonic Moor of Shakespeare's earliest tragedy, *Titus Andronicus*. Early in the play, the ambitious Aaron seeks to cast off his "slavish weeds and servile thoughts" (2.1.18), yet when he calls the child of his adulterous liaison with the Empress a "thick-lipped slave" (4.2.181), it is as though he instinctively recognized the baby as marked for servitude by its appearance. At the same time, wishing only to "have his soul black like his face" (3.1.208). Aaron celebrates his own color as the badge of a wickedness he shares with almost all the other Black characters of early Elizabethan drama.

When Iago, in the course of the tirade with which he opens *Othello*, snidely refers to the protagonist as "his Moorship" (1.1.35), he immediately highlights the ethnic tensions in the play. Not once in the scene do the other characters refer to Othello by name; instead he is simply "the Moor," "the thicklips," and "an extravagant and freewheeling stranger" (1.1.151).

From the perspective established in the play's first scene, what we nowadays call "race" would appear absolutely central to the tragedy of *Othello*.

Race has been among the most fiercely debated social issues of our times. Othello's blackness has come to dominate any interpretation of the play. In Shakespeare's *Othello*, Othello's race and color do not simply determine the reactions of other characters to him, they also explain his actions. In other words, Shakespeare suggests that Othello behaves as he does because he is Black. And to suggest that a person's behavior is racially determined is, by definition, racist.

In today's real world, it is easy to see how racism is alive and well in digital online comment sections. Today, the digital age is "the real world." Polls and studies that measure racism are hotly debated because most people will not acknowledge their prejudice to a stranger. The topic is so subjective and politically charged, and many people, of all races, may not recognize their own biases. In a world of racial profiling, systematic inequalities and extreme prejudice are abundant in too many people who are sworn to serve and protect. Such disrespectful treatment of people of color is simply being in the wrong place at the wrong time.

Contrast the 2017 incident in Las Vegas involving football player Michael Bennett, with recently-surfaced dash camera footage showing a Cobb County, Georgia, Officer, Lt. Greg Abbott, comforting a nervous white woman who had been pulled over, and expressed her fear. On Saturday, August 26th 2017, Seattle Seahawks football star Michael Bennett was among of group of people attending the Mayweather vs. McGregor boxing match in Las Vegas. Bennett and others began fleeing what sounded like gun shots when police officers brought him down to the ground, dug a knee into his back and threatened to blow his "f---ing head off" (Mather). Lt. Abbott, in contrast, told the terrified woman, "But you're not Black. Remember, we only kill Black people." In the wake of the furor, Abbott retired—with full benefits (Hauser and Fortin).

African American high school students, particularly in depressed urban and rural communities in America, need to understand that the same conversations about race that have been relevant for generations still apply in 2018. How do the visuals of prison bars in film director Oliver Parker's 1995 *Othello* resonate with the surveillance and criminalization of Black men and women in twentieth-century America? How do the racial tensions that accompany Othello's presence in Venice relate to the students' experiences in and out of school?

The continuing immediacy of the issue that is played to the worst fears of whites for example, black crime, or black male super-sexuality deflowering white womanhood, was made apparent by the nationwide reaction to the O.J. Simpson scandal in 1994. When the African American football star and sports broadcaster was arrested for the murder of his white wife, journalists across the country immediately drew comparisons with Othello. By providing an explanatory template for Simpson's crime, Shakespeare's tragedy even seemed to confirm the accused's guilt. Observers claimed to recognize in Simpson the symptoms of a particular jealous psychosis known as "Othello syndrome."

When issues of race, language, and culture are prominent in national conversations, the reading and writing students engage in can present both opportunities and challenges. In the age of Black Lives Matter and DACA (Deferred Action for Childhood Arrivals) teachers can use *Othello* as a basis for discussion on how race plays out in current images seen today. Othello can be used with students of color and their white counterparts as they learn to understand one another in and out of the classroom. Othello can be used for students to work through difficult perspectives as they try to understand racism today. The assumption of black violence and also Black naiveté that is played out to its logical conclusion in *Othello* haunts people of color in their own neighborhoods, still choreographs their steps, and motivates full body searches by police when they stop a car for a missing headlight. The fear of being judged less than—which we all face at different times of our lives—plays out particularly for first generation, low income students of color. These students do not understand that asking questions or even asking for help is a sign of curiosity and interest, and not of weakness.

Students spend a lot of time learning academic skills, but rarely do they talk about the emotional reactions they may have to what they read, which may address deeper themes. Students in school are pushed to become clinical crafters of arguments and masters of academic language. While these are essential skills, students appear perfectly comfortable not acknowledging and discussing emotional responses to literature. Characters are fictitious abstractions, and, without actors to bring them to life, and makeup and digital tricks to make the drama feel real, students are blocked and may strictly do the analytical work without a significant emotional response. In my opinion, this is a bad thing. An emotional response to drama and literature should be part of the curriculum.

In the right hands, the important stories, grim plots and all, can help students cope with real life. A work like *Othello* becomes a way to address the corrosive legacy of racism that continues to haunt society. The process of entering imagined worlds of fiction builds empathy and improves one's ability to take another person's point of view.

Since the number of Black teachers is declining significantly, and the population of all minorities is rising, it is important to ponder those implications for Black students. Shakespeare's Othello lives and works in a white environment. The play concerns itself with shame, humiliation, and a sense of betrayal. It is crucial for students to explore the nuances of these feelings.

Discussions can be led about the subject of social isolation, and what can happen when supportive familial, friendship, and organizational ties are not available to help one be prevented from achieving his or her goals. Students of color understand that to navigate in white environments one has to have a strong racial awareness and coping skills necessary for survival. Individuals react differently to the negative, stressful emotional impact of racism, and its resulting social isolation. Social isolation can lead to internal stress, which often manifests itself in physiological disorders even to the extent of suicide. Much of Othello's psychological cohesion is destroyed by the manipulations of Iago.

Possible prompts for students can include what are the high school courtship patterns and the insecurities on which they thrive? How do the issues of surveillance and racial tensions that accompany Othello's presence in Venice relate to their own experiences in and out of school? Are there any implications crossing boundaries between cultures, religions, and races?

Is *Othello* a racist play? To be fair to Shakespeare he did not invent the play, but he was committed to using the same plot (from the novella *Hecatmmithi*, written by Giraldi Cinthio in 1565). The play is problematic in that the assumptions contained within the short story, the conventions both literary and theatrical that Shakespeare and Cinthio used, suggest that Black people behave as they do because of their ethnicity.

It is arguable then that although Shakespeare was constrained by the original short story, in plot terms, he was liberated when he came to introducing the racist language. I know it is a mistake to attribute the views of a character to an author necessarily, but when Shakespeare had Iago say that Moors "are changeable in their wills" (1.3. 390) and then goes on to demonstrate precisely that, I think it is fair to ask if Shakespeare isn't being a bit of a bigot?

In Shakespeare's time, the popular contemporary view of Moors was given expression by John Leo, known as Leo Africanus, in his *Geographical Historie of Africa*, translated from the Italian by John Pory, and published in London in 1600: "No nation in the world is so subject unto jealousie; for they will rather losse their lives, than put up any disgrace in the behalfe of their women."

Including the character of the villainous Moor, Aaron, in *Titus Andronicus*, Shakespeare exploited the conventional view of Moors in other plays. In *The Merchant of Venice*, Portia is relieved to get rid of the Prince of Morocco and "all of his complexion" (2.7. 87). Hamlet denigrates his mother's choice when, comparing pictures of his father, he puns "Could you on this fair mountain leave to feed, and batten on this Moor? Ha, have you eyes" (3.4. 77). In *The Tempest*, the King of Naples, in the eyes of his court, has brought disaster on himself because he was foolish enough to marry his daughter to the King of Tunis, or "lose her to an African" (2.1. 133). As Virginia Mason Vaughan notes in her book *Othello: A Contextual History*, "Black skin signified in addition to visual ugliness an ingrained moral infection, a taint in the blood often linked to sexual perversion, and the desire to possess a white woman—her body, her status, her wealth, or her power" (62).

The question also arises did Shakespeare know any Black people? Could he have known any Black people? Miranda Kaufman's *Black Tudors: The Untold Story* establishes through scholarly research that in parish records there were hundreds of Black people in Elizabethan England. There was an ambassadorial visit in 1600-1 to Queen Elizabeth's court by Abd el-Ouahed ben Messaoud Anoun Mohammed and his entourage from the Barbary Coast, to discuss their common enemy, Philip II of Spain. It was in the interests of the North African states to form an alliance with Elizabeth I. So, yes, Shakespeare could have known some Black people. The question is, did he do his homework? Did he bother to get to know any Black people? If he didn't, was he being lazy? If he did get to know some Black people, and still wrote the Othello of the second half who becomes an obsessive murderous honor killer, was he being a bigot?

Students must be made aware that the Black presence in Britain has been rigorously historicized: harking back to Roman times. It includes the African entertainers in the Tudor court, the servants, valets, extending to the grooms of Hogarth's time, seamen, hostel keepers, the African American anti-slavery campaigners, and such nineteenth-century greats as the composer Samuel Coleridge-Taylor, to the earliest Black Shakespeare performers, Ira Aldridge, and after him, Paul Robeson. Aldridge and Robeson both challenged the virulent racial assumptions of their respective time.

Teachers can use the lessons from *Othello* to talk about how people in contemporary society live authentic lives despite the narrative of racism. How do we face our fears and self-doubt? What happens when we confront institutional forms of racism? The weak, minority, and the poor are targeted recipients of racism that is being politically endorsed. Different groups of immigrants are played off against each other. In the twenty-first century, Black students are still called names like "nigger," "pickaninny," and "chocolate mousse." They have been discouraged from taking STEM course, though their parents are doctors and scientists. Some white teachers still feel Black students aren't capable of handling advanced courses.

It is necessary for these uncomfortable conversations to be pushed forward in this historical moment. One of the biggest conditions of impossibility that people of color face everyday is the isolation and self-destruction felt by

Othello. Is Othello a warrior, wife murderer, gullible dupe, or victim of a campaign of hate?

Teachers of Shakespeare in high schools and colleges can initiate discussions of how people of color navigate public spaces. How might the Latino or African American student who has been adopted and raised by a white family in a white culture be both similarly a part of and separate from that culture in their everyday lives? How might Iago's alienation be felt in the current political climate of disgruntled working class white voters, and the issue of immigration and DACA?

Students can be taught to choose to cross the ancient line of racism to find common ground for social change, or we can continue to allow the color line as Langston Hughes noted in his poem *A Dream Deferred*, "to fester like a sore" and to "sag like a heavy load" on the nation until it explodes.

No wonder that Vaughan, in the course of her contextual history of the play and its reception, should find herself oscillating helplessly between the two positions: "I think this play is racist, and I think it is not." But Vaughan goes on to warn against the impossibility of escaping this conundrum, since "Othello's example shows me that if I insist on resolving the contradiction, I will forge only lies and distortions ... the discourse of racial difference is inescapably embedded in this play just as it was embedded in Shakespeare's culture and our own" (70). Like *Othello* itself, we may resist this discourse, but, as the play's reception and performance histories demonstrate, learning to think outside its parameters in the Age of Black Lives Matter and DACA is a much more difficult matter.

Works Cited

All textual citations refer to: Folger Shakespeare Library. *Shakespeare's Plays,* from Folger Digital Texts. Ed. Barbara Mowat, Paul Werstine, Michael Poston, and Rebecca Niles. Folger Shakespeare Library, 11 April, 2017. www.folgerdigitaltexts.org.

Hauser, Christine, and Jacey Fortin. *The New York Times,* https://www.nytimes.com/2017/08/31/us/Black-kill-police-georgia.html?smid=tw-nytimes&smtyp=cur.

Mather, Victor. *The New York Times,* https://www.nytimes.com/2017/09/06/sports/football/michael-bennett-seattle-seahawks-police.html

John Todd and Kenneth Dewhurst. "The Othello Syndrome: A Study in the Psychopathology of Sexual Jealousy." Journal of Nervous and Mental Disorder 122 (1955): 367.

G.R. Bullough. *Narrative and Dramatic Sources of Shakespeare,* 8 vols. Routledge, 1957-75. Vol. II, 1973. p. 209.

Kaufman, Miranda. *Black Tudors: The Untold Story.* Oneworld Publications, 2017.

Vaughan, Virginia Mason. *Othello: A Contextual History.* Cambridge UP, 1994.

5. "He that plays the King shall be welcome"

ARMIN SHIMERMAN

It is common knowledge among actors that when playing a villain of any sort, you cannot simply play evil. Rather, you must empathize with your character and find out what drives him/her and makes her/him do what they do. You must look for motivating needs that compel an Iago or a Don John to jeopardize their eternal souls in order to reap revenge or gain a crown or murder an innocent. Doing otherwise is to give a rather flat performance with no insights into the human psyche. You must love your character despite his faults as much as you love yourself.

This was my objective when I twice played Claudius in *Hamlet*. Killing the reigning monarch is a crime most foul compounded by the oldest sin in the bible, fratricide. What causes this man to commit the worst of Elizabethan crimes, that of regicide, and conspiracy to murder the old king's son? Notice I do not say "rightful heir." It is usually surprising to moderns to learn that Denmark did not follow the rules of primogeniture and that Hamlet is not the "rightful" next king. He himself cites the explanation in the text, "Why, what a King is this! / He that hath ... / Popp'd in between th'election and my hopes" (*Hamlet*, 5.2.70-75). Thus, Claudius did not steal the Danish throne from prince Hamlet. Did he maliciously murder his brother to create an opportunity? Yes. But neither Claudius nor the Danish court can be seen to be at fault for subsequently winning an election, especially as Prince Hamlet has not campaigned, but been away at university. Like Hamlet, Claudius is a wonderful collage of human complexity. He has committed murder, but suffers at the thought of that murder. He can be loving, charming, and powerful, and then appear hateful, odious, and weak. He is a character worthy of examination, with a conscience on display at various key moments of the play, weighing his past against his future.

The play suggests that ambition in moderation is not a fault, but only intolerable when it exceeds the moral compass. Hamlet praises Fortinbras for his ambition. The Prince tells us, "I am myself very proud, revengeful, ambitious" (3.1.135). But, in the prayer scene (Act 3, scene 3) one of the most revealing moments in the play, Claudius lets us know how much he suffers for the one heinous act he has ambitiously committed, "O, my offense is rank / It smells to heaven" (3.3.40). What has prompted this self-loathing? We have but to listen and, nineteen verse lines later, we are given the answer. He has sacrificed his eternal peace for "my crown, my own ambition, and my queen" (3.3.59).

Let us look at the first of these reasons, "my crown." My sympathy for Claudius prompts me to remember that many of Shakespeare's most noteworthy characters seek elevation to Kingship: Bolingbroke, Richard of York, Edmund Mortimer, Julius Caesar, and arguably Henry V, who is victorious in securing the French crown. To strive to reach the pinnacle of human hierarchy can be seen as a heroic thing. So, I can defend to myself that my role's desire to achieve greatness is admirable. But to commit regicide in order to attain it? That is the question. Elizabeth and her government (and her players) were constantly on the lookout for threats against the monarch. Several attempts were made on Queen Bess' life and she escaped them all. But the threat and the possibility of a successful attempt were ever-present in the national conscience. The government saw the brunt of the threat coming from recusant Catholics. They had been given permission by the Pope to assassinate the English monarch, who was (according the the Catholics) born a bastard of an unsanctified marriage. A papal bull, or edict, from Pope Pius V had told them that their souls would not go to Hell for such a murder. So this atrocity had a very religious connotation to the original playgoers and they would have been quick to see Elizabeth in the figure of slaughtered King Hamlet. Subsequent audiences would be horrified at the thought of such an unholy act as killing a king whom Shakespeare often entitled "God's deputy." In 1604, King James, his family, and a hall-full of aristocrats narrowly escaped being torn asunder by the recusants' Gunpowder Plot to blow up Parliament. Whether it was in Elizabethan or Jacobean times, regicide and its horrors played on the national conscience.

As to the second – "my ambition"– it is part and parcel of the first. One assumes Claudius is the younger brother to King Hamlet. The natural order of primogeniture suggests that, but then an election of King Hamlet to king may speak in opposition to that. But whether Claudius is younger or older, the fact remains that his royal brother was a man who inspired others, as Hamlet informs us: "The front of Jove himself, / An eye like Mars to threaten and command, / A station like the herald Mercury" (3.4.66-8).

It is an enormous burden to live in the shadow of your sibling. Never measuring up can cause jealousy, resentment, and rivalry. It can drive you to try harder and/or forego niceties. Every human has felt "lesser than" in comparison with someone else, either because of psychic or material disadvantages. The feeling never fades when you are a sibling with an enormously successful brother. I tapped these feelings of inadequacy along with a need to surpass former indignities when coloring my first speech:

> CLAUDIUS. Though yet of Hamlet, our dear brother's death, the memory be green
> And it us befittst to bathe our hearts in grief
> And our whole kingdom to be contracted in one brow of woe.
> Yet so far hath discretion fought with nature that we
> With wisest sorrow think on him
> Together with remembrance of ourselves. (*Ham*. 1. 2.1-7)

And there is a sweet irony in these words. Claudius is cutting short any ceremonies of court mourning because of remembrance of past indignities. This is just ambiguous enough to sound like a fitting and reasonable explanation. "Discretion" was for me an interesting choice of words, an equivocating word. I remember always pouncing on it when I arrived at that part of the speech. Firstly, it signifies the political acumen that it is wiser to cut short national mourning and move on. After all, it has been at least a month since the death of King Hamlet. The king is dead, long live the king! But it also alludes to the idea that one must be thoughtful and circumspect. I conceived King Hamlet to be a more "natural" man, a ruler who let his instincts drive him. My Claudius is informing the court that my rule will be more about discrete reason than natural feeling. I was suggesting that the Danish court must be discrete from now on. This is ironical from a man who arguably is intrinsically "passion's slave." I must confess that at first I was a little baffled by the pronouns "we, us, and our." Early on in my first stab at the role, I was not sure that the meaning of these words was to indicate that I was addressing the Danish court or referring to myself in the royal "we." In my second outing in the role, I chose to think the latter. The royal privilege of speaking of oneself that way seemed a reward for the character's ambition and a satisfying acknowledgement of attaining the highest position in the land.

The first and second causes of Claudius' deed are really subservient and intertwined with the third – "my queen." There is no doubt in my mind that Claudius truly loves Gertrude and has coveted his brother's wife for quite some time. Is this also a symptom of sibling rivalry? I would venture to say that Gertrude has feelings for Claudius as well. The ghost seems to think so too. "Won ... / The will of my most seeming-virtuous queen" (1.5.53). Is she in love? Is she in lust? No matter. Gertrude wants him as much as he wants her. The motivating force of his love and the distracting sweetness of her desiring him has overwhelmed the man and pushed him to commit an abominable murder. To quote another Shakespearian character, "It is the cause. It is the cause" (*Othello*, 5.2.1). I think this is why Claudius almost immediately brings his newly married wife into his opening remarks, "Therefore our sometime sister, now our queen ... / Have we ... / Taken to wife" (1.2.8-14). He is proud of their marriage and eager to boast about it, despite any Biblical prohibitions. He is, however, politically careful to address any qualms the court might have about this sudden marriage with measured, parenthetical phrases that acknowledge and balance the country's loss of their king and his brother with his marital happiness. His doing so indicates to me that Claudius is politically skilled, a well-trained rhetorical speaker, and well aware of the probability of court gossip and the dissention it might inspire. In my last performance, I gave Gertrude (played by my real-life wife) such a show of love and adoration that no one could mistake my feelings for her. In the play-within-a-play scene, Gertrude and I chose to flirt and neck despite the fact that the scene is rather a public one. It had the secondary effect of pushing the actor playing Hamlet to such extremes that his rude behavior to Ophelia seemed like a psychotic response to our public lovemaking on stage.

Love in Shakespeare can be one of two things, either "merely a madness" (*AYLI*, 3.2.407) or "a spirit all compact of fire" (*Venus and Adonis*, 149). It can inspire folly or, as Shakespeare writes in *Troilus & Cressida*, "Hot blood begets hot thoughts, and hot thoughts beget hot deeds, and hot deeds are love" (*Tro.* 3.1.127). Such is Claudius' yearning for Gertrude that he madly lets his passion overwhelm his conscience, his reason, and his political know-how. Again, to quote another quasi-villain/hero, Macbeth, to accomplish our heart's desire "we would jump the life to come," (*Mac.* 1.7.7). In other words, forego the joys of Heaven.

In his first scene, Claudius accedes to the wishes of his beloved by requiring Hamlet to stay at Elsinore and not return to Wittenberg. It is most foolhardy to allow him to stay as it must be obvious on a personal level that the Prince has no liking for his father's replacement and, from a political point of view, it is always wise to keep your political rivals at arm's length, "... for let the world take note, / You are the most immediate to our throne" (1.2.90). Surely, allowing him to stay at court is an ardent wish of Gertrude's that Claudius is catering to. Next, one may question Claudius' outpouring of affection for Hamlet in Act 1, scene 2.

> CLAUDIUS. And with no less nobility of love
> Than that which dearest father bears his son
> Do I impart toward you. (*Ham.* 1.2.90)

As the new father has not yet learned the full antipathy of his stepson, it is only human to have spoken thus, making an attempt both to bring Hamlet out of his melancholy and appear kindly towards him. Surely, he is also seconding his Queen's motherly plea to "cast thy nighted color off" (1.2.70). If Claudius has killed for love, there is no reason to believe he holds any ill will for his nephew at this early stage of the play. Those that argue otherwise are mistakenly seeing Claudius from Hamlet's point of view and not Claudius'.

The king's next scene is Act 2, scene 2. There he welcomes Hamlet's old schoolmates, Rosencrantz and Guildenstern to Denmark, with perhaps some wine-pouring, perhaps the shaking of hands. More, he asks or perhaps orders them to spy upon their old friend and report back what they can glean. I see nothing insidious about this. Hamlet is manifestly suffering from depression and though psychiatry as a science will not occur for centuries to come, people knew enough to try to divert melancholics with 'pleasures' and look for ways to bring the mentally disturbed back to peace of mind. Claudius has already attempted this in the prior scene where assuming it is the loss of a father that has gotten Hamlet down, he counsels Hamlet on how fathers' deaths are common and, though the loss is sad, must be accepted as the natural course of events. Again, the actor playing the King can choose to play this request to Rosencrantz and Guildenstern as Claudius' own idea, or perhaps fulfilling a request from Gertrude, the worried mother, who is as eager to press these gentlemen on her son as Claudius is. They leave and Polonius enters with the prospect of revealing the source of Hamlet's despondency.

> GERTRUDE. I doubt it is no other but the main,
> His father's death and our o'er hasty marriage.
> CLAUDIUS. Well, we shall sift him." (*Ham.* 2.2.59-61)

I am always struck by this curt and short response. It is not the reference to King Hamlet's death that bothers Claudius, but the intimation from Gertrude that they married "o'er hastily." Does Gertrude find fault in that? Does she anguish over whether or not her actions have caused Hamlet's affliction? It always gave me pause when I heard it on stage. Was she having second thoughts about the speed of their wedding? But certainly, as the widowed

Queen, she would have postponed the wedding day out of propriety if she had not wanted to marry Claudius as much as he wanted to marry her. The scene continues and Polonius, the Court's chief advisor (perhaps modeled on Elizabeth's own chief advisor, Sir William Cecil) suggests, "loosing his daughter" on the Prince and spying out his reactions. The assumption is that Hamlet is mad with love. Mother, stepfather, and possible future father-in-law all agree to the stratagem which Polonius calls "boarding" and Claudius calls "lawful espials" (3.1.34). If there is villainy here, I do not detect it. The scene ends with a rather awkward speech by Claudius to the audience; in other words, an aside:

> CLAUDIUS.   How smart a lash that speech doth give my conscience.
> The harlot's cheek, beautified with plastering art,
> Is not more ugly to the thing that helps it
> Then is my deed to my most painted word.
> O heavy burden! (*Ham.* 3.1.58-62)

Claudius for the first time in the play reveals that he is not what he seems, indicating that the quondam king, who may have been sent by Heaven or Hell to either inspire Hamlet to a just revenge or tempt him to damnation, is telling the truth. But I think more importantly, Claudius is also saying that he has a conscience that lashes him for the murder. Love unattained prompted him to kill, but having attained his love, his sublimated moral center is beginning to re-emerge.

I can't help thinking that this aside is somehow not part of the original text, but rather appended on later in the writing process. It seems to come out of nowhere and crudely stops the action of the scene. Could Sir Edmund Tilney, Elizabeth's Master of the Revels, have required it? It was his job to censure plays and add moral language? In a play of soaring language and tight plot construction, this passage seems an outlier. Nevertheless, the "boarding" scene ends with Claudius fully convinced that Hamlet is not in love. Rather, unlike Polonius, Claudius has noted Hamlet's subtle threat to his life. "Those that are married already, all but one, shall live. / The rest shall keep as they are" (3.1.160-61).

> CLAUDIUS.   There is something in his soul
> O'er which his melancholy sits on brood,
> And I do doubt that the hatch and the disclose
> Will be some danger ... (*Ham.* 3.1.178-81)

Despite Gertrude's solicitous desire to keep her son close, Claudius orders Hamlet to vacate Denmark, and will put him as far away from himself as his foreign relations can extend, i.e. to England. As I said earlier, it is politic to move your enemies as far from you as you can. And the just finished scene has made Claudius aware, for the first time, I think, that Hamlet is his enemy. The play within a play, (referred to as "the Mousetrap"), occurs next for Claudius. Listening to the Player King, Claudius must hear his own inner misgivings being spoken aloud.

> CLAUDIUS. What to ourselves in passion we propose
> The passion ending, doth the purpose lose.
> The violence of either grief or joy
> Their own enactures with themselves destroy.
> Where joy most revels grief doth most lament. (*Ham.* 3.2.217-21)

Taken with the perspective I have proposed (that the new King of Denmark is shaken by the act he has committed out of passion for Gertrude) the Player King's words must be the very echo of Claudius' guilty conscience. I always thought in performance that it was these words, plus the Player King's poisoning, that strike so much fear into the King's heart. Not being able to bear another word, he bolts away to ask forgiveness from God, but finds much to his regret, that he cannot pray - or rather he cannot in all good conscience ask God to forgive him if he will not foreswear the kingship, and most importantly Gertrude. What can lip service to Heaven do "when one cannot repent? O wretched state!" (3.3.69) O, wretched state indeed! Claudius must acknowledge out loud the hellish pathway his eternal soul must take, and it harrows his soul. He is in a desperate state and the rest of the play is his desperate reaction to his downward spiraling fortunes. Like Macbeth, the other regicide, Claudius foolishly hopes to combat the consequence of his own sinful acts by eliminating any imagined avenging angel. In his case it is the Prince of Denmark. From here on Claudius thrashes about, allowing his fears to overshadow his conscience. At the beginning of Act IV, Claudius takes pains to satisfy Gertrude that her desire to keep Hamlet at home is dangerous:

> CLAUDIUS. His liberty is full of threats to all-
> To you yourself, to us, to everyone ….
> It will be laid to us, whose providence
> Should have kept short, restrain'd and out of haunt
> This mad young man. But so much was our love
> We would not understand what was most fit. (*Ham.* 4.1.15-21)

In this passage it is evident that Claudius is being as clear and simple as he can be. Notice the number of monosyllabic words, an implicit stage direction for the actor to slow down and make every word count. This is said even as the ghastly information of Hamlet's rash killing of Polonius is still sinking in. It is patently obvious the intended victim was Claudius. The "us" in this passage is definitely not the royal 'us." He is appealing to Gertrude's sense of duty and responsibility as a co-governor or "jointress of this warlike state" (1.2.9). Polonius is beloved of the multitude and their thoughts will become "muddied" by his death. The mob's thoughts may lead to revolution, to civil unrest. The statement says to me that they *both* should not have allowed Hamlet to roam free to slay the beloved Polonius. But if the "our" in "our love" means both of them, then he is also saying that both of them are guilty for loving Hamlet too much. Obviously, this is a ruse on his part. But, there is a grain of truth to it. For such is Claudius' loving –not for Hamlet, but for Gertrude - that he has allowed her wishes to outweigh his political judgment in permitting Hamlet to be at liberty. And such is his love for her that he must lie in order to soften the blow of Hamlet's forthcoming departure. He shares his plan for Hamlet's banishment with the boy's mother, who makes no attempt to dissuade him from doing so. Seeing her political responsibility and understanding the threat to peace, Gertrude speaks not a word of argument against her son being sent away. Claudius' full attention is now on his crown and preserving peace and stability in the kingdom. As his last words indicate, "My soul (his conscience) is full of discord and dismay" (4.1.29).

As his next scene starts, Claudius is concerned about how to deal with a "distracted multitude" who adore the Prince as well as Polonius, and who must not be incited to revolt. Is this out of personal fear? Perhaps. But some of Shakespeare's most dire passages describe a nation thrown into civil war. The theme is rampant through the *Henriad, King Lear, Macbeth, Julius Caesar,* and even *Antony & Cleopatra.* Critics will suggest that Claudius egoistically fears for himself, but given this dominant theme in Shakespeare, I think, if we are to play him successfully, we must give him some credit for fearing for his country's well being. Moreover, the mob has found a leader in Laertes who is infected by the rabbles' discontent. They wish to overthrow the recent election and elect Laertes as their new King. Claudius' growing desperation is obvious even to himself, "Diseases desperate grown / By desperate appliance are relieved / Or not at all" (4.3.9-11). As he says, the uneasy King has a "hectic in his blood."

Claudius knows that both Hamlet's perceived vengeance and the growing insurrection will sour all, and that he will neither be able to enjoy his royal power nor his royal queen. Having seemingly found a remedy for the former, Claudius now gives full attention to the latter. His arguments to Laertes are neither self-serving nor nefarious. Claudius has had no hand in the murder of Polonius and he must assure Laertes, the would-be rebel, of his innocence. Once convinced of that, Polonius' son will be able to quell the mounting discord among the "multitude" over the death of his father. Further, he promises to explain all not only in private, but also in front of others of Laertes' choosing. Claudius' policy toward the death of Polonius is a response to a political miscalculation, not the shady dealings of a villain. His option was either to pay great homage to Polonius, who is beloved of the people, or minimize the national ceremonies so as to not magnify the focus on Hamlet's murderous action. Hamlet, too, is beloved of the people. It is an unenviable choice to make. I can't help but think his decision was prompted by Gertrude's wishes. Claudius wishes not only "content" for Laertes' soul, but peace for the country. In fact, Shakespeare has given the King a rather heroic nobleness, words I always thrilled saying, "There's such divinity that doth hedge a king / That treason can but peep to do what it would" (4.5.139-40).

Act IV, scene 7 reaffirms my primary theme that Claudius has done all for love. When Laertes pointedly questions the King why he has not taken action against Hamlet for killing his father, Claudius reveals the extent of his love for Gertrude.

> LAERTES. But tell me
> Why you proceeded not against these feats
> So crimeful and so capital in nature ...
> KING. O, for two special reasons
> Which may to you perhaps seem unsinewed
> But yet to me they're strong. The Queen his mother
> Lives almost by his looks, and for myself
> (My virtue or my plague, be it either which),
> She is so conjunctive to my life and soul
> That, as a star moves not but in his sphere,
> I could not but by her." (*Ham.* 4.7.6-18)

I loved this moment of two formidable men talking intimately. When the one asks the other about why he didn't have the gumption to do something, the older, more worldly man sheepishly admits that it was out of love, a reason perhaps 'unsinew'd" or unmanly. He goes further saying his love may be a "virtue or a plague" but, like celestial commandments, he *could not* move against his amour's desire to protect her son. This comes out of so much conviction that even the aggrieved Laertes makes no objection to the King's explanation why he did not do more for Polonius' obsequies.

At that moment, Hamlet's return to Denmark is announced and, with this, the former political enemies now join forces, once again proving the old adage that "the enemy of my enemy is my friend." And here, late in Act IV, begins Claudius' despicable behavior, which condemns him as a villain. It is the King's plot to have a public fencing contest between the adept swordsman, Laertes, and the supposedly amateurish Hamlet. All that follows is a conspiracy to murder. Perhaps a less guilty soul might have found a less Machiavellian solution to Hamlet's threat, and Laertes thirst for vengeance, and Gertrude's love for her son. But the story of Hamlet or Amleth is an old one, with several literary sources familiar to the Elizabethan public (including an assumed lost ur-*Hamlet* play). But Shakespeare provides the King one more heart-revealing passage that again glances at his regret at what Love has kept him from doing, that of banishing Hamlet at the beginning of the play, despite Gertrude's desires:

> CLAUDIUS.   That we would do
>   We should do when we would; for this "would' changes
>   And hath abatements and delays as many
>   As there are tongues, are hands, are accidents;
>   And then this 'should' is like a spendthrift sigh
>   That hurts by easing. (*Ham.* 4.7. 134-40)

The character of the love-wounded King must eventually succumb to the parameters of the plot of previous source materials. The many-layered Claudius must now put on his destined livery as a villain. But as in all Senecan tragedies, this villainy twists and turns and prompts a self-lacerating wound for the conniver. Fierce animal passion has led to regicide, and the ensuing soul-sickening guilt has maimed a once capable man. In an attempt to assure Hamlet's demise, Claudius devises a poisoned chalice meant for the Prince, but is eventually used by the Queen. I think there is no more painful moment in the play for Claudius than his seeing his Love poison herself with his prepared potion. For me that moment in the acting of it was truly more horrifying and more unwanted than his own death by stabbing and poisoning.

But to give Claudius credit, he has moved purposefully throughout the play, striving determinedly to possess those things he covets. He is purposefully aggressive to hold on to what he has won, experiencing a panoply of feelings as he courses through the halls of Elsinore. He is a fitting foil to literature's most compelling hero. I venture to suggest that if Claudius were a lesser creation, Hamlet's exertions and victories would be less meaningful.

Claudius' merciless deeds are villainous, but Shakespeare has given him reasons and vulnerabilities that can at times mitigate his villainy. The master playwright has written a character who is both calculating and conscience-ridden, authoritative and pitiful, detestable and charming, aggressive and put upon, and both filled with hate and loving. These contradictions of character, his guilt, and his over-riding desire for Gertrude are complexities that make this "villain" wonderful to play. Like the indomitable Richard III, or the too moralizing Macbeth, his conscience will hobble him with his heavy burden, but the struggle - though insurmountable- is a joy to take on. It is often surmised that Shakespeare himself acted the Kings when the larger role in a play went to the lead actor, Burbage. Perhaps with creating Claudius, Will took great care to write himself a really good role. One he could sink his teeth into!

Works Cited

All textual citations refer to: Folger Shakespeare Library. *Hamlet,* from Folger Digital Texts. Ed. Barbara Mowat, Paul Werstine, Michael Poston, and Rebecca Niles. Folger Shakespeare Library, 15 January, 2019. www.folgerdigitaltexts.org.

6. Through Hamlet's Eyes

TIMOTHY HARRIS

Two years ago,[1] Peter Brook's version of *Hamlet* for eight players and a musician was performed at the Setagaya Public Theater in Tokyo, where I saw it, and subsequently at the Young Vic in London. The original performances were at Brook's base, Théâtre des Bouffes du Nord in Paris. I was very impressed by certain aspects of the production, particularly the performance of Adrian Lester as Hamlet, but had some reservations; reservations that have been reinforced by the high definition video of this *Hamlet* now available: (www.youtube.com/watch?v=XSfRZmNPHoE).

By denying Brook the strengths that spring from live performance, the video brings out the weaknesses of the production more clearly. The principal weakness lies in Brook's conception, and this weakness may be summed up by Harley Granville-Barker's remark about the play as a whole, which is that Hamlet so dominates the play that we are too apt to see things "through his eyes." In the interview that accompanied the showing of the video on Japanese television, *Peter Brook Speaks About 'Hamlet'* (www.youtube.com/ watch?v=_MgjX9qw9uI), Brook said that "many, many great authorities have said that *Hamlet* is an artistic failure," and that this was so because Shakespeare did not conceive of the play as a whole since he was reworking an older and "not very good . . . melodrama."

Granville-Barker certainly thought that Shakespeare had been unable to assimilate character and story so that "no incongruities appear," but equally certainly he did not judge the play an artistic failure (his Preface on *Hamlet* is by far the longest of the *Prefaces*). That was left to T.S. Eliot, recycling the opinions of some academic critic in *The Sacred Wood*. I do not know who the many other "great authorities" that Brook refers to are. Voltaire, perhaps, was one? Whoever they are, they are used to justify removing two hours of what has become "Romantic and rhetorical staging" or "what for today is no longer as important as it was at other moments of history," in order to extract, according to Brook, "a very pure, essential myth in which the essential elements are a father, his brother who murders him, a wife who comes into an incestuous relationship with her brother-in-law, a son and a very pure young girl that the son loves." This "essential pattern," says Brook, "speaks to us directly without any decoration." It speaks "straight to the heart of everyone's interests and preoccupations." It speaks to us "today." And as soon as an audience sees Adrian Lester, they recognize him as a young man of "today" (Brook Speaks).

There can be few directors who are Brook's equal at creating a charged theatrical space. His most famous book is entitled *The Empty Space*, but that emptiness is replete and vibrant with possibilities before any actor sets foot in it. The "stage" for his *Hamlet* was something that resembled a large, square exercise mat, though refined in quality, and lit at the beginning so that it seemed to glow a warm, light orange. The proximity of the first rows of the audience, sitting on cushions on the floor, made the otherness and inviolableness of the performance area more distinct. Around the other three sides of the mat was a penumbral region in which actors would wait and from which they would emerge. From the first entrance, of Horatio through the audience, every entrance and every exit compelled attention. The Japanese have recognized better than anyone else the theatrical power of exits and entrances and refined the art of making them, and Brook has surely learnt from their theater, as well as from Indian theater. As in Noh or the Indian Kathakali, the performance of the actors was accompanied by music, which seemed largely Asian in provenance and was sometimes extraordinarily expressive. I still can't forget the terror of the dry rustle and chirping of the sistrum that accompanied the appearances of the Ghost. There was one musician, Tsuchitori Toshi, who is Japanese, with a grand array of instruments. Like the musicians in the Noh and Kathakali, he was at all times visible and on occasion came completely on stage. But, apart from the sound of the music, all this is lost from the video, and it is not compensated for by the certainly beautiful old red walls of the Théâtre des Bouffes du Nord, where the video was filmed. The video begins not with Horatio's slow, solitary and electrifying entrance through the dusk of the auditorium towards the glowing and expectant performance space and his "Who's there?", which seemed not only to be calling up a ghost, but calling on all of us to be truly present and to attend on a rite. It begins instead with Hamlet, in place, speaking very slowly and softly, and at the outset in the somewhat toneless tones of today, "O that this too, too sullied flesh" (1.2.113).

The cutting and reordering of the "score," for both stage and video versions (they are a little different), has been cunningly done, if not quite so cunningly and effectively as in the case of some of the tailoring in the often maligned First Quarto. It is an interesting idea, and one suited to the character of this production, from which Fortinbras has once again been excised, to put "To be or not to be" on the eve of Hamlet's departure from England instead of "How all occasions," whose last line and a half, "O, from this time forth / My thoughts be bloody, or be nothing worth!" (4.5.67–8) replaces the last two and a half lines of the former speech, "Soft you now, / the fair Ophelia" (3.1.96–7). But what cutting all too often does, as I know from experience, having put on a number of such "reduced" versions of Shakespeare plays with a few actors, is to make of the play a chamber piece, a kind of lyrical variation on the original; a variation that is in fact dependent on the audience's knowledge of the original.

"Lyrical," because the outcomes of action tend to be presented through juxtaposition, without enough of the action that leads to them: turning points and climaxes without the development that justifies them. "Lyrical" also because the multiple viewpoints of the play tend be reduced to that of the protagonist alone. There is nothing necessarily wrong with this, but I think it needs to be recognized, in this case and others, that it is not so much that "a very pure and essential myth" is being allowed, "with respect and delicacy," to emerge from the well- or ill-hewn block of the play, as Brook proposes, as that the varied articulation and tensions of drama are being foregone in favor of a refined singleness, a sort of *Lamb's Tale* for stage and screen.

Perhaps the word "myth" (which originally meant a "tale") has a special meaning for Brook, but myths, as they have come down to us and particularly as they are presented in the work of collectors and myth-mongers like Frazer, Freud, Jung, Lévi Strauss, O'Flaherty and Campbell, are often schematic; they are not necessarily in themselves so interesting or profound. It is usually the "decoration" given to them by great artists like Aeschylus, Sophocles, Euripides, Ovid and Shakespeare, exploring the possibilities they present and using them to make discoveries, that renders them both interesting and profound.

One of the most compelling moments in *Hamlet*, I feel, occurs when Horatio makes what clearly comes across to Hamlet as an accusation: "So Guildenstern and Rosencrantz go to't" (5.2.63). Horatio is seeing a new and ruthless Hamlet, someone quite unlike the Hamlet of old, and he is shocked, as the audience should be if the moment is acted well. Something changes here between the two men. Hamlet responds chillingly with "They are not near my conscience." And he goes on to say "'Tis dangerous when the baser nature comes / Between the pass and fell incensèd points / Of mighty opposites" (5.2.65–69). The "mighty opposite" of Hamlet is Claudius, and by the end of the play, many lives have fallen between their "fell, incensèd points." But this brief exchange, with its glance into and away from giddy depths and its sense of recognitions too disturbing to be fully expressed, has been cut, perhaps because in Brook's version, Hamlet has no "mighty opposite," no real antagonist.

We are back with Granville-Barker's point that we are too apt to see things through Hamlet's eyes. Myth or no myth, the true problem for any director of the play, it seems to me, lies in finding ways to ensure that Hamlet's antagonist is a worthy one, and that it is not only "through Hamlet's eyes" that we see the play's events.

If you excise the whole political dimension of the play, the sense of the vast Northern world where the "fell kings" of Basil Bunting's *Briggflatts* engage in single combat and smite "the sledded Polacks on the ice" (1.1.74), and within which Claudius conducts his diplomatic maneuvers; if you remove the opportunities for Claudius to display his power publicly in the presence of a full court; if you reduce the scenes in which Claudius magisterially brings Laertes to heel and tempts him to a treacherous revenge so that they amount to a few perfunctory exchanges in which all drama is lost and Claudius' success becomes a foregone conclusion; if Hamlet is not allowed to stake the claim "This is I, Hamlet the Dane" (5.1.270–1), and if at the end you make Claudius agree meekly and "nobly" to his fate and cut his last gambler's words, ("O, yet defend me, friends! I am but hurt" (5.2.355)), then there is no foil for Hamlet, there is nothing for him to push against, and consequently no real drama, whose "double demand," to paraphrase Granville-Barker, is not solely for action or for the revelation of character, but for *character in action*. There is no reason, apart from poor direction, why the staging of the court and other scenes should be "Romantic and rhetorical." They certainly are not in Grigori Kozintsev's brilliant and politically astute version, which remains by far the best film of *Hamlet* ever made.

Aristotle, in the *Poetics*, pointed out that tragedies are focused on family relations (as, incidentally, are many detective stories, which revenge tragedies in some ways resemble), but he did not mistake a bare paradigm for the thickness and complexity of a particular human situation, whether real or imagined. The particular situation in *Hamlet* includes the facts that Claudius is a powerful king, that Hamlet is a powerless prince cheated of his right, and that something is rotten in the whole state of Denmark and not merely in the predicament of one family.

The First Quarto returns *Hamlet* to a form closer to the kind of action-packed revenge tragedy that Shakespeare was clearly seeking to go beyond. Brook domesticates the play, which surely is not a presentation of a pure and essential myth, but tells of rottenness, offences that smell to Heaven, jigging whores, rank sweat, enseaméd beds, copulation over the nasty sty, worms, the guts of beggars, dust and pocky corpses; and, despite his talk of "today," he gives to it a form that seems to encapsulate some late Nineteenth or early Twentieth-century idea of the play, in which character is conceived in isolation from situation. "*Hamlet* is about Hamlet," Brook remarks in the interview, a statement which, though not wrong, is inadequate and certainly nothing new. His approach is fundamentally lyrical and Romantic, and never more so than in his use of Asian, or quasi-Asian, practices. This use derives obviously from a deep and justified respect for Asian theater, but also, I suspect, from a more questionable belief that Asian theater is somehow more wise and profound than European theater, and that a Noh play, for example, is less a piece of theater than some kind of mystical insight in theatrical form. In this *Hamlet*, it is as though Brook wants the refinement, or what he supposes to be the refinement, of certain forms of Asian drama (Kabuki and Peking Opera are often splendidly and unabashedly vulgar, and Kathakali has a grand and very physical energy). It is as though he is trying to interpret *Hamlet* in terms of *rasa* (the sentiment evoked in the spectator), which is the essence of Sanskrit drama, or of the *yugen* ("elegant simplicity" or "subtle profundity") of certain Noh plays. The costumes and stage furnishings, too, are vaguely Asian in character, in what still strikes me as a slightly too tasteful, self-conscious and Age of Aquarius sort of way, though on stage the few furnishings were certainly used in wonderfully imaginative ways to create different scenes before the audience's eyes, drawing the audience into the "play" of the play more deeply by making them co-creators, something that, again, does not happen with the video.

I do not know enough about Sanskrit drama to judge, but in the case of Noh at least, an elegant simplicity or subtle profundity does not preclude the building and release of strong physical and emotional tensions, and it is this that is lacking in Brook's, though not in Shakespeare's, *Hamlet*. The second half of Brook's version, particularly as filmed, is almost all on one elegiac note (the first half is rather more various). But the building and release of tension in Noh is not achieved in the same way as it is in the case of a kind of drama that depends strongly upon "character in action," and upon the interplay and clash of characters whereby the action develops. It is achieved largely through the interplay between dancer and music. This music, though doubtless more refined, does not depart in a fundamental way from the folk music out of which it was developed, and which still exists in, for example, the mountains of Aichi Prefecture, where the festival known as *hanamatsuri* ("Flower Festival") preserves some of the forms that went into the making of Noh. The music, with its repeated melodic patterns and fluctuating tempo and pitch, its intensifyings and slackenings, tends to create in the dancers as well as in the spectators a state of mind that the Danish composer Vagn Holmboe, speaking of the round dances of Romania and the Faroes, described as either ecstatic (with loss of ego-consciousness) or magical (with a kind of heightened awareness).

The music of Noh retains this characteristic, and is used at times to create a hypnotic and almost unbearable tension, as during the final fast dance in *Atsumori*. But though the music in Brook's *Hamlet* was often used, as in Noh, Kathakali, and Kabuki, as counterpoint to the action, it tended to be more evocative than energetic, and, particularly towards the end, became an elegiacally soothing accompaniment that colluded with the lack of strong dramatic articulation to soften, and sweeten, the grimness and pain of true tragedy. It seemed more suited to the character of "The Murder of Gonzago" (what we have of it) than to that of *Hamlet*. All this is even more true of the video, which lacks the physical presence of the musician, than it was of the stage version.

The desire for an Asian refinement perhaps lies behind what comes across, except in the case of Adrian Lester, as the largely generic nature of the acting, a quality that again denies any real contention as well as any profound meeting between the characters. Natasha Parry's Gertrude seems no more than the idea of a "great lady," quite beyond any sexual life. Bruce Myers as Polonius is a dapper nonentity, and his gravedigger, who sings, for no good reason that I can think of, a Dublin children's skipping song instead of the song Shakespeare wrote for him, is no creature of clay, bones, stinking corruption and gallows humor, but a slightly different dapper nonentity with an Irish accent. Shantala Shivalingappa was chosen to play Ophelia because Brook felt that a girl with her upbringing in a high-class Indian family was closer to a girl brought up like Ophelia than any modern Western girl could be. Brook may well be right. But being well brought up does not preclude the possession of a character. Oddly, Shantala Shivalingappa, who is clearly very gifted, comes across far more strongly in the video than she did on stage, but here, too, I have the impression that she has not been allowed to exert her full powers, particularly in the scenes of madness where at first you think, ah, something's going to come alive, but then the music (not Ophelia's) is used to turn all to favor and to prettiness, and the presence within her and the situation of "thought and afflictions, passion, hell itself" (4.5.211) is simply suppressed.

The actors playing Horatio, Rosencrantz and Guildenstern are good and competent, though the one who doubles as Laertes is wholly unconvincing with Laertes' laments and rantings. But, again, one wonders how much this is the actor's fault and how much is due to a directorial desire to avoid the naked expression of strong feeling, or furious bluster. Claudius has of course been left little that is dangerous to play with, but that little could still have been used better. The great speech "O, my offense is rank" (3.3.40) is done, as all too often it is, as a simple, self-pitying expression of guilt and despair, and not as a dramatic and desperate wrestling in which Claudius (who is a brilliant and heartless gambler, with all the gambler's improvisatory nerve) speculates as to whether he might be able to trick Heaven as well, before concluding that, no, he can't.

Shakespeare's may not be, but Brook's *Hamlet* certainly is, all about Hamlet, and in Adrian Lester Brook has a wonderful actor: physically attractive, as Zeami thought actors should be, playful, dangerous, and with a powerful energy and physical presence, a good sense of comedy, and, despite a tendency to put too much weight on adjectives and other less important words, the ability to speak the verse in a lively and improvisatory way that is readily understandable to the ear.

On stage, he had superb clarity of focus, and used the audience masterfully, breaching the fourth wall for soliloquy and aside to great effect, and reinstating it with a simple gesture or movement. This was never better done than in the grave-digging scene, where he set a skull on a stick so that it took on a life of its own, and through interplay with the audience created some brilliant and macabre comedy that suddenly turned chill. This episode, which requires the presence of an audience, does not appear on the video. And the soliloquies, which also require the presence of an audience, suffer in the video version, though even on stage "To be or not to be" (3.1.64) was far too much an introverted set piece, lacking energy and bite, a mere expression of J. Dover Wilson's stage direction ("Hamlet enters, in deep dejection"), as opposed to what Christopher McCullough discovered when performing the speech as it appears in the First Quarto:

> "To be or not to be,—aye, there's the point," actually only made sense if I said it to the audience. In fact I was using the soliloquy as a way of putting an argument to the audience as to what was going on in the narrative . . .[2]

The Second Quarto or Folio versions of the speech are no less an argument, a wrestling, and here, for once, I do not feel that, in Brook's words, Adrian Lester is using "Shakespeare's language in such a way that at every moment you feel it is the language of his thoughts, that he's thinking and finding the only words that correspond at the moment to his experience." Brook is mostly right in his praise of Lester, but he goes on to make what seems to me a hugely, and characteristically exaggerated claim when he speaks of "the false tradition of Shakespeare that has lasted for many hundreds of years all through Europe," and says that, "at last you have an actor who can be so at ease with this complex language that he can make you feel he is inventing it." Declamation, which is always with us, is simply bad acting, as is the overly informal, throwaway, streetwise style that has become fashionable of late. Good actors are, and surely always have been, able to make formal language like Shakespeare's sound improvised, as if it were springing from a succession of fresh impulses; they make it new. That is why they are good. But of course this claim is not only about Adrian Lester, it is about Brook's production as a whole, which is supposed to have stripped away all false traditions, all Romantic and rhetorical staging, all mere decoration, in order to speak directly to us "today."

If only "today" were so straightforward a category. But rather than bringing a great play of the past into the frame of "today," would it not be more challenging, both as a task and a service, to take people out of their limited views of what "today" is, and to allow them to enter into the otherness of an imagined world, and into the otherness of those who inhabit it? Would this not enrich "today"? I think of Marguerite Yourcenar speaking, in her reflections on the composition of the great *Memoirs of Hadrian*, of "that sympathetic magic which operates when one transports oneself, in thought, into another's body and soul," and reminding herself of the importance of a kind of self-abnegation before otherness: "Keep one's own shadow out of the picture; leave the mirror clean of the mist of one's own breath."[3] Hamlet speaks in not dissimilar terms of the discipline of holding the mirror up to nature. Words for the interpreter.

Brook's version of the play strikes me not as a true interpretation but as a fascinating curiosity, a reworking of an old play, just as Shakespeare's tragedy is a reworking of an old play, but in terms of a philosophical and theatrical conception that does not measure up to Shakespeare's greater vision, and is at odds with it.

Notes

1 This essay was written some years ago (*PN Review* 153, Volume 30 Number 1, September/October, 2003), and when the editor of this volume asked if it could be reprinted here, I looked at it with an eye to revising it a little so that it might address more explicitly the themes of monarchs and monarchy, but quickly determined that this would be an impossible task. I decided, therefore, to append the

following brief note, whose assertions, for reasons of space, I cannot make an argument for here. The principal reason why most British (and, I suspect, American) productions of *Hamlet*, including the production discussed above, are unsatisfactory, is that they do not recognize the importance of its politics, as Grigori Kozintsev's great film of it definitely does. This may be due in part to stage tradition, in part to a residual Freudian influence, and in part to the valued and supposedly a-political "individualism" of the modern Anglo-American world. Hamlet returns from his "sea-change" a different man, having demonstrated, in his sending of Rosenkrantz and Guildenstern to their deaths, a ruthlessness that, however much it may shock us moderns, as it did Horatio, was proper and necessary for a monarch in those days if the state and commonweal were to survive (think of Elizabeth I and Mary, Queen of Scots). He also shows a studied determination to bring Claudius publicly to book, which is what the deaths of Rosenkrantz and Guildenstern on, apparently, Claudius's orders may permit. Finally, in giving his "dying voice" to Fortinbras, as Elizabeth gave hers to James I, he assumes the status and prerogatives of a monarch. The consensus still seems to be that Fortinbras's words about Hamlet, that "he was likely had he been put on / To have prov'd most royal" (5.2.442–5), are risible in the light of the events of the play. I think the consensus is wrong.

2 Christopher McCullough's remarks on "To be, or not to be, I there's the point." Quoted in *The Tragicall Historie of Hamlet Prince of Denmark*, ed. Graham Holderness & Brian Loughrey (Hemel Hempstead: Harvester Wheatsheaf, 1992). (Intro., pp. 25 & 26)

3 See: Bayart, Jean-Francois, "Comparing from below" in *Societes Politiques Comparees: Revue Europeenne d'Analyse des Societes Politiques*. No. 1, Jan. 2008. http://www.fasopo.org/sites/default/files/papier1_eng_n1.pdf.

Works Cited

All textual citations refer to: Folger Shakespeare Library. *Shakespeare's Plays* from Folger Digital Texts. Edited by Barbara Mowat, Paul Werstine, Michael Poston, and Rebecca Niles. Folger Shakespeare Library, 15 January, 2019. www.folgerdigitaltexts.org.

Bunting, Basil. *Briggflatts*. Bloodaxe Books Ltd. 2009.

Eliot, Thomas S. "Hamlet and His Problems". *The Sacred Wood*. Methuen, reprint. 1960, pp. 95–103.

Granville-Barker, Harley. *Preface to 'Hamlet'*. A Drama Book. Hill and Wang Publishers, 1962.

Holmboe, Vagn. *Experiencing Music: A Composer's Notes*. Boydell & Brewer, 1991.

Shakespeare, William. *Hamlet*, ed. Wilson, John Dover. Cambridge University Press, 1934.

Yourcenar, Marguerite. *Memoirs of Hadrian*. FSG Classics, Farrar, Strauss and Giroux, 2005.

7. "In Boy, go first. You houseless povertie …": Social Justice and Transformation in King Lear

Charles Duff

Introduction[1]

As well as working in the professional theater for forty years, I have been teaching Shakespeare to students from seven to seventy, from secondary schools in underserved communities to privileged colleges and universities, for one reason only: I believe that the plays of Shakespeare help people to lead better and happier lives. This is my *belief*, but I also have the *knowledge* that Shakespeare is always boring if you sit down at a desk and study him, and never boring if you get up on your feet and speak him aloud. To have his thoughts in your head and his words in your mouth is transformative.

Today, in these strange and terrible times, all of us as teachers have a huge responsibility but also a unique opportunity. Every generation recreates their Shakespeare in reaction to the fashions that have gone before. These plays are deep and wide and true enough to take (almost) any interpretation. What remains constant is that great Shakespearean virtue: Tolerance.

Shakespeare's own presence is so quiet. He never takes up a moral attitude (although he shows the consequences of characteristics and actions). Each of his over one hundred leading characters speak with their own voice and have their own point of view. This is given in a language so instantly memorable, that whenever we have similar feelings, or experience related situations, we remember his words.

Yet these words were written over four hundred years ago. Even the greatest Shakespearean scholar has the need for a glossary. But bear in mind that the English language has changed surprisingly little in the last four hundred years. Largely due, I would submit, to Shakespeare and the King James Bible, both providing the standard and benchmark, and thus holding back its progress. Just think how enormously the English language changed in the previous two hundred years between Chaucer and Shakespeare.

As you know, in 1623, seven years after Shakespeare's death, two of his colleagues edited a complete edition of thirty-six Shakespeare plays known as the First Folio. "Folio" is a printer's term and it means a pretty sizable book. Eighteen of these plays had already been printed during Shakespeare's lifetime in smaller, cheaper individual editions called Quartos (another printer's term meaning a small book, about the size of a modern paperback). There were "bad" Quartos (which we needn't bother about here) and "good" Quartos which, you must allow me to believe, were taken from Shakespeare's longhand manuscript, written with a quill pen (confusingly known as "Foul Papers"), which Ralph Crane, the scribe of Shakespeare's company, The King's Men, transcribed into "Fair Copy."

When the same eighteen plays appeared in "the Folio" (the collected works) there were frequently differences. In the case of both *Hamlet* (which had been in the company's repertoire for nineteen years) and *King Lear* (now called a Tragedy rather than a History) for fifteen years, there were many, and notable, differences. The versions in the Folio were surely the plays as they were being performed *circa* 1620. The alterations might have been made by Shakespeare (and in *King Lear* obviously some were authorial rewrites) or by the actors. The differences are usually those of clarification and simplification. The Folio text is, I believe, what the company thought worked best in theatrical terms.

I declare myself, unequivocally, a Folio man.

Because of the differences, which will be examined shortly between the Quarto and Folio *King Lear*, most modern editions (and by modern I mean since Nicholas Rowe's edition in 1709), have been a cumbersome conflation of the two texts. In the last thirty years, some editors have chosen to treat them as two entirely separate plays. I also believe that the First Folio was most carefully printed. (Unavoidably there are many typos, slips, and some mislineations, although far fewer of these than many academics would like to think). I believe that if you know how to read the Folio, clues can be found in the printed text as to how it should be spoken. As strictly as a musician can read a musical score. This jars on some, as it seems the exact opposite of "the Method" way of approaching a role, that is, finding the truth of character and situation first, and then pegging the words on to that truth. Without knowledge of an observance of this form, Shakespeare will ironically, always sound artificial and unreal. Dumb him down and try to make the verse conversational, and we just think, "Why are they talking funny?" If you know the "prosody," the way it is written, it will sound as natural and spontaneous as it did in the mouths of a Gwen Ffrangcon-Davies, Vanessa Redgrave, Irene Worth, or Anton Lesser.

In order to do that, you need to know something about a subject that all educated Elizabethan men, and some (not enough) women, were familiar with: Rhetoric; Public Speech designed to persuade, to get people to change their minds. And in order to grasp Rhetoric, you need to know about punctuation, which to the Elizabethans, was solely a means to help you speak out loud.

For the moment, there is only one punctuation mark that I would like you to hold in your heads: the period or full stop. *A period denotes a thought change.* Unless there is a period or a question mark there is no thought change. Villainous modern editors change Folio colons (which are in lieu of "therefore") or semi-colons (in lieu of "and") into periods, and thus Shakespeare seems to be thinking in short thoughts when he isn't. Unless he has good reason not to, Shakespeare thinks in long thoughts.

If a period comes at the end of a line of blank verse, you can obviously take your time changing thought, but if it is placed in the middle of a line of verse you can't, because you have to keep the rhythm going. Why does the character change thoughts so quickly? Is s/he emotionally and mentally excited? Or maybe s/he just doesn't want to be interrupted?

I have open a First Folio (only facsimile, unfortunately) at the first page of *The Tragedie of King Lear* (p. 283 actually) (791). Copies of the play which you order through Amazon or buy in bookstores may be a conflation, like the Penguin or 2nd Arden series, or editions based on the Quarto (Oxford) or Folio (New Cambridge). The Folio cuts about three hundred lines from the Quarto. It also adds one hundred lines of its own. As in *Hamlet*, some well-loved passages and familiar readings are not present in the Folio. However, I believe that the Folio is the more authoritative text. With *King Lear*, the much poorer printed Quartos (both the 1608 and, almost identical, 1619) are to be referred back to, and used or not, according to your pleasure and good judgment.

Shakespeare, as we all know, writes in verse and prose. Verse for the higher-ups (kings, nobles, and so on), with prose for the lower lot (peasants and those who serve the well-born). But is that so here?

The Play

Actus primus. Scoena Prima.

Enter two Earls (senior noblemen), Kent and Gloucester, and they are talking in prose, providing information and a few laughs about sex. As *As*

You Like It and *Twelfth Night* start off as tragedies, and *Romeo and Juliet* a low comedy, the way into *King Lear*, this most shattering and cataclysmic of all tragedy, is a high, light comedy: fun, games, and a bit of exposition. We shall look at the first scene more closely than we will any scene again until the last.

The date (according to Dr. Steve Sohmer's fascinating *The Lunar Calendar in King Lear*) is 23 February, the Festival of The Boundaries (7). The Earl of Kent, the younger of the two Earls, declares that he thought that "the king had more affected the Duke of Albany than of Cornwall" (1.1.1–2), namely that he inclined towards his loyal son-in-law rather than the treacherous Cornwall, but we learn from the Earl of Gloucester that he is equally poised between the two, thus heralding the battle between light and darkness to be waged throughout the play (29).[2] We suspect too that Gloucester's preference is for his illegitimate and amoral son Edmund (who has rather modestly accompanied them onstage) rather than for his strange but true legitimate son, Edgar. It is this failure to discriminate between True and False, this ignorance of values, that is going to lead *him* on to his own ultimate fate.

Then a sennet (quite a long fanfare, which only signified the entrance of royalty) sounds and a procession enters. In the Quartos preceded by one bearing a coronet. Then an order of entrance in both Quartos and Folio, headed by the King himself, Lear. Silly directors want to change this order, with Lear coming on last because they think it gives him more pomp, power, and grandeur. Clearly in the Quartos, he is not wearing a coronet, as it is being carried, and in the Folio he is. He takes this off his own head for his sons-in-law to part between them. So you have a choice.

The scene switches from prose into verse and the moment that a scene or a speech switches from one to the other is *the key moment* of that scene or speech. Monitor closely.

Now look at Lear's opening speech and see why he must head the procession and come first. He is in a hurry, a great hurry: all the periods, the thought changes, are in the middle of lines.

> LEAR.   Give me the map there. Know that we have divided
> In three our Kingdom: and 'tis our fast intent,
> To shake all Cares and Business from our Age,
> Conferring them on younger strengths, while we
> Unburdened crawl toward death. Our son of Cornwall,
> And you our no less loving son of Albany,
> We have this hour a constant will to publish
> Our daughters' several Dowers, that future strife

May be prevented now. The princes France and Burgundy,
Great Rivals in our youngest daughter's love,
Long in our Court have made their amorous sojourn,
And here are to be answered. Tell me, my daughters--
(*Lear*, 1.1. 36–48)[3]

And in the Folio, at least, where he has seven extra lines, (40–44 and 48–49) he *is* talking too much. We do, in the Folio, get the reason why he wishes to split up the kingdom today, this minute (which is not in the Quarto) "that future strife may be prevented now" (43–44). These mid-line thought changes continue during Lear's following speeches. His mind is running quickly (too quickly). He is going to brook no argument, and he wants everything done and dusted now!

It is clear from the opening conversation between the two Earls that everyone knows why they have been summoned to the meeting. But what Lear springs on them next takes them completely by surprise, and a look of disbelief passes between Goneril and Regan. He requires a ceremonial love competition; standard fare in the eulogies of Kings and Emperors, and familiar to all students of rhetoric. Goneril, commanded as the eldest born speaks first, what rhetoricians call "the topic of inexpressibility," (Kermode 185). "Sir, I love you more than word can wield the matter ..." (54). And she does it pretty well: formal, if a bit practiced. Regan follows with what Curtius called "the outdoing"- the *cedat* formula ("Let her yield" (Kermode 185)). Her sister has expressed Regan's sentiments quite well "only she comes too short" (71). Now Cordelia has the impossible task of topping both. Put on the spot, she is furious. Lear can never get enough love from his favorite daughter, and there is nothing *ever* passive about Cordelia.

CORDELIA.   Nothing my Lord.
LEAR.   Nothing?
CORDELIA.   Nothing.
LEAR.   Nothing will come of nothing, speak again. (*Lear*, 88–91)

The two extra "nothings" only found in the Folio, are surely essential. "Nothing" is the key word of the play. Only by having nothing will Lear find himself. Cordelia's eloquent and appropriate explanation, "So young my lord and true," (106) is met by Lear's grandiose loss of temper, calling down pagan deities in this pre-Christian play: "For by the sacred radiance of the Sun, / The miseries of Hecate and the night" (108–109).

It is "miseries" not "mysteries" in the Folio. A neat antithetical reading which I like.

When Kent starts to protest, Lear launches into a speech which to his mind wraps the matter up (120–133). Midline thought changes forestall any further interruption. All the news, which he must know will go down badly: "our self by Monthly course" to "this coronet part between you" (131–138) is delivered in one sentence of tightly controlled syntax, eight lines long.

What else to note in this opening scene? Kent suddenly addressing Lear in the familiar "thou": "What woulds't thou do old man?" (145), rather than by the respectful "you." Throughout, Kent advises from spiritual values while the Fool advises from expediency, chiding Lear for his folly, while Kent rebukes him for the harm that he does (Pogson 45).

After the exit of Cordelia and the King of France (who is always referred to as choleric and hot blooded, so why is he always played as such a bland young man?) Regan suddenly switches into cold prose "That's most certain, and with you. Next month with us" (285).

Now the atheist Edmund appears for his apostrophe to his goddess, Nature, and to Bastards in general. He has never been given an exit so, surely, has been lurking and observing all the previous scene. His speech (1.2.1–22), so loved by student actors, is in prose in the Quarto and verse in the Folio. It is obviously a verse speech, and one with its snappy midline thought changes to be taken quite fast.

The Folio variants from the Quarto for the rest of Act 1 seem to me to be a sensibly trimmed and edited prompt script. The additions seem sensible too: Gloucester's lament on the fate of the world: "there's son against Father, the King falls from bias of Nature, there's Father against children. We have seen the best of our time" (1.2.105).

"Who is it that can tell me who I am?" (1.4.140) says Lear and, in the Quarto answers himself with "Lear's Shadow." In the Folio (far better) the answer is given by the Fool. And in the Folio, Goneril again gives a sound reason for her desire for her father to "disquantify" his hundred knights: "he may enguard his dotage with their powers / And hold our lives in mercy" (1.4.315). The act ends with Lear, "let me not be mad not mad sweet heaven" (1.5.41), leaving for Regan's house, where he will find her absent.

I'm not going to plough through the whole play like this, as I see the Folio as an edited version of the Quarto. I shall select eight moments where Quarto and Folio diverge and argue, but not in every instance, the case for the Folio. But I do regret the Folios omission of "Dost thou call me fool boy?" and "All thy other titles thou has given away; that thou wast born with" (1.4.140).

In Act 3, scene 1, Kent's speech to the Gentleman has been re-written. In the Folio (22–29) he tells of Albany and Cornwall having servants who are in the pay of France. In the Quarto (30–42) that there's an advance party of a French invasion. You take your pick, but I don't think we need both.

In Act 3, scene 2 (79–96), the Fool's prophecy is only in the Folio. After a ranting sonnet, he says, "This prophecy Merlin shall make; for I live before his time." I think this almost the most wonderful moment in the play. G.K. Chesterton said, "This is one of the Shakespearean shocks or blows that take the breath away," and "The Fool juggles with time and space and tomorrow and yesterday" (Chesterton 93–94). Kiernan Ryan comments, "It takes the breath away because of the sudden sense of temporal vertigo it introduces. It takes the play out of all time. It juxtaposes utopian possibilities with dystopian actualities, encapsulating the battle between the way things are, and the way they could be that rages at the core of the tragedy" (*Lear*, Lxiii).

In Act 3, scene 4, line 37 is only found in the Folio: Edgar's "Fathom and half, fathom and half, poor Tom." This is a boatswain sounding the depth, and then shouting over his shoulder to the Mariners behind him. "Nero is an angler in the lake of darkness," as Fraterello tells Edgar (3.6 6–7), the entrance to Hell (Sitwell 48).

Edgar's entrance follows immediately after Lear, for the first time in his life, puts another before himself: "In Boy, go first. You houseless povertie." (3.4.26). This is only to be found in the Folio. Lear, of all people being considerate!

Then the great turning point for Lear in his extraordinary journey; his pleas for the homeless:

> LEAR.   Poor naked wretches, where so e'er you are
>   That bide the pelting of this pitiless storm,
>   How shall your House-less heads and unfed sides,
>   Your looped and windowed raggedness, defend you
>   From seasons such as these? O I have ta'en
>   Too little care of this: Take Physic, Pomp.
>   Expose thyself to feel what wretches feel,
>   That thou mayst shake the superflux to them,
>   And show the Heavens more just. (*Lear*, 3.4.186-194)

The famous mock trial of Act 3, scene 6 (17–55), is only to be found in the Quarto. This is quite a huge chunk, which shows the extent of Lear's insanity, (and the weirdness of Edgar's feigned insanity). It can be a useful way of getting rid of the Fool too, if Lear stabs him in a frenzy mistaking him for Goneril, which I have seen in more than one production. The Fool's haunting final line, "I'll go to bed at noon!" (83) is only in the Folio. But I think the play can easily do without the mock trial. I feel it is a sensible theater cut, magnificent material that doesn't quite serve the play well enough. What I would regret far more, in fact the only piece of the Quarto not in the Folio that I would strive to keep, would be Edgar's sonnet which ends Act 3, scene 6.

> EDGAR.　　When we our betters see bearing our woes,
> 　　　　　　We scarcely think our miseries our foes. . . .
> 　　　　　　He childed as I fathered! Tom, away! . . .
> 　　　　　　Lurk, lurk. (*Lear*, 3.6.111–126)[4]

It depends where you want to put the intermission. If here, you need Edgar's heartbroken and heartbreaking, sonnet to conclude the first half; perhaps discovering the murdered or self-killed corpse of the Fool at its conclusion. If the intermission comes here and the blinding of Gloucester in Act 3, scene 7 is the first scene of the second half, I would be tempted to keep the short exchange between the two servants (3.7.94–106) found only in the Quarto, arranging for Tom to lead the blinded Gloucester to Dover and treat his poor bleeding face with the whites of eggs. But, should the intermission come after Gloucester's blinding (which is usual, but it does make for a long first half), I think I would follow the Folio and cut the servants. "Go thrust him out of the gates and let him smell his way to Dover," says Regan (3.7.90).

Dover, as we know, is the English seaport nearest to France. But here, it is also non-geographical: a place of resolution that all in the play converge towards. (*Dwfr* in middle Welsh, from which the name comes, means "water": the domain of the Celtic sea god, Llyr.)

Gloucester, the loyal but sensuously selfish man, goes on an extraordinary journey too, one parallel to Lear's. But, in his case, giving a purse to the "Poor naked fellow," his disguised son, he realizes:

> GLOUCESTER.　Let the superfluous, and Lust-dieted man,
> 　　　　　　　　That slaves your ordinance, that will not see
> 　　　　　　　　Because he does not feel, feel your power quickly:
> 　　　　　　　　So distribution should undo excess,
> 　　　　　　　　And each man have enough. (*Lear*, 4.1.73–77)

Like Gonzalo in *The Tempest*, he has become a communist. That is only the beginning of his path, and his guide and mentor is his rejected and traduced son, Edgar, whose own journey through hell and darkness into a dazzling spiritual light moves me as much as any character in all world drama. The avenger of his father, sure, but also his father's parent. He teaches him that suicide is never the answer:

EDGAR.   What in ill thoughts again?
                Men must endure
                Their going hence, even as their coming hither,
                Ripeness is all come on.
GLOUCESTER.   And that's true too. (*Lear*, 5.2. 75-80)

And earlier:

GLOUCESTER.   You ever gentle Gods, take my breath from me;
                Let not my worser Spirit tempt me again
                To die before you please. (4.5.470-473)

The director Barry Kyle encapsulates the character of Edgar:

Whenever Poor Tom began to talk about who he was seeing, there was never any doubt that he was having genuine visions of a schizophrenic nature, and that some of these were to do with the devil, and were to be completely feared. It clearly goes beyond being a disguise. This is not Rosalind dressing up in pants in the Forest of Arden. It is somebody who, like Hamlet, enters a disguise and the disguise becomes a pathway to psychosis. He puts on the antic disposition and then can't get it off. (Croall 115)

Until he is entrusted by the old tenant with the well-being and guidance of his father and he says, "I cannot daub it further" (4.1.53), which, in the Quarto reads, "I cannot dance it further"! Edgar will earn his kingdom. Act 4, scene 3, between Kent and the Gentleman, is in the Quarto only. Nice, I suppose to hear about Queen Cordelia's tearful reaction to Kent's letters. But it is really not needed, and the scene holds up the momentum of the play. Let it go!

The great awakening scene of Act 4, scene 7, the reconciliation of Lear and Cordelia, surely the most moving in all Shakespeare, is different in the Quarto and Folio. In the Folio, there is no Doctor, "Madam do you, 'tis fittest" (4.7.43), no music and a short regrettable cut for Cordelia: "to watch, poor perdu! / with this thin helm …" (35–36).

Severe depletions? Perhaps. The healing music can make the scene, but if it is poor music, can mar it, and it is the Gentleman, not the Doctor, who says the absolutely vital line, "Be comforted good madam; the great rage, you see is kill'd in him" (78–79).

Far too many King Lears of my experience have never had that great rage in the first place. Laurence Olivier and Anthony Hopkins did. It is much better for the scene to end with Lear and Cordelia's exit, "Pray you now, forget and forgive. I am old and foolish" (84). Otherwise it tails off with yet another little chat between Kent and the Gentleman.

The whole awakening scene is almost entirely written in words of one syllable: "You do me wrong to take me out o'the'grave" (45). When Shakespeare writes a line in words of one syllable it is to be taken slowly:

LEAR.   Thou art a Soul in bliss, but I am bound
             Upon a wheel of fire, that mine own tears
             Do scald like molten lead. (*Lear*, 4.7. 596–598)

I don't think that Edgar's description of Kent's heart-attack (only in the Quarto) in Act 5, scene 3 (203–220) is wanted. It is more effective for Kent to follow his master by offstage suicide at the end, "I have a journey, Sir, shortly to go / My Master calls me, I must not say no" (5.3. 320).

And now for the final scene: Act 5, scene 3 from line 256, the entry of Lear carrying the dead Cordelia. I like him commanding the onlookers to "Howle" four times, as in the Quarto. There are only three in the Folio. But the Folio's fivefold "Never," ("Never, never, never, never, never" (307)) is a stroke of genius, even if it was, as possible, thought up by an actor!

Lear's death in the Quarto is very simple and beautiful. He says in prose, "pray undo this button, thank you, sir, O, o, o, o, o." These are known as the "O Groans." (That's how Hamlet dies in the Folio of *Hamlet*). But "O" means "Nothing," the key word of the play. Of course, in *Hamlet* they are nearly always cut, but when Mark Rylance, at the rebuilt Globe, died on four dwindling "ohs," I have never been so convinced that I was in the presence of a spirit leaving a body. The body is now Nothing. Nothing. Nothing will come of nothing. But then nobody who is not a woman or man of stone would lose Lear's vision of Cordelia coming back to life, which is only in the Folio: "Do you see this? Look on her? Look her lips, / Look there, look there. *He dies*" (309–310).

It does make a great difference to Lear's state of mind at his moment of passing. Dwindling into the Nothing, which is the key of the world, or glimpsing in joy something beyond.

Once, when I directed the play with students, Albany and Edgar shared the final speech, (which is given to Albany in the Quarto, Edgar in the Folio). They both came downstage, faced each other and Albany started:

ALBANY.   The weight of this sad time we must obey,
            Speak what we feel, not what we ought to say:
            The oldest hath borne most . . .

Then Edgar took it up:

EDGAR.   ...we that are young,
              Shall never see so much, nor live so long. (*Lear*, 5.3 430–433)

Then everyone on stage froze around the *pièta* of the dead Lear cradling Cordelia, as in the distance the rumble of a storm was heard (an effect I cribbed shamelessly from Peter Brook's 1960s production). But I wouldn't do this now. Albany has abdicated his authority, and we are not as emotionally engaged with him as we are with Edgar. It's nice that Albany has found a bit of spunk, told his horrible wife what he thinks of her, and shown responsibility for the country, but we haven't followed him on anything like Edgar's extraordinary psychological and spiritual journey. And, anyway, Albany isn't all that young, is he? Not young as Edgar is young. Edgar has earned the final speech!

In the Quarto, there is no stage direction at the end of the play. In the Folio, *"exeunt with a dead March"*! The real King Edgar (some centuries later) as Harold Bloom points out, rid Britain of wolves (479). Perhaps wolves should howl in the distance as the bodies are, with solemn ceremony, taken off. A pause for breath before the world goes savage and mad again.

Bear free and patient thoughts. (4.6.96)[5]

Notes

1 This essay is based on a talk given in July 2020 (via Zoom) for the Los Angeles Shakespeare Institute, a joint project of the Shakespeare Center of Los Angeles and the UCLA William Andrews Clark Memorial Library. I have tried to keep as much of the conversational tone of that lecture in this paper as possible.

2 The lineation used here (and in all following in-text quotations) is of the Arden text of *King Lear*, edited by Kenneth Muir (Methuen, 1972). Most subsequent editions which conflate Q and F use this text, in particular *The Oxford Schools Shakespeare* (ed. Roma Gill O.U.P., 1994), which I recommend to teachers.

3 This and all subsequent Folio quotations from: Shakespeare, William. *The Applause First Folio of Shakespeare in Modern Type*. Ed. Neil Freeman. Applause Books, 2001. I have used this text for capitalization, punctuation and line numbers. However, for modernized spelling I have used *King Lear (Modern Folio Edition)* from The Internet Shakespeare. Ed. Michael Best. July 21, 2021. https://internetshakespeare. uvic.ca/doc/Lr_FM/complete/index.html.

4 Shakespeare, William. *King Lear* from The Folger Shakespeare. Ed. Barbara Mowat, Paul Werstine, Michael Poston, and Rebecca Niles. Folger Shakespeare Library, July 18, 2021. https://shakespeare.folger.edu/shakespeares-works/king-lear/Internet Shakespeare Editions.

5 Ibid.

Works Cited

Bloom, Harold. *Shakespeare: The Invention of the Human.* Fourth Estate/Harper Collins, 2010.

Chesterton, G. K., and Dale Ahlquist. *The Soul of Wit G.K. Chesterton on William Shakespeare.* Dover Publications, 2012.

Croall, Jonathan. *Performing King Lear: Gielgud to Russell Beale.* Bloomsbury Publishing Plc, 2015.

Kermode, Frank. *Shakespeare's Language.* Penguin Books, 2009.

Pogson, Beryl. *"In the East My Pleasure Lies": and Other Esoteric Interpretations of Plays by William Shakespeare.* Haskell House Ltd., 1974.

Ryan, Kiernan. "Introduction." Shakespeare, William. *King Lear,* edited by George Hunter. Penguin Classics, 2015.

Shakespeare, William. *Mr. William Shakespeares Comedies, Histories, & and Tragedies: a Facsimile of the First Folio, 1623.* Ed. Doug Moston. Routledge, 1998.

Sitwell, Dame Edith. *A Notebook on William Shakespeare.* Bloomsbury, 1961.

Sohmer, Steve. "The Lunar Calendar of Shakespeare's King Lear." *Early Modern Literary Studies* 5.2 (Sept. 1999): 1–17.

8. *My Poor Fool: Dramatic Implications for Single, Double and Dual Casting Cordelia and the Fool in* King Lear

JESSIE LEE MILLS

The parallels between Lear's Fool and his youngest daughter, Cordelia, abound. Within the narrative, they both serve as the two truth-tellers and prove to be Lear's most loyal devotees. They each bravely oppose Lear when his reasoning appears faulty, and both strive to uphold the King's dignity as he spirals into madness. Fittingly, productions often take care to highlight the commonalities between the two characters. Though rarely, some productions choose to further underscore the connection between Cordelia and the Fool by double casting the characters, including the 2019 Broadway revival starring Glenda Jackson as Lear and Ruth Wilson as Cordelia and the Fool.[1]

This doubling is supported by many Shakespearean scholars, who "near the turn of the [twentieth] century, [proposed] the hypothesis that the actor playing Cordelia doubled as the Fool in early productions of *King Lear*."[2] This argument, presented as early as 1894 by Alois Brandl, "arose as a means to explain the disappearance of the Fool in Act III, as well as for his failure to appear or even be mentioned in the first scene of the play."[3] Combing through the archives, scholars have hotly debated this hypothesis throughout the twentieth and now into the twenty-first century. Shakespearean scholars Thomas Stroup and Richard Abrams both trace the discourse quite succinctly in a footnote and endnote, respectively, noting that while some scholars dismiss the proposal outright in favor of single casting, others believe the doubling premise quite plausible and focus the debate on whether Robert Wilson or Robert Armin (two members of The Chamberlain's Men) took on the paired roles.[4]

Other scholars further speculate that this doubling was not only logistically possible, but artistically intentional as a *dualling* of characters. Just three years after Brandl posited that Cordelia and the Fool were doubled, Arthur J. Stringer extended the argument and "adopted what ... is now an unhesitatingly accepted belief: that is, that the Fool in Shakespeare's *King Lear* is none other than Cordelia herself."[5] Stringer's sentiments were later echoed by H. L. Anshutz,[6] however both scholars' hypotheses have been widely dismissed. Indeed, Richard Abrams lists this assertion as the least plausible possibility for the relationship between Cordelia and the Fool.[7] Thomas Stroup, similarly, notes that Stringer's theory comes by way of "disregarding the text."[8] Stringer would unabashedly agree with Stroup's assessment, and opined on the matter quite glibly:

> In attempting to give my reasons for believing that Cordelia and the Fool are one, it will be unnecessary to deal at length with the literary history of the text: for if the dramatic and artistic evidences fail, it is quite useless to rely on the probability of mere textual evidence.[9]

If we take on Stringer's provocation, what can be gained if we think about possible casting options through the lens of the dramatic and artistic?

From an historical standpoint, these three modes of casting possibilities – single, double, and dual casting – each offer a fascinating glimpse into Shakespeare's troupe, performance trends, and writing. From a purely literary lens, these casting hypotheses invite a flurry of exploration and analysis. From a *staging* perspective, as Stringer urges us to consider first and foremost, we must ask how these interpretations affect our audiences' experience. As theater-makers, we are tasked with understanding the corporeal, theatrical implications of such casting choices. Be it performers, directors, designers, technicians, dramaturgs, administrators, educators, or practitioners, our job is to lift the words beyond the page and into the community. As such, I shall present a case for each casting possibility with a theater-maker's and audience's experience in mind. In assessing the artistic significance, each case will consider both practical and thematic rationales for the creative team and audience.

A Case for Single Casting

The Practical: The Difference Between a Bitter Fool and a Sweet One

Given the sizeable discourse on the doubling of Cordelia and the Fool, it seems curious that so few productions have done so. Within the past century alone, of the nine productions of King Lear on Broadway, only the 2019 production doubled Cordelia and the Fool.[10] Beyond the artistic merit, there are practical benefits to leaving Cordelia and the Fool as separate entities. While Shakespeare tied these two characters together thematically, they ultimately embody very different energies, physicalities, and sentiments. Of the eight non-doubled Broadway productions, all cast men (often older) as the Fool, and women (often younger) as Cordelia.[11]

Considering the ways in which each character is described throughout the play, there is reasonable value behind this trend of single casting. When Cordelia describes herself, often in asides, she mainly speaks about her trouble in finding the right words to say. In Act I, when her father demands she articulate her filial love and devotion, she worries in an aside that "my love's / More ponderous than my tongue" (1.1.86-87). And when tasked to speak in front of her father and sisters, she admits "I cannot heave / My heart into my mouth" (1.1.100-101) and muses that,

> CORDELIA.   If for I want that glib and oily art
>   To speak and purpose not—since what I well intend,
>   I'll do't before I speak—that you make known
>   It is no vicious blot, murder, or foulness,
>   No unchaste action or dishonored step
>   That hath deprived me of your grace and favor,
>   But even for want of that for which I am richer:
>   A still-soliciting eye and such a tongue
>   As I am glad I have not, though not to have it
>   Hath lost me in your liking." (*Lear*, 1.1.258-268)

Cordelia is thoughtful and straight to the point. She is not magniloquent, nor does she aim to be. She says plainly and confidently that such grandiloquence does not indicate love or honor. Other characters recognize this trait as a virtue. Kent, while counseling Lear, reminds the King that "Thy youngest daughter does not love thee least / Nor are those empty-hearted whose low sound / Reverbs no hollowness" (1.1.171-173). Even Lear, upon Cordelia's death, finally sees the beauty in her eloquence, lamenting that "Her voice was ever soft, / Gentle, and low" (5.3.328-329).

The Fool, on the other hand, is described as quite the opposite. Goneril rages that he is Lear's "all-licensed fool" (1.4.206). Where Cordelia is soft-spoken, the Fool is loud-mouthed; where Cordelia is thoughtful, the Fool is brash; where Cordelia is gentle, the Fool is blunt. Moreover, Cordelia is described as fair (1.1.290), virtuous (1.1.292), and kind (4.7.35), while the Fool is described as a knave (1.4.43), a mongrel (1.4.50), and bitter (1.4.140).

The King of France defies Lear by claiming that Cordelia "is herself a dowry" (1.1.278) when he wishes her to be his wife. The Fool, on the other hand, is lashed about. Lear belittles him by calling him "boy" and is scorned and embittered by the Fool's (once appreciated) mockery and buffoonery.

Perhaps the biggest, and most nuanced, discrepancy between the two characters is their awareness of how "truth" affects their king. Cordelia believes honesty to be an extension of duty. When she tells her father,

> CORDELIA.   You have begot me, bred me, loved me.
> I return those duties back as are right fit:
> Obey you, love you, and most honor you." (*Lear*, 1.1.106-108)

She explains that her love will always sit with her father, but also extend to her husband and family. Lear, unable to see that her virtue in honesty matches her virtue in love, asks, "So young and so untender?" (1.1.118) To which Cordelia responds, "So young, my lord, and true" (1.1.119).

The Fool, on the other hand, understands the tense nature of truth, knowing that some members of Lear's household (Goneril and Regan, namely) believe "Truth's a dog that must to kennel. / He must be whipped out" (1.4.115-116). The Fool, in his brash and blunt ways understands, implicitly, the danger in truth-telling. In fact, the Fool wishes he knew how to lie. He sings:

> FOOL.   *Then they for sudden joy did weep*
> *And I for sorrow sung,*
> *That such a king should play bo-peep*
> *And go the fools among.*
> *Prithee, nuncle, keep a schoolmaster that can*
> *teach thy fool to lie. I would fain learn to lie.* (*Lear*, 1.4.179-184)

Here, the Fool paints a painful picture of Lear's status – a child and a fool – and begs for someone to teach him to lie so that he might not be forced to articulate such truths. Cordelia, in her fairness and virtue, does not calibrate how the truth may ultimately harm her, nor the great personal tragedy that will ensue from her honesty.

Additionally, much can be mined in the distinct ages and lived experiences of these characters. Though some scholars believe that the doubling of Cordelia and the Fool was written for a younger performer on the basis that "the two roles call for the same kind of voices ... to [sing] the whimsical songs required,"[12] many productions have cast Lear's Fool as a much older man. This casting may highlight the distinct relationship that Lear and his

Fool have developed throughout a lifetime of service and companionship. Practically speaking, there is real value in distinguishing the two roles by casting different actors, especially if the goal is to highlight markedly different ages. In this case, single casting would help to clarify that the two characters hold different spaces in Lear's ears and heart. What he can understand intellectually from the Fool he cannot bear emotionally from Cordelia, and this is a dramatic distinction worth watching.

The Thematic: Hearing and Mishearing, Tethering and Untethering

The more we separate Cordelia and the Fool via casting, the more we continue to understand Lear's unique relationship with each of them. Richard Abrams notes that "during Cordelia's absence the Fool takes over her function of telling Lear the painful truth about himself."[13] These painful truths, regardless of the speaker, are often met with Lear's demand for clarification and rearticulation (or, perhaps, a hope that he misheard).

When Lear asks Cordelia what she can say about her love and devotion to draw land and a title "more opulent than [her] sisters'," (1.1.95) she responds, "Nothing." (1.1.96). "Nothing?" (1.1.97) Lear asks – surprised, hurt, hoping he had misheard. And when she clarifies that she cannot outdo her sisters' (falsely) professed love, Lear appeals with, "But goes thy heart with this?" (1.1.116). Similarly, when the Fool spends considerable time mocking Lear's poor decision-making, the King seems unable to fully take in the Fool's words, only finally realizing "Dost thou call me 'fool,' boy?" about 50 lines into the exchange.

However, when Lear does understand the truths spoken by Cordelia and the Fool, his response could not be more different. With Cordelia, the King is soft in his initial questioning ("But goes thy heart?"). He is heartbroken, and the pain is uniquely tender. But this initial reaction ratchets up and quickly spirals out of control.

> LEAR.　Thy truth, then, by thy dower,
> For by the sacred radiance of the sun,
> The mysteries of Hecate and the night,
> By all the operation of the orbs
> From whom we do exist and cease to be,
> Here I disclaim all my paternal care,
> Propinquity, and property of blood,
> And as a stranger to my heart and me
> Hold thee from this forever (*Lear*, 1.1.120-128).

Lear calls upon Hecate, an enraged and powerful force, as he violently disowns his most beloved daughter. When Kent tries to pacify him, Lear warns "Come not between the dragon and his wrath" (1.1.136). Lear's blood boils and nothing can calm him.

When the Fool speaks equally (if not more) painful truths, Lear has an inverse reaction. The King might begin in rage, but he settles into tranquility or pontification. In his rage, Lear twice reminds the Fool that a whipping is in order (1.4.114; 1.4.185), but never makes good on the threat. Rather, the King's frustration is redirected where it belongs: to Goneril, Regan, and to himself,

> FOOL.   If thou wert my Fool, nuncle, I'd have thee
>   beaten for being old before thy time.
> LEAR.   How's that?
> FOOL.   Thou shouldst not have been old till thou hadst
>   been wise.
> LEAR.   O, let me not be mad, not mad, sweet heaven!
>   Keep me in temper. I would not be mad! (*Lear*, 1.5.34-46)

The Fool, perhaps compassionately, perhaps mockingly, jokes about whipping Lear for becoming old before becoming wise. Lear's senility is showing, and the Fool is not shy about pointing it out. Lear, in response, prays to the heavens to stave off his dementia. Where Cordelia was banished for speaking a truth about herself, the Fool, in directly addressing Lear's faults, is held closer and with more regard.

Separating these two characters into different actors allows an audience to truly see how Lear hears one and cannot hear the other. A fair amount of this may have to do with gender discrimination and social contract,[14] and some of this has to do with *when* Lear can process the truth. As he spirals closer and closer to madness, it seems that the truth becomes more palatable. Structurally, it makes sense that the Fool accompanies Lear into madness. It is, potentially, only in the King's madness that he is able to hear and understand clearly. And if the Fool is tethered to Lear's madness, then it is only the Fool who can truly make the King hear the truth.

Cordelia, on the other hand, is banished while Lear is still stable and then reunites with her father as he is coming out of his fog of madness. When cast as a single role, the audience watches her character return to her weakened father in a devastating reunion. She nurses him back into health and stability and he clings to her more dearly, now, than he ever did his Fool. His Fool, after all, served his part. The Fool was tethered to his King's mind. Cordelia, his daughter, is tethered to his heart.

In this way, separating the two characters into two different performers allows the audience to see the depth and richness of these relationships. While the Fool and Cordelia perform similar actions and occupy parallel roles, they are ultimately uniquely distinct. Perhaps, without doubling, we not only see the Fool and Cordelia more clearly, but we are better able to understand Lear himself.

A Case for Double Casting

The Practical: Quick-changes and Honoring History

The doubling of roles can, undoubtedly, illuminate a number of interesting thematic and textual parallels. In a fully realized production, however, this decision is often enabled or defeated by logistics. A costume designer will be the first to point out the complications of a costume change, especially one concerned with period or intricate clothing. In *King Lear*, the text offers ample space for this changeover, even inviting the possibility. Cordelia and the Fool never overlap onstage and, more to the point, Shakespeare offers a buffer of time between one's exit and the other's entrance.

Lear disowns and dismisses Cordelia at the end of Act I scene 1, when her newly avowed fiancé, The King of France, beckons her to "come, my fair Cordelia" (1.1.328). In the Folio, it is not until Act I, scene 4, with 343 lines to spare, that the Fool enters. Similarly, the Fool's final spoken line rests in Act III, scene 6, announcing that he will "go to bed at noon" (3.6.90), though he does not exit until Gloucester's invitation to "come, come away" (3.6.110). Cordelia reemerges in Act IV, scene 4, with 419 lines in between. This timing, scholars argue, is no accident. Indeed, Stroup observes that "Between Cordelia's exit and the Fool's entry the same number of lines are spoken [in the Quarto[15]] as between the Fool's final exit and Cordelia's re-entry. Time is ... meted out for some reason, probably for the change of costume and make-up."[16]

Perhaps it is, similarly, no accident that both characters are beckoned away from their King. Unlike Lear's other servants and daughters who often leave of their own, fraught accord, both Cordelia and the Fool leave at the summoning of another. One might argue that this is the only way these two characters would leave their King. The act of leaving, then, is open-ended. Even as Cordelia is disowned and the Fool exhausted, both leave with unfinished business and with a connective thread still attached to Lear. In this way, their doubling allows one character to pick up where the other fell away.

For a director, producer, and costume designer, these exits and entrances make a Cordelia/Fool doubling not only possible, but compelling. If 100 lines equals approximately five minutes of stage time, an actor has 15–20 minutes for both changeovers. This may be time enough to lace or unlace a corset, remove and reapply any distinguishing make-up, and even provide a performer time to prepare their physical and psychological change in performance. More to the point, if this was the practice of Shakespeare's troupe, there is a silent honor paid to The Chamberlain's Men and the Bard himself. Conceptually speaking, this is a fascinating way to hook into the spirit and intentions of the original, historical productions.

The Thematic: Fools and Foolishness as a Dramatic Arc

Thematically, doubling the role of Cordelia and the Fool illuminates the arresting parallels between the two characters and, therefore, has the potential to unlock deeper truths about the play. While scholars and literary experts have mined the plethora of minutia in the shared language and values of these two characters, I will focus on an audience's experience of this doubling. A potential theater-goer who has little familiarity with this text may only have a first blush, if rich and embodied, experience of this language and these characters. As such, an intriguing benefit to this doubling is the way in which it primes the audience to better understand the depth and beauty of the arc of King Lear. If the audience knows that Cordelia and the Fool are played by the same actor, a thematic link is formed, and both Cordelia's lines and the Fool's lines have a deeper meaning. For the audience, this experience can be tracked through the use of the word fool, as it takes on considerable double meaning.

Shakespeare takes care to introduce the Fool before his arrival. Lear asks for him several times, beginning with a request to his court to, "Go you and call my Fool hither" (1.4.44), noting that he hasn't seen his Fool in two days (1.4.72). His First Knight replies that since Cordelia's banishment, "the Fool hath much pined away" (1.4.74). As Stroup notes, "the deliberate and painstaking association of the Fool with Cordelia, the stress laid upon his devotion to her, prepares the audience for his bitterness."[17] Moreover, knowledge of the Fool's distress over Cordelia's banishment prepares the audience to meet a Fool who is "sympathetic to Cordelia who will assume her defense and also remind them of her person."[18]

The Fool, upon his arrival, promptly takes Lear to task for what he's done to Cordelia, admonishing anyone who follows Lear to,

> FOOL.   There, take my coxcomb.
>   Why, this fellow has banished two on's
>   daughters and did the third a blessing against his

will. If thou follow him, thou must needs wear my
coxcomb. (*Lear*, 1.4.104-108)

The Fool offers his own status and title to all those in accord with Lear's rash decision. In a case of doubling, the audience sees the same truth in juxtaposing sentiments. Where Cordelia diplomatically points out the King's foolishness and inability to see clearly by asking "Why have my sisters husbands if they say / They love you all?" (1.1.109-110), the Fool assertively offers his cap to wear to anyone who supports Lear's foolish resolution.

And then the Fool goes a step further than Cordelia could: In response to Lear carelessly relinquishing his Kingdom and titles, he directly refers to his King as a fool. When Lear asks, "Dost though call me 'fool,' boy?" (1.4.152) the Fool responds, cutting to the core, "All thy other titles thou hast given away. That / thou wast born with." (1.4.153-154). Or, without the titles of his birth, "fool" is the only status inherent to Lear that remains. Through the lens of doubling, the same actor playing Cordelia strips Lear of his title, just as he did to her.

The use of the word fool is, indeed, used liberally throughout King Lear. Julian Markle notes:

> [In] King Lear Shakespeare ... make[s] the very word "fool" a blessing and a sanctification. All of the good characters in the play, all who sooner or later stand up for Lear, in their purity or their purification are nevertheless called "fool." The Fool, who always speaks true, calls Lear "fool" ... When Lear wakes up in Cordelia's tent, he confirms this judgement: in his earned humility he calls himself a fond and foolish old man."[19]

But the most potent use of the title is Lear's solemn line spoken upon announcing Cordelia's death, "And my poor fool is hanged" (5.3.369). In Lear's deepest grieving, he assigns the affectionate term to his youngest daughter; a term that he at first resented, then to which he capitulated, and ultimately a term that held his most devoted affection. Indeed, Lear's relationship with the very word "fool" itself parallels the trajectory of his relationship with Cordelia.

A Case for Dual Casting

The Practical: Suspending Disbelief Anew

For a literary historian, the sentiment that Cordelia is the Fool in disguise may be pure blasphemy. Indeed, this disguise would go against the structured formula that Shakespeare uses for every other disguised character throughout his oeuvre. As P.V. Kreider calculates,

> Shakespeare's purpose in bringing a disguised figure onto the stage is never to mystify or deceive and later surprise his audience; his intent is always to conceal the identity of one or more characters from other persons in the play. A contingency more or less serious demands that certain personages operate incognito, but the dramatist takes care that the spectators derive that passive, complacent delight which comes from acquaintance with all the details of the situation ... he tells [the audience], in plain terms, exactly what he is about to do."[20]

At no point in *King Lear* does Shakespeare elucidate to the audience, in plain terms, that Cordelia is donning the disguise of the Fool. More tellingly, Shakespeare *does* conspicuously clarify both the intents and mechanisms of Kent and Edger's disguises within *King Lear*. Even so, for a theater-maker, this notion of Cordelia dualling with the Fool is quite intriguing. As noted, Stringer, who originally proposed this hypothesis, boldly asserted that the success of a production of *King Lear* relies primarily on the dramatic staging, rather than the literary interpretation. What are the dramatic implications, then, of this casting choice?

One challenge in dualling Cordelia as the Fool is the particular suspension of disbelief needed to keep the audience engaged. In the doubling proposal, the audience merely needed to suspend the disbelief that the same actor is two different roles, a relatively commonplace experience in Shakespeare's other productions. In this dualling hypothesis, however, a new cognitive dissonance may arise: an audience member might ponder how Lear or Cordelia's sisters could not see their daughter or sibling through her mask. Shakespeare, one step ahead, has already written to the strength of his familial characters' disguises in *Twelfth Night* and *As You. Like It*. In *Twelfth Night*, Viola was so convincing as Cesario that Antonio could not distinguish between her and her twin brother, Sebastian. Furthermore, when Sebastian meets Cesario, he can see a resemblance, but does not immediately know who she is. Sebastian asks, "Of charity, what kin are you to me? / What countryman? What name? What parentage?" (*TN*, 5.1.241-242). Sebastian is actively looking for his sister and still cannot see through her costume. Goneril and Regan, on the other hand, have no interest in finding their banished sister and are less likely to seek out or notice such a resemblance.

As for Lear, *As You Like It* lays the groundwork for a father's inability to see his daughter in disguise. Upon seeing his daughter, Rosalind, in the dressings of Ganymede, Duke Senior remarks, "I do remember in this shepherd boy / Some lively touches of my daughter's favor" (*AYL*, 5.4.27-28). Similar to Sebastian, Duke Senior can sense a resemblance, but he cannot see through her convincing mask. Lear, on the other hand, does not have complete control over his faculties. While Lear certainly spends far more time with his daughter disguised as the Fool than Duke Senior does with

Ganymede, the King's wits are not about him, and he cannot fully take in the world around him.

That said, further questions percolate: how does Cordelia conceal her identity from Lear's full cadre of personnel? Has Cordelia always been the Fool, or did she only take over once banished? If the former, to what end? If the latter, what happened to the Fool before she took over? Do those two days that Lear has not seen his Fool now take on a deeper meaning? Did the Fool and Cordelia hatch this plan together? Did the Fool pass away within those two days, leaving a space for Cordelia to seamlessly step in? Logistically, this suspension of disbelief relies on the audience overlooking some substantial questions. That said, if we take Stringer at his word, this proof is in the thematic and artistic interpretation.

The Thematic: Sir, do you know me?

To consider the full impact of this dualling, we must consider how the audience would experience Cordelia anew through her disguise. In the doubling proposal, the audience has access to a deeper thematic link between the two characters, and ultimately more information about Lear's connection and relationship to each character. In this dualling hypothesis, the focus shifts to center on Cordelia as the audience bears witness to her psyche and experience. Through her disguise as the Fool, the audience now watches as Cordelia forcibly observes her father in decline. A heart wrenching experience, certainly, and one that Cordelia may feel a duty to uphold. Stringer writes of Cordelia's choice to follow her father,

> "She makes the well intended *[sic]* but necessarily unfortunate sacrifice to check her father in his foolish exhibition of vanity and childishness: and is it not strange that she should selfishly desert him, when she knew, as a result of her unfortunate attempt, he would certainly end in misfortune and misery? It seems to me she was scarcely of nature to live contentedly and happily with the King of France, in the consciousness that the father she loved was suffering both mediately and immediately because of an act of her own. She was tender, but she was daring—else how that first opposition? She determines to cleave to her father in his unhappiness, as Edgar cleaves to Gloster *[sic]*. To do so openly would be impossible. Not only would it be dangerous to her personally, but the enraged King would refuse to receive her, so she becomes his Fool. She adopts the only possible disguise and remains with her weak and helpless father, to attempt to shield him from the selfish cruelty of her sisters, and to endeavor to check his growing madness by bitter speeches and caustic irony, even as she has failed to do by candor and uprightness."[21]

It is the very same duty that prompted Cordelia to speak the truth in Act I that motivates her to follow her father in disguise through Act III. As

Stringer notes, an interesting parallel is now drawn between Edgar and Cordelia, which deepens "the lunatic trial of Regan and Goneril," where Poor Tom and Poor Cordelia, together, help Lear see the truth of his treacherous daughters.

With Cordelia concealed as the Fool, the audience is now "in" on the doubling. Through this dramatic irony, their experience and perspective has changed significantly, as they now actively watch the Fool through the lens of Cordelia's experience. An audience is not only primed to understand the parallels between characters, but every word spoken by and to the Fool is now spoken by and to Cordelia. Likewise, every word spoken by or to Cordelia is now spoken by or to the Fool. When Lear says to the Fool "I did her wrong" (1.5.24), for instance, the audience must watch Cordelia grapple with his apology, even as she must stay the course as the Fool.

And when Cordelia returns as herself, we interpret her lines as someone who has seen the entire trajectory of the King's madness. When she asks Lear,

> CORDELIA.   Sir, do you know me?
> LEAR.   You are a spirit, I know. Where did you die?
> CORDELIA.   Still, still far wide!" (*Lear*, 4.7.55-57)

Cordelia notes that he is "still" far wide, as though she was hoping Lear would have snapped back to lucidity by now. In this artistic lens, we see a full journey in Cordelia's character. She was the daughter that refused to be banished, but later abandons her father at the height of his madness. Now, racked with guilt, she begins by begging her father to be healed ("O, my dear father, restoration hang / Thy medicine on my lips, and let this kiss / Repair" IV.7.31-33), and ends by begging Lear to bless and, perhaps, heal her ("O, look upon me, sir / And hold your hands in benediction o'er me" (4.7.65-66).

Perhaps this casting option ultimately offers a creative route where Lear is the most deeply connected to Cordelia. If Lear moves in and out of his madness, then perhaps in his more lucid moments he can see who his Fool truly is. Perhaps Stringer was wrong in his assessment that "the enraged King would refuse to receive her," and it is, indeed, Cordelia seen through her disguise that guides Lear back to sanity. When the Fool rages against Goneril, Lear takes note. In the exchange where the Fool says,

> FOOL.   For you know, nuncle,
>   The hedge-sparrow fed the cuckoo so long,
>   That it's had it head bit off by it young.
>   So out went the candle and we were left darkling. (*Lear*,
>   1.4.220-223)

And Lear responds,

> LEAR.   Are you our daughter? (1.4.224)

The assumption is that this line is spoken to Goneril. A distressed question, wondering where his once devoted daughter went. In this staging, however, perhaps this line is delivered to Cordelia as a moment where Lear remembers who he is, and who his Fool might be. Perhaps Lear turns to Cordelia with clarity in his eyes, looking gratefully to the daughter who defends him, supports him, and truly loves him, to ask if she is truly with him, as he always hoped she would be, "[a]re you our daughter?"

And once Lear emerges from his fog of madness, there is a chance that he knows what his daughter has done for him. When he and Cordelia are carted off to prison, Lear calms her by musing,

> LEAR.   Come, let's away to prison.
> We two alone will sing like birds i' th' cage.
> When thou dost ask me blessing, I'll kneel down
> And ask of thee forgiveness. So we'll live,
> And pray, and sing, and tell old tales, and laugh
> At gilded butterflies, and hear poor rogues
> Talk of court news, and we'll talk with them too—
> Who loses and who wins; who's in, who's out—
> And take upon 's the mystery of things,
> As if we were God's spies. And we'll wear out,
> In a walled prison, packs and sects of great ones
> That ebb and flow by th' moon. (Lear, 5.3.9-20)

Just as he did with his Fool, Lear and Cordelia will pray, sing, and tell old tales. And when his Cordelia is ultimately taken from him, Lear's famous line now cuts more deeply than ever: "My poor fool is hanged." It is his final honor, and the culmination of Lear's anguished lament, paid to the daughter and companion he loved above all else.

Conclusion: Artistic Considerations or, the Trial of Daughters, Fools, and Madmen

Artistically, there is much to be gained in highlighting the parallels and distinctions between Cordelia and the Fool, whether portrayed in a single, double, or dual casting. In each case, theatrical choices abound, and a creative team might want to begin by deciding the aesthetic and appearance of both characters (be it costume, lighting, sound, relationship to space, etc.), and how those elements might create or subdue distinctions in gender, age, or other distinguishing characteristics between the two roles.

There is a middle ground, however; a liminal space where Cordelia and the Fool share and exchange space, or morph into and out of one another. Given Lear's descent into madness, the opportunity for the hallucination of Cordelia in place of the Fool (and vice versa) seems ripe, especially at the crescendo of Lear's decent into madness during the storm in Act III. Though scholars debate the exact onset of Lear's madness, and scholar Josephine Water Bennett does a fine job chronicling this discourse,[22] most agree that its height occurs in what Barker-Granville famously calls, "the lunatic trial of Regan and Goneril."[23]

In this trial, Edgar (or Poor Tom) serves as the judge, and the Fool as Lear's wise counsel. Regan's imagined examination follows Goneril's, and neither are spared Lear's searing wrath. Lear speaks of Goneril:

> LEAR.   Arraign her first. 'Tis Goneril. I here take my
>   oath before this honorable assembly, she
>   kicked the poor king her father. (Lear, 3.6.50-52)

And of Regan,

> LEAR.   And here's another, whose warped looks proclaim
>   What store her heart is made on. (3.6.56-57)

In no uncertain terms, Lear denounces Goneril for her abuse and Regan for her corrupt and hardened heart.

If the parts of Cordelia and the Fool are single cast, the Fool would sit with Lear as the King imagines his daughters brought into the court room. Further, if this scene is staged through Lear's eyes, a director may decide to bring on the actors playing Goneril and Regan so that the audience sees what Lear sees. In this instance, the Fool represents both himself and Lear's third daughter, highlighting the parallels between the two. Or perhaps a director might opt to also bring on the actor playing Cordelia to sit in counsel beside her father with the Fool. In this space, at the height of his lunacy, his two dearest companions and fiercest allies share space at his side.

If the parts are double cast, the Fool has the potential to appear, aesthetically, to morph into a clearer resemblance Cordelia in this scene. This artistic rendering not only invites the audience to thematically link Cordelia and the Fool, but it also highlights Lear's lunacy as he struggles to understand who is in the room and who is not. As Lear hallucinates the traitorous Regan and

Goneril on trial, it stands to reason that he would imagine his beloved youngest daughter at his side in solidarity against her sisters. Indeed, as this scene's dynamics echo the play's opening where the three sisters are on trial for their devotion, imagining Cordelia as his counsel allows Lear to finally position her where she rightfully belongs: at, and on, his side.

Last, if the roles are dual cast, then Cordelia as the Fool would finally hear her father condemn her sisters. In this casting, Lear truly amends his wrongs and, not only does he seek justice for himself, but he also restores justice to Cordelia. Artistically, there is an additional layer in Lear's three trial companions – Kent, Edgar, and Cordelia – all in disguise to serve their King. Perhaps these three share a knowing recognition of this benevolent deception. Perhaps all three, taking advantage of Lear's lunacy, can even momentarily discard their masks as they help their King seek justice.

No matter the casting choice, the relationship between Cordelia and the Fool is critical in the staging of this trial. The two are inextricably linked, and their connection engenders deep heartbreak in Lear: for it is only in Lear's madness that he can have all his allies at his side. Although Lear wishes often throughout the play that he not succumb to his madness ("O, let me not be mad, not mad, sweet heaven!" 1.5.45), perhaps it is only in madness that he can see his world restored. At the closing of the play, the audience may hold a compassionate, if complicated, wish for Lear to become mad again, so that he can see the world as it should be.

Ultimately, following Stringer's invitation to assess the artistic merit of each casting choice reveals three unique opportunities to heighten the themes in *King Lear*. Shakespeare's words, in their intended form, exist in the corporeal and ephemeral medium of theater, and the audience is the truest arbiter of their success. Therefore, any invitation to consider how we might impact an audience more deeply is a welcome one, indeed.

Notes

1 Previews ran February 28 – April 3, 2019. Official production ran April 4 – June 9, 2019, Cort Theater, New York, NY.
2 Richard Abrams, p. 354.
3 Brandl, p. 179.
4 Both Stroup and Abrams agree that Alois Brandl was an early advocate for this hypothesis. Abrams credits Wilfred Perrett (*The Story of King Lear*) as an early adopter of the doubling, where Stroup credits Brander Matthews (*Shakespeare as Playwright*). Stroup credits Brander Matthews with the proposal that Wilson doubled as Cordelia and the Fool, and Tucker Brooke with the proposal that it was, in fact, Armin. Both Stroup and Abrams eschew the assertion that Cordelia, herself, also plays the Fool, but where Stroup cites Arthur Stringer's 1897 paper, "Was

Cordelia the King's Fool?", Abrams references H. L. Anshutz's 1964 essay, "Cordelia and the Fool."

5 Stringer, p. 4.
6 Anshultz, pp. 240–260.
7 Abrams, p. 366.
8 Stroup, p. 127.
9 Stringer, pp. 2–3.
10 https://www.ibdb.com/broadway-show/king-lear-5064
11 https://www.ibdb.com/broadway-show/king-lear-5064
12 Thomas Stroup credits Janet Spens with this argument in "Cordelia and the Fool," p. 127, though he does not supply a specific citation to follow up on her analysis.
13 Abrams, p. 354.
14 Much has been brilliantly written about the issues of the patriarchy and misogyny in King Lear, most notably, Lesley Catherine Kordecki and Karla Koskinen's *Re-visioning Lear's Daughters: Testing Feminist Criticism and Theory*, 1st ed., Palgrave Macmillan, 2010, where they position each daughter on trial under the thumb of the patriarchy.
15 Stroup notes that, in the Quarto, there are 356 lines before the Fool's entrance and 357 lines between the Fool's exit and Cordelia's reentrance.
16 Stroup, p. 127
17 Stroup, p. 129
18 Stroup, p. 129.
19 Markels, p. 76.
20 Kreider, p. 167–168.
21 Stringer, p. 4.
22 Josephine Water Bennett outlines several hypotheses as to the onset of Lear's Madness in "The Storm Within: The Madness of King Lear." This includes, but is not limited to, A. C. Bradley's proposal that Lear's madness begins upon seeing Edgar, whereas Kenneth Muir and Norman Maclean assert that the King's madness occurs upon seeing Poor Tom. According to Water Bennett, authors Joseph Wharton, Samuel Taylor Coleridge, and Sholom J. Kahn precisely pinpoint the onset of Lear's madness with specific lines or stage directions in Act III scene 4.
23 Granville-Barker, p. 120 (footnote).

Works Cited

All textual citations refer to: Folger Shakespeare Library. *Shakespeare's Plays*. from Folger Digital Texts. Ed. Barbara Mowat, Paul Werstine, Michael Poston, Rebecca Niles. Folger Shakespeare Library, 1 April 2019. www.folgerdigitaltexts.org

Abrams, Richard. "The Double Casting of Cordelia and Lear's Fool." *Texas Studies in Literature and Language*, vol. 27, no. 4, The English Renaissance and Enlightenment, 1985, p. 354–368.

Anshutz, H.L. "Cordelia and the Fool." *Research Studies*, Washington State University, vol. 32, pp. 240–260.

Barker-Granville, Harley. "King Lear." *Shakespeare Criticism 1919–1935*, edited by Anne Bradby, Atlantic Publishers & Distributors, 2004, pp. 95–129.

Brandl, Alois. *Shakespeare*. Berlin: Hoffman, 1894.

Kreider, P. V. "The Mechanics of Disguise in Shakespeare's Plays." *The Shakespeare Association Bulletin*, vol. 9, no. 4, 1934, p. 167–180.

Markels, Julian. "Shakespeare's Confluence of Tragedy and Comedy: Twelfth Night and King Lear." *Shakespeare Quarterly*, vol. 15, no. 2, 1964, p. 75–88.

Stroup, Thomas. "Cordelia and the Fool." *Shakespeare Quarterly*, vol. 12, no. 2, 1961, p. 127–132.

Stringer, Arthur J. "Was Cordelia The King's Fool?" *The American Shakespeare Magazine*, vol. 3, 1897, p. 1–11.

Water Bennett, Josephine. "The Storm Within: The Madness of King Lear." *Shakespeare Quarterly*, vol. 13, no. 2, 1962, p. 137–155.

Wear, Keziah. (April 1, 2019). "Glenda Jackson as King Lear Puts Classic Power Struggles in a Freshly Gilded Frame," *Vanity Fair*. Online.

King Lear. By William Shakespeare, directed by Sam Gold, June 1 2019, Cort Theater, New York, NY. Performance.

League, The Broadway. "IBDB.com." *IBDB*, https://www.ibdb.com/

Additional References

Kordecki, Lesley, and Karla Koskinen. *Re-Visioning Lears Daughters: Testing FeministCriticism and Theory*. Palgrave Macmillan US, 2010.

Matthews, Brander. *Shakespeare as Playwright*. Charles Scribner's Sons, 1913.

Thaler, Alwin, and Alwin Thaler. *Shakespeare's Silences*. Books for Lib. Press, 1970.

Lawrence, William John. *Pre-Restoration Stage Studies*. Bloom, 1967.

Shakespeare, William, and William Lyon. PHELPS. *The Yale Shakespeare . . . New Edition Revised by Tucker Brooke*.

Spens, Janet. *Elizabethan Drama*. Nabu Press, 2010.

Perrett, Wilfrid. *The Story of King Lear: from Geoffrey of Monmouth to Shakespeare*. Wagner, 1903.

Bradley, A.C. Shakespearean Tragedy. Macmillan Publishers Ltd, 1904.

Muir, Kenneth: Shakespeare's Sources I. Methuen & Co Ltd, 1957.

Maclean, Norman. "Episode, Scene, Speech, And Word - The Madness Of Lear." *The Journal of General Education*, vol. 5, no. 3, 1951, p. 186–201

Warton, Joseph. "The Adventurer." *Shakespeare Criticism: A Selection 1623–1840*, p. 52–69.

Coleridge, Samuel Taylor. "The Lectures." *Shakespeare Criticism: A Selection 1623–1840*, p. 213–272.

Kahn, Sholom J. "Enter Lear Mad." *Shakespeare Quarterly*, vol. 8, no. 3, 1957, p. 311–329.

9. Measure for Measure

ELAINE TURNER

"For if you forgive men their trespasses, your heavenly Father will also forgive you."

Matthew 6:14 (KJV)

"Judge not, that ye be not judged. For with what judgment ye judge, ye shall be judged; and with what measure ye mete, it shall be measured to you again."

Matthew 7:2 (KJV)

The enactment of power and its consequences are addressed in virtually all of Shakespeare's plays—in some more directly than others, of course. Sometimes they are matched for comparative discussion. For example, in two of the plays a usurper murders the ruler, and his reign is elaborated through the dramatic action. At least three rulers give away their kingdoms while still expecting the benefits of power. Leaving *King Lear* aside, we find two more rulers handing over the job to a second in command. One, Prospero, so that he can go to his library; the other, the Duke in *Measure for Measure*, cannot bring himself to enforce the draconian laws he himself has created. The Duke fears his popularity may be at stake if he enacts these laws. His solution is to appoint a deputy, Angelo, to take his place and enforce the laws while he, the Duke, observes in the background, his reputation for kindliness intact.

If all rulers have fools, at first glance one might expect that Angelo, the recipient of the Duke's poison chalice, is the Duke's fool. But Shakespeare is more clever than that. Angelo turns out to be more victim than fool, floundering in a situation well over his head. It seems that the Duke in his self-admiration casts *himself* as the classical fool, the character who is outside the action, able at once to be both critic and commentator. Too bad for the Duke, then, (given that the essence of his new role is disengagement), for as soon as he sees the virginal Isabella he is taken with her, and before we know it, the Duke is attempting to manipulate the action to his own benefit, trans-gressing his self-imposed role of observer/commentator. The Duke becomes a genuine fool, trapped in his own machinations, unable to save himself.

It is unavoidable that our perspectives on all works of art are formed through the social, political and cultural experiences of our time. The Victorians, apparently comfortable and secure at the center of an empire, were reverent and supportive of those in power. Their responses to Shakespeare's plays centered on beneficent (or well-meaning but misunderstood) rulers. A "duke of such a mild and gentle temper" begin Charles and Mary Lamb in their Victorian elaboration of *Measure for Measure* (https://www.bartleby.com/1012/14.html). Critic A.C. Bradley, writing over a hundred years ago, sees the play as one of forgiveness, in which a "good" Duke pardons all.

"Forgiveness" is an interesting point here. The Duke, in the end, does forgive. He forgives everyone except Lucio, one of the few characters who interacts with him; the man who saves him by exposing his disguise. The Duke remains a genuine fool, who acts without knowledge, understanding, or a sense of responsibility, and consequently finds himself in unexpected difficulties. But he is also the Duke and he is a dangerous ruler. In *Measure for Measure* the misuse of power is elaborated in detail to the humiliation and near-punishment of the enactor, but also, and more importantly, to the final silencing of those who are powerless. In our time, when the clay feet of the powerful have, for better or worse, been horribly exposed, it is difficult to see the Duke as anything more than a man who craves power without responsi-bility, who wants credit without taking risks, and who sees personal benefit as a just reward for his position. Ultimately he will take what he wants and mold the world to his desires.

With Isabella, we can see what happens to those without "voice" or power. Isabella, who only desires to be a nun and live in a convent, is manipulated by three different men, but fights courageously until she comes face to face with the highest authority. "To whom can I complain?" (2.4.185), she asks. When she confronts the Duke, however, he uses his position to absorb her. This exceptionally articulate woman is struck dumb. When power is absolute and used for personal gain, there is nowhere to turn. Simultaneously, the role of the fool is also elaborated. Its sacred untouchability, created through dis-tance, insight and lack of personal engagement, is disrupted. You cannot be your own fool. One needs a fool to be able to say that one's affections would become tender, "were I human" (*Tempest*, 5.1.24–27). Playing the classical fool is the last chance one has to gain perspective and self-knowledge.

I find *Measure for Measure* a shocking play. In its quiet, unprepossess-ing way, it examines the machinations of power in several forms, and its conclusions are not encouraging. There is much in the Duke that is familiar to us: a ruler who casts himself as a "fool" to gain sympathy, attention, and to mask the consequences of his actions. Power permits and exonerates everything. This Duke is the ruler of an enclosed city. Imagine if he were to rule an entire country!

I

Measure for Measure is traditionally referred to as a "problem play," generally because it is considered neither a comedy nor a tragedy in the canon. However, *Measure for Measure* can be seen as a genuine "problem play" in that its entire purpose is to investigate a specific problem: given human frailty, how can we mete out justice so that it is equitable, so there is a "measure for measure"? *Measure for Measure* offers more opportunities than most plays for observation through a personalized lens. After all, no reading of any play can be totally objective. Underlying assumptions cannot help but color our responses. Nor can a reading be entirely personal, for our own prejudices and predilections are formed and influenced by the social, political and cultural preconceptions and assumptions of the world in which we live. Interest in power would focus our attention on the Duke. In today's "#MeToo" world, Isabella might take center stage. The difficulty lies in giving each character his or her full value, as Shakespeare does, and then arriving at the end of the play with a sense of dramatic coherence. The following is an attempt to provide a coherent approach to this remarkable but often troublesome play.

As the Duke is the character with the largest part, the most knowledge of what is going on, and the most power, it is the Duke we must first interrogate. He does have a name, Vincentio, but it is never used. His position is his identity. The Duke opens the play with an almost incomprehensible speech ("Of government the properties to unfold" (1.1.3)) that boils down to telling an associate, Lord Escalus, that he is going away and leaving Angelo in charge. They agree that Angelo has a spotless reputation. Angelo arrives and modestly argues that he is not ready for such responsibility, but the Duke insists, telling Angelo he may "enforce or qualify" the laws, as he sees best.

However, the Duke, two scenes later, in the process of disguising himself as a monk, tells Friar Thomas that he expects his laws to be enforced. He himself has neglected them, he admits. However, they are so severe that he feels the public will turn against him if he revives them, so he has set Angelo to enforce them. The Friar disapproving, quite rightly, objects:

FRIAR THOMAS. It rested in your Grace
   To unloose this tied-up justice when you pleased,

> And it in you more dreadful would have seemed
> Than in Lord Angelo.
> DUKE. I do fear, too dreadful.
> Sith, 'twas my fault to give the people scope. (*MM*, 1. 3. 33–88)

The Duke fears this would damage his reputation for kindness and make him politically unpopular. He then explains there is another reason, which he describes with somewhat more passion than the first:

> DUKE. Lord Angelo is precise ... / scarce confesses
> That his blood flows, or that his appetite
> Is more to bread than stone. Hence shall we see,
> If power change purpose, what our seemers be. (*MM*, 1.3.54–8)

Perhaps it is our sensitivity to psychological nuance that makes us flinch at the Duke's rather excessive and bitter description of Angelo. Is it hatred? Jealousy? Whatever the cause, it is clear that this is personally set up by the Duke to discredit Angelo. Ironically, of course, the Duke could never have foreseen the appearance of Isabel, who actually proves to be Angelo's undoing.

There are several Shakespearean rulers who leave their kingdoms in the hands of others, and the result is never good. We could discuss the limits and possibilities left to a second-in-command, but suffice it to say the deputy can never exercise the full scope of an absolute ruler. Caught between a rock and a hard place, Angelo must carry out the tasks obligatory to the role, while at the same time be aware that these actions, and the manner by which he carries them out, will be scrutinized and judged by his superior.

Angelo has a reputation for fastidiousness, and prides himself on it. Hence the idea that he has ice water in his veins. But Angelo initially does not plan to do anything disreputable. Yet, both Escalus and Isabel later suggest that Angelo might have violated the law in his youthful past, putting the audience on guard against hypocrisy:

> ESCALUS. Whether you had not some time in your life
> Erred in this point which you now censure him,
> And pulled the law upon you. (*MM*, 2.1.15–21)

And ...

> ISABELLA. Go to your bosom,
> Knock there, and ask your heart what it doth know
> That's like my brother's fault. (*MM*, 2.2.166–8)

Angelo's transgression is not sex outside marriage, but breach of promise of marriage. He was contracted to marry Mariana, but because her dowry was lost at sea, he did not marry her. Breach of promise is a civil crime, not a capital crime, and a good lawyer could probably argue that the dowry was part of the contract, so Angelo is not in breach of the contract. So far he certainly cannot be judged as either a hypocrite or felon.

The "bed trick" of switching bodies, by which Angelo is caught, was a common enough Renaissance dramatic trope, but Shakespeare never uses any trope without purpose. This "trick" has sinister implications regarding the Duke, who is not only acting as a pimp, but also forcing Angelo to break the law. All this casts doubts on the concept of a "good Duke." His behavior is manipulative and outrageous. By this point in the play the Duke cannot be seen as a detached observer in any way. He wants Isabella. It is difficult to see how those who found him beneficent a century and more ago could excuse not only his embroiling her in his nefarious plot against Angelo, but also, more shocking, telling her that her brother had been executed in order to gain her unmerited gratitude. To see the Duke as excusable, one needs to see Isabella as cold-hearted. It is challenging for a modern reader to entertain this position. Of all the characters, it is probably Isabella who comes across most passionately today. Those against her are turned so mostly by her insistence on her "chastity," and feel it is cold and churlish of her to choose an ideal over the actual life of her brother. Many feel it is her duty to sacrifice herself, a suggestion that implies a relative value between brother-and-sister/man-and-woman which is unpalatable today.

Isabella intends to be a nun. True, it is not a common occupation these days, but it is her desire. She responds readily to Lucio's request to plead with Angelo for her brother's life. Arguably, there is no heroine in all of Shakespeare who can hold a candle to Isabella when it comes to an argument. When she confronts Angelo, she begins hesitantly, but with Lucio urging from the sidelines, she becomes increasingly passionate:

> ISABELLA. How would you be
> If He which is the top of judgment should
> But judge you as you are? Oh think on that,
> And mercy will then breathe within your lips
> Like man new-made. (*MM*, 2.2.99–103)

Isabella's words flow from her deep-seated Christianity and mirror St Matthew's description of justice. It will be important to remember these words in the last act.

Angelo has seemingly never before been tempted by sex. It is Isabel's goodness that undoes him:

ANGELO. What's this? What's this? Is this her fault or mine?
    The tempter or the tempted, who sins most, ha?
    Not she, nor doth she tempt; but it is I . . .
    . . . Never could the strumpet
    With all her double vigor, art and nature,
    Once stir my temper, but this virtuous maid
    Subdues me quite. Ever till now
    When men were fond, I smiled and wondered how. (*MM,* 2.2.220–224)

Is Angelo evil? It is difficult to credit that. First, there is limited premeditation. Second, he does not aim to harm, although he must do so to achieve his own desire. Third, as Isabel later says, he did not, in the end, do anything. Is he wrong? Of course! Moreover, he commits Blackmail, which is a serious crime. This blackmail is never mentioned by any of the characters; it is a secret Angelo and Isabel share with the audience. Like the Duke, Angelo takes advantage of the power of his position. Power and responsibility are ever in Shakespeare's sights, and here we have two men, each with unquestioned power, using it for their own ends.

II

The second meeting between Angelo and Isabella rings with passion, its language is rich with sexual innuendo. Isabella, perhaps, is unconscious of the intimations behind her words. Angelo thirsts, making them explicit. He tells her outright "I love you" (2.4.152), and that he will exchange her brother Claudio's life for her body. Isabel threatens to tell the world "what man thou art" (2.4.165), and Angelo retorts that his unsullied name will speak for him, even though "my false o'erweighs your true" (2.4.184). "To whom should I complain" (2.4. 185), cries Isabella at the end of the scene; a clear and desperate cry that rings through the remainder of the play. There is only one person from whom she might obtain justice. The audience waits in expectation.

    I suspect most women today would identify with Isabella and see the issue not as one of chastity, but of violation. Chastity is the language by which it is discussed, but violation is the subject. "Soul" is the description of the integral person in this play. For Isabella, her body and her integrity, her soul, are neither separable nor dispensable.

    The dead center of the play rests in Isabella's meeting with her brother, Claudio. Here, too, our preconceptions are called upon. Do we feel with Claudio that sex between his sister and Angelo would be a small price to pay to save him from death? Or do we feel with Isabella that this violation is too great a price to pay? She cannot dispense with her 'self', even for her brother.

Shakespeare increases the scene's tension with Claudio's interruptions, in a rhythmic exchange:

> CLAUDIO. O Isabel—
> ISABELLA. What says my brother?
> CLAUDIO. Death is a fearful thing.
> ISABELLA. And shamed life a hateful.
> CLAUDIO. Ay but to die, and go we know not where ... (*MM*, 3.1.129–33)

There is no justice in this scene. It is the Duke's law, not Angelo's, that Claudio is debating.

The Duke's manipulations against Angelo are unnecessary; Angelo has lost himself. I suggest that Angelo's reaction in Act V is not horror in having been discovered as Mariana's former betrothed, but shock at the shattering of his self-image. An entirely different person has burst from the pristine shell of which Angelo was so proud. He stands before himself as a man driven by passion; lustful, secretive and deceitful. Angelo has become the perfect image of human frailty: a man undone by his passions. Add the fact that he has been manipulated, betrayed and publicly exposed by his employer and liege. No wonder he wants to die! How will he live with the new Angelo?

Fortunately, he has Mariana. She has had the good fortune to somehow run into the Duke, who, disguised as a Friar, uses her in his plot. The "bed trick" is more than a mere dramatic solution, it also reveals the Duke to be morally suspect in contrast to his own self-image as the wise and loving ruler. The Duke may have absolute power, but the audience is in a position to assess him and his actions. Take, for example, his discussion with Claudio, where he attempts to convince Claudio that death is preferable to living:

> DUKE. Be absolute for death.
> ... Thy best of rest is sleep,
> And that thou oft provok'st, yet grossly fear'st
> Thy death, which is no more. (*MM*, 3.1.18–20)

There are several critics, including Knight, who see the play as an illustration of Christian faith, and this monologue in particular as a confirmation of sacred values. It is unlikely that the average 21st Century audience member will entertain this idea. Instead we are faced with a set of more complex responses. We know the Duke made the law himself. He is in a position to call a halt to its proceedings and save Claudio. Why doesn't he? Given that the Duke engendered this law, doesn't his attempt to encourage Claudio to embrace death come across as not only hypocritical but cruel? The scene offers us the opportunity to assess both the law and the Duke. Similarly, the Duke's interrogation of Claudio's lover, Juliet (a choice of name perhaps meant to conjure memories of an earlier Juliet, also punished for love), provides another such opportunity. The heavily pregnant Juliet is humble and gracious in her expression of love for Claudio, as well as her acceptance of her situation. When the Duke hears that she willingly made love with Claudio, he tells her that her sin was of a "heavier kind than his" (2.3.31). Juliet replies:

> JULIET. I do repent me as it is an evil,
>   And take the shame with joy. (*MM*, 2.3.39–40)

Again, it is difficult to assess the Duke's intentions here. There is nothing we can take for granted as the play progresses. We are kept on our toes!

III

So far, we have concentrated on the "better-off" characters of status; the characters who make the action, so to speak, and whose decisions others need to live by. But Shakespeare also treats us to a pimp and his mistress, and their concerns for their business. Brothels are being closed in the suburbs of Vienna, but these two know there is no chance of cleansing the city of sexual activity! Much Jacobean fun is had when constable Elbow brings tapster Pompey and his client Froth before Lord Escalus. Pompey, in grand style, accuses Froth of violating his wife. Shakespeare seems to have a fondness for these energetic reprobates. Their language is hearty and Shakespeare gives them some of his best jokes.

However, Pompey is arrested, sent to prison, and then given a job as an assistant executioner; a series of actions which might be seen to express a "measure for measure." In the prison we meet the irrepressible Barnadine. Despite its shadow of death, this play consistently calls our attention to the value of life through vibrant characters like Barnadine. The Duke's law focuses on the significance of life and the naked opposition between physicality, the life force, and the finality of the death penalty. Juliet's pregnancy makes this visually explicit. Claudio's plight, Angelo's choices, Isabella's resistance, the Duke's conversations about death all focus our attention on the precious gift of life, which Barnadine literally embodies. He absolutely refuses to die!

Again, we cannot escape the assumptions we bring with us. If one is an advocate for capital punishment this consistent focus on life/death choices (and its natural bias towards life) encourages us to see the Duke in a positive light. If one feels that the law is absolute (regardless of its viability), then Juliet, Claudio, Pompey and Barnadine must face their punishment. But if one seeks justice in the law then one has to consider human frailty and the ways that humans can be sabotaged by their own emotions. Juliet and

Claudio were in love and were prevented from marriage. Angelo is turned inside out by his overwhelming passions. There will always be prostitutes and brothels, and justice is not served by the death penalty. (If you believe this, though, you will never become Duke!).

IV

Before we come to the last act, we need to have a look at Lucio, who is the link between the two halves of this world. He is a good friend to Claudio and moves to help him when he is arrested. He has a certain social status, but he is also a friend to Pompey and Mistress Overdone and frequents their establishments. He has a certain sensitivity. He seeks out Isabella, is aware of her qualities, and he is able to convince her to confront Angelo. He stimulates her courage, cleverly coaching her from the sidelines. However, he has little discretion and is too full of himself for his own good. He cannot prevent himself from promoting himself, defaming the Duke to his face, when he believes he is the Friar. Ironically, Lucio several times bemoans the absence of the Duke, emphasizing the Duke's precious reputation for kindness and beneficence.

> LUCIO. Would the Duke that is absent have done this?
> . . . He knew the service, and that instructed him to mercy. (*MM*, 3.2.117–21)

And later:

> LUCIO. By my troth, Isabel, I loved thy brother. If the old fantastical duke of dark corners had been at home, he had lived. (*MM*, 4.3.168–71)

Double irony! Ironic, also, that it is Lucio's bravado that reveals the Duke; a rare, humiliating moment for him. During Act IV, the Duke is heavily occupied with his own machinations. He sets Isabella and Mariana to "trick" Angelo who, in his panic to protect himself, has ordered Claudio's early execution. The Duke, to save Claudio, decides to substitute a prisoner, but Barnadine refuses to be executed. Luckily, another prisoner has recently died. They will present the head of this unfortunate to Angelo as if it were Claudio's. These are all familiar dramatic tropes, but in context, surely, they signify something more to the audience. How does an audience member relate to them? Are these human lives merely chess pieces to be manipulated as it suits those who are in positions to play? In Act V, of course, all must be resolved.

The Duke has warned Isabella that he may be harsh with her, but to take no notice of it. The memory of Isabella's plaintiff "to whom should I complain" rings in the air as she indeed complains to the Duke, now himself, of

Angelo's advances. Angelo claims she is mad, and the Duke, surprisingly, has her taken away. Mariana enters veiled. Through a series of oblique, innuendo-laden questions, it is revealed that Angelo has unwillingly, and unknowingly, been Mariana's lover. Isabella calls the Friar as her witness. The Duke is obliged to go offstage and change, returning as the Friar. Lucio denounces him to the point where Escalus orders the Friar to be taken to the prison, and the Duke seems caught in his own disguise. Lucio furiously pulls off the Friar's hood and ... lo and behold! When the Duke is revealed, he settles down to sorting everyone, and everything, out. To Angelo he says:

> DUKE. Being criminal in double violation
>   Of sacred chastity and of promise-breach
>   Thereon dependent, for your brother's life—
>   The very mercy of the law cries out
>   Most audible, even from his proper tongue,
>   "An Angelo for Claudio, death for death."
>   Haste still pays haste, and leisure answers leisure;
>   Like doth quit like, and measure still for measure. (*MM*, 5.1.460–68)

But is this really what St Matthew is saying? Is this Justice? An eye for an eye? Those who have found the Duke to be a kind and compassionate ruler have taken it for granted that he can do whatever he likes, because secretly he has everyone's best interest at heart. If one's image of the Duke is less accepting, one may well be disturbed by his quiet vendetta against Angelo, his manipulating and interfering in the lives of others, his relish of his power, and his disguise. As I have said before, it is actually Isabella, not the Duke, who undoes Angelo. The Duke could never have imagined he would gain such an asset when he planned his absence!

And what of Angelo? The Duke condemns him to death and the devastated Mariana begs Isabella to plead for his life. Many critics have seen Isabella's agreement here as the warming up of a cold woman, or proof of her learning about compassion. I would like to present a different approach: Isabella is a committed Christian and has shown herself to be so throughout. Charity, compassion, forgiveness, are central to Christianity. "Forgiveness," as exemplified here, is central to the Christian ethos. Indeed, when Isabella first met Angelo she offered him a definition of justice that echoed St Matthew. Now she does so in a specific context:

> ISABELLA. I partly think
>   A due sincerity governed his deeds
>   'Til he did look on me. Since it is so,
>   Let him not die. My brother had but justice,
>   In that he did the thing for which he died.

For Angelo,
His act did not o'ertake his intent ...
Thoughts are no subjects,
Intents but merely thoughts. (*MM*, 5.1.510–19)

For Isabella, justice has always been informed by mercy.

Isabella plays well in our world. She is intelligent, feisty, passionate and arguably the most verbally adept of all of Shakespeare's women. Moreover, she is gentle and compassionate. And she knows what she wants. She wants to be a nun. All the more shocking, then, is the Duke's capture of her. The Duke stale-mates Isabella by telling her Claudio is dead and then producing him at the right moment, telling her, almost in the same breath, that she can marry him. Is the silence of this unusually loquacious woman the silent pleasure of agreement? Or, more likely, is she literally struck dumb? Again, her former plea rings in our ears: "to whom should I complain?"

By our final tableau, all the loose ends have been neatly tied. Indeed, all the couples firmly matched to each other, manipulated into marriage by this over-active, gloating Duke, a visual image of absolute power. The Duke goes his own way. He disguises himself, manipulates others, rearranges their lives and tricks them into breaking the law. He deceives them and takes what he wants. To whom can *we* complain when there is no limit or responsibility to power? The stated purpose of the Duke is to make sure that an unpopular law is enforced. Has it been? No. Has the law been vindicated? No. One might even contend that the law has been proved impossible to enforce. The Duke could repeal it at any point. Does he? No.

Is the audience satisfied? Does marrying everyone off solve any problems? I think we can see how, at one time, especially with a happily married Victorian Queen on the throne, multiple marriages at the end of a play might have seemed a loving, satisfying idea, but in the 21st Century this is unlikely to be comforting. Rather, this tableau exposes the Duke and highlights one of Shakespeare's favorite issues, the limits of power and responsibility.

This Duke gave us a disturbing picture of unlimited power in his manipulation of private lives for his own benefit against a background of draconian laws. Shakespeare is indeed "for all times." He speaks to each time in its own language. We may be hard-pressed to see the kindly Duke that 19th and early 20th century critics did, but our 21st Century Duke serves as an apt and serious warning for our time.

Works Cited

All textual citations refer to: Folger Shakespeare Library. *Shakespeare's Plays.* from Folger
   Digital Texts. Ed. Barbara Mowat, Paul Werstine, Michael Poston, Rebecca Niles.
   Folger Shakespeare Library, 1 April 2019. www.folgerdigitaltexts.org

Bradley, Andrew C. "From Shakespearean Tragedy." *Measure for Measure,* Norton
   Critical Editions, 2009.

Chambers, Raymond W. *Man's Unconquerable Mind.* Jonathan Cape, 1952.

Knight, G. Wilson. *The Wheel of Fire.* Methuen, 1965.

Miles, Rosalind. *The Problem of Measure for Measure: A Historical Investigation.* Vision
   Press, 1976.

Shakespeare, William, and Eccles, Mark, editor. *Measure for Measure (New Variorum
   Edition).* Modern Language Association of America, 1980.

Wells, Stanley, editor. *Shakespeare: A Bibliographical Guide.* Clarendon Press, 1990.

10. Caliban in Love

SUSAN GAYLE TODD

Caliban and Miranda are lovers—well, ex-lovers. Believe it or not, the text, subtext, and historic context of Shakespeare's *The Tempest* support this interpretation.

Having benefitted from recent decades' postcolonial criticism of *The Tempest*, I am surprised that so many productions still stick to the European characters' take on Caliban as a deformed, subhuman rapist. On occasion, Caliban appears sympathetically as a conquered native, or exotically as a "noble savage," but he is still most often depicted as intrinsically evil, based on the idea that his mother is a witch, and he is the devil's son. These are unexamined notions, introduced through the perspectives of Prospero the patriarch, his daughter Miranda, and various nobles and commoners who, in the course of the play, encounter objects and individuals that are outside their usual Western experience.

In traditional productions, Caliban is presented according to the European characters' descriptors of him: a monster, "a mooncalf" (2.2.115), "a fish—he smells like a fish" (2.2.26), and other bestial terms. Actors traditionally delight in being cast as the foolish, filthy villain who speaks in verse. Costume designers dress him in fangs, fur, and scales, while directors have him growling, limping, pissing, and slobbering around the stage. When we think of lovers, this typical depiction of Caliban is not what comes to mind, and the image is certainly no match for Miranda, the daughter of the island's patriarch. As a response to this reading of the play, I staged Caliban and Miranda in 2010 as lovers in my play *Sycorax*, a prequel adaptation of *The Tempest*. The atypical representation of Caliban, as neither an exotic native nor a monstrous beast, but a young man in love, challenged traditional interpretations of *The Tempest* that are, frankly, non-rigorous because they rely on preconceptions of the play and merely skim the surface of Shakespeare's deeply textured, complex work.

I grew up during the Civil Rights Movement in the southern United States, and at first brush with *The Tempest*, I recognized immediately the European characters' descriptors of Sycorax and Caliban. The islanders are referred to in the same kinds of bestial and degrading terms I heard throughout my youth, when people of color were routinely characterized as violent, sexually deviant, and intrinsically evil. The slurs that Shakespeare's characters bestow on Sycorax and Caliban in *The Tempest* are rooted in the same racist, patriarchal attitudes that were the norm during my upbringing. Back then, women and people of color in our Texas town who ventured beyond the realms of domesticity or labor were often considered "uppity" or presumptuous. The oppression was real, persisting from the same attitudes that for centuries drove slavery in the Americas and prevailed in European culture during Shakespeare's time—along with the popular pursuit of misogynistic "witch" persecution.

Puzzlingly, however, Shakespeare subverts the Europeans' assessments of Caliban and his mother Sycorax with mystery and ambiguity. They are referred to disparagingly as witch and villain by the other characters, but their stories are sympathetically appealing. The playwright's subversion of the obviously favored perspective is crucial to any full appreciation of the play.

It wasn't until I taught *The Tempest* to high schoolers that I came to that deeper appreciation. I am a longtime devotee of Donald Finkel's *Teaching With Your Mouth Shut* approach, whereby teachers reserve their interpretations and students submit their questions about texts—not answers based on instruction. I should add that Finkel avoids textbooks in order to eliminate pontificating editors whose opinions influence students' raw impressions of original texts. Year after year, I presented *The Tempest* to high school students using these methods, and with no prompting from me, they overwhelmingly hated Prospero and complained that he enslaves, tortures, manipulates, and lies. They were horrified that he puts his daughter to sleep at whim and spies on her, enslaves and tortures Caliban, threatens Ariel while also calling him by endearing terms, and terrorizes innocent shipwrecked victims. They dubbed Prospero a hypocrite, racist, and manipulator, among more colorful expletives. Uninitiated in Shakespeare, they also saw textual and sub-textual suggestions that run counter to the traditional interpretations of Caliban's character as frequently trotted out on stage. Even my youngest students pointed out that Caliban is educated alongside Miranda, speaks in verse the same as other characters of elevated status, and is trusting to a fault. They often cited Prospero's accusation and asked incredulously, "Did Caliban really try to rape Miranda?" I would reply, "We don't know. What do the words mean? Go back and explore the text. Find evidence, one way or the other." Armed with only the text the students argued *ad infinitum* for and against Caliban's guilt.

Like many of my students, I have been struck that Caliban reads not as an evil monster but a victim of violent patriarchy. In spite of his outcast state, and even after Miranda rails against him in alliance with her father, Caliban continues through the rest of the play to speak of her with awe and tenderness. And so, in re-imagining Caliban as a lover in the "Prologue" and "Epilogue" of my play *Sycorax*, I relied upon Shakespeare's sympathetic characterization of him, along with telltale ambiguities and reverberations in the text that cast doubt on the notion of Caliban as a rapist and a brute.

In Defense of Caliban

If the character Caliban could be called into a court of law under the charge of attempted rape, what would an audience of jurors need in order to convict him? An explicit charge, witness accounts, character testimonials, or even a confession of guilt? Traditionally, readers claim that Shakespeare provides all of this tidily in Act 1, scene 2: Prospero charges Caliban; Prospero and Miranda deny Caliban's veracity and disparage his character; Miranda corroborates; and Caliban admits guilt. In truth, however, none of this explicitly exists in the play.

In examining the text as my students did, independent of the historical productions and interpretations that overwhelmingly favor Prospero, I find the idea of Caliban attempting to rape Miranda inconsistent with his characterization. To the contrary, stronger evidence points to Caliban being wrongly accused and convicted by a confirmed deceiver and manipulator with absolute control over his compliant, misled daughter. My examination of Caliban's case begins with the altercation between the Prospero family and Caliban, in Act 1, scene 2:

> PROSPERO. We'll visit Caliban my slave, who never
> Yields us kind answer.
> MIRANDA. 'Tis a villain, sir,
> I do not love to look on.
> PROSPERO. But as 'tis,
> We cannot miss him. He does make our fire,
> Fetch in our wood, and serves in offices
> That profit us. —What ho, slave, Caliban!
> Thou earth, thou, speak! (*Tem.* 1.2. 368-376)

Given the opening of the stormy exchange, I wonder that any enlightened scholar or director blindly accepts Prospero's claims as reliable. For one thing, Prospero's expectation that an incarcerated, tortured slave should respond kindly to the insults of his oppressor shows his arrogance and sense of undeserved entitlement. For another thing, the statement casts doubt on Prospero and Miranda's character and veracity because here Prospero explicitly and conspiratorially reminds Miranda that their reason for abusing Caliban is their comfort and profit—not as punishment for attempting to "violate the honor" of Miranda. As the ensuing lines show, once they are face-to-face with Caliban, Prospero justifies Caliban's enslavement in the name of comeuppance, and Miranda tells Caliban he was "deservedly confined unto this rock, / Who had deserved more than a prison" (1.2.435-6). This kind of punishment by slavery for vague offenses is an age-old practice among patriarchal oppressors, and it has long served as a convenient justification for getting free labor out of the accused.

Amid the volley of curses that follows between Caliban and his master, Shakespeare handily interjects an entrance by Prospero's other slave, the spirit Ariel. In one breath Prospero calls the obedient Ariel "Fine apparition! My quaint Ariel," and the non-compliant Caliban "Thou poisonous slave, got by the devil himself" (1.2.380-83). The interruption calls up the ages-old "good slave-bad slave" trope, a dichotomous notion commonly held about slaves in the New World. This contrasting dynamic between Prospero and his two slaves is a running theme in *The Tempest*, with Caliban of course cast in the role of "bad slave." As the altercation proceeds, Caliban restates his claim to the island based on his mother's original occupation of it. He reminisces about the days when Prospero and Miranda were kind to him—when he loved them and helped them survive. Finally, though, he curses himself and them—himself for helping them and them for enslaving him (1.2.395-410). This is when Prospero lashes out with the accusation that is traditionally accepted as evidence that Caliban tried to rape Miranda:

> PROSPERO. Thou most lying slave,
> Whom stripes may move, not kindness, I have used thee—
> Filth as thou art—with humane care, and lodged thee
> In mine own cell, till thou didst seek to violate
> The honor of my child. (*Tem.* 1.2.412-16)

This passage is widely accepted as evidence that Caliban attempted to rape Miranda, although, as I will argue, there is no such explicit accusation. Prospero is certainly capable of naming the sex act as he does later in the play when he gives Miranda to Ferdinand and cautions him not to "break her virgin-knot" before marriage (4.1.16). For Prospero, violation of Miranda's honor could be anything from hand-holding, to kissing, to full-on sex, or simply the batting of eyes—as evidenced later in the play when he sharply admonishes Ferdinand, "Be more abstemious" (4.1.58), while Prospero is himself fully present as chaperone. The vague charge against Caliban and the severity of its punitive outcome in the play echo the grim fact that white patriarchy has historically cast dark-skinned and colonized native men as a sexual threat to white women. The examples of the trend are excruciating and plentiful.

Journalist Morgan Jerkins' succinct calling-out of the trend resonates with Prospero's accusation:

> White men have spent centuries upholding the sanctity of white womanhood as a way of maintaining their control of white women's sexuality. And racist white men have long been terrified that white women will end up in black men's arms. During slavery, racist men and women thought of black men as animalistic and overly sexual. Lynching was the punishment for black men who were thought to have defiled a white woman's body—or merely to have desired it. (Jerkins)

If Prospero's hazy accusation is not enough to convict Caliban, Caliban's response is nearly always viewed as an admission of guilt: "O ho, O ho! Would't had been done! / Thou dids't prevent me—I had peopled else / This isle with Calibans" (1.2.419-21), but again, the ambiguous, subjunctive reply is not an explicit confession of attempted rape. Caliban's "O ho, O ho!" implies surprise or derision and rings of incredulity. The exclamations are followed by what I interpret as an incredulous, sarcastic quip in response to an outrageous accusation. And at any rate, it would be natural, retrospectively, for Caliban to wish he and Miranda had consummated their courtship and that he had won the day, with her and his own brood by his side. This bitter expression of regret is no confession of attempted rape. At this point, Caliban knows that to deny the charge and defend himself is futile. His parting conclusion, "I must obey. His art is of such power / It would control my dam's god, Setebos, / And make a vassal of him" (1.2.449-50), echoes yet another historical trend in Shakespeare's day when European slaveholders resembling Prospero were infiltrating the New World and enslaving even the most powerful leaders of native lands.

More evidence to support the notion of Caliban as Miranda's former lover is Caliban's function as foil to the suitor Prospero handpicks for his daughter. To retrace Prospero's revenge plot in the play up to this point, he has fake-wrecked the ship carrying his enemies and transported them, unharmed, to the island where they are trapped. One of the victims is Ferdinand, son of

King Alonso; Prospero aims to punish Alonso for his complicity in Prospero's banishment and set Miranda up to marry Prince Ferdinand in the bargain.

Prospero prefaces Miranda's first glimpse of Ferdinand strategically, on the heels of their visit to Caliban, where Miranda has been reminded of the grave consequences of her prior relationship with a man. The recent image of the debased Caliban, incarcerated in squalor and spitting vengeful curses strikes a sharp contrast between one suitor and the other, whom she will soon meet—a melancholy prince dressed, miraculously, in fine, fresh garments. This new encounter is permeated with situational and dialogic similarities and contrasts between Caliban and Ferdinand, which implies that Caliban is viewed by both Miranda and her father, not as a beast, but as a man and a suitor. Here Prospero performs a bizarre re-enactment of what happened pre-textually, before the action of the play, when Caliban and Miranda's relationship was disrupted. This time, however, Prospero is only pretending to disapprove of the young man, and this time the young man is Ferdinand.

As the exchange begins, Prospero appears to have put his daughter to sleep (yet again) as he and Ariel coax the grieving Ferdinand, who assumes his father is dead. Baited by an enchanting song about the drowned king, Prospero sets the stage by placing Ferdinand where Miranda may view him. Here Prospero's manipulation of Miranda plays out in a sinister way. First he wakes her and calls her attention to Ferdinand, saying, "The fringéd curtain of thine eye advance, / And say what thou seest yond" (1.2.486-7). As Miranda opens her eyes and gazes on Ferdinand, the ensuing dialog and action provide a complex window, showing both the inner and outer workings of Prospero's scheming. One frame of that window is an artificial masque, performed openly by Prospero to manipulate Miranda's emotions to fall for Ferdinand. When Miranda admires Ferdinand as "a thing divine," we are also privy to the other frame, Prospero's authentic private thought, which he murmurs in an aside, "It goes on, I see, / As my soul prompts it" (1.2.501-2). From this point until the end of the scene, Prospero attacks Ferdinand in a belligerent sham that echoes his treatment of Caliban.

In this strange re-enactment, Prospero's threats are idle ones, intended to motivate Miranda to spring to the young man's defense, which she does. In the process, both Miranda and Prospero evoke the memory of Caliban in this context of conventional courtship—not of sexual assault. When Prospero gets surly with Ferdinand, Miranda sees what is coming and recalls Caliban. This is not an aside, and Miranda is quick to reassure her father she never "sighed for" Caliban, and to beg him to agree with her choice. She pleads,

> MIRANDA. Why speaks my father so ungently? This
> Is the third man that e'er I saw, the first
> That e'er I sighed for. Pity move my father
> To be inclined my way! (*Tem.* 1.2.445-8)

Ignoring Miranda's pleas, Prospero explodes in faux anger. He disarms and enslaves the man, just as he has done with Caliban, threatening,

> PROSPERO. Come,
> I'll manacle thy neck and feet together.
> Sea-water shalt thou drink; thy food shall be
> The fresh-brook mussels, withered roots, and husks
> Wherein the acorn cradled. (*Tem.* 1.2.557-61)

As Prospero's fraudulently concocted conflict escalates, Miranda is desperate, physically grabbing her father and pleading with him not to harm Ferdinand, as she has witnessed what he did to Caliban. Prospero responds by going so far as to equate Ferdinand with Caliban as just another suitor:

> MIRANDA.   Beseech you, father—
> PROSPERO.   Hence! Hang not on my garments.
> MIRANDA.   Sir, have pity;/ I'll be his surety.
> PROSPERO.   Silence! One word more
> Shall make me chide thee, if not hate thee . . .
> . . . Thou think'st there is no more such shapes as he,
> Having seen but him and Caliban. Foolish wench,
> To th' most of men this is a Caliban,
> And they to him are angels. (*Tem.* 1.2.575-85)

Echoing the good slave-bad slave model, Prospero presents his daughter with a good suitor-bad suitor pairing. Having only just ushered Miranda to the debased Caliban's sty, he now sets before her an honest-to-goodness prince. The suitors are foils to each other; they appear to be opposites, but they are not so different. Both men are attracted to Miranda, and both scenarios center on Miranda's nubile state and a young man's overtures. The trumped-up accusation and enslavement of Ferdinand casts suspicion on Prospero's pre-textual accusation and enslavement of Caliban.

The re-enactment continues violently with Prospero threatening Ferdinand as Miranda begs her father in desperate terms, "Make not too rash a trial of him, for / He's gentle and not fearful"; "Beseech you, father"; and "Sir, have pity; / I'll be his surety" (1.2.567-8). But Prospero finally squelches Miranda's attempt to defend the young man. He does so with the ultimate parent's threat—to hate her:

> PROSPERO.   Silence! One word more
> Shall make me chide thee, if not hate thee. What,
> An advocate for an imposter? Hush!
> Thou think'st there is no more such shapes as he,
> Having seen but him and Caliban. Foolish wench. (*Tem.*
> 1.2.579-83)

After his cruel outburst and reminder of Caliban, Miranda responds humbly. She is her father's daughter, however, and in spite of the curses and cruel treatment she has witnessed her father dole out to Caliban, she exits the scene, disingenuously telling her new suitor to "be of comfort."

> MIRANDA.   My father's of a better nature, sir,
> Than he appears by speech. This is unwonted
> Which now came from him. (*Tem.* 1.2.604-7)

Miranda's reassurance is a blatant contradiction of what she knows about her father's cruel tendencies. Even if Prospero has hidden from her his threat-laden abuse of Ariel, she has seen firsthand his maltreatment of Caliban. Miranda knows very well the cruelty and violence her father is capable of. In the course of Act 1, scene 2 she, Ariel, Caliban, and Ferdinand are all introduced as subjects of his abuse or manipulation, or both. This very scene opens as Miranda herself, horrified at the sight of a ship splitting to pieces with its passengers screaming and perishing, pleads, "If by your art, my dearest father, you have / Put the wild waters in this roar, allay them" (1.2.1-2). Upon seeing the violent, deadly offshore scene, she immediately assumes it is the work of her father.

Miranda's little white lie that Prospero's current behavior is "unwonted" is perhaps meant to encourage Ferdinand, but it also exemplifies her willingness to turn a blind eye to her father's violent, abusive behavior. She contradicts herself later, erasing her former relationship with Caliban—and erasing Caliban entirely, as her courtship with Ferdinand intensifies. Earlier, Miranda has acknowledged Caliban's existence and manhood, reminding her father that Ferdinand is "the third man that e'er [she] saw" (1.2.534), but later, to Ferdinand's face, she coyly says, "Nor have I seen / More that I may call men than you, good friend, and my dear father" (3.1.60-2). Miranda's veracity is as questionable as her father's, whose manipulative tricks and threats bend her to align herself with Prospero and to malign Caliban.

Caliban's active role as a lover ended before the play began, pre-textually, and for the entirety of the play, he is oppressed, cursed, and threatened by Prospero and Miranda, or drunk in the company of fools, desperately plotting to murder Prospero. Caliban is obsessive in his hatred of Prospero. But, in spite of the harsh tongue-lashing he has just received from her in the altercation scenario, Caliban never disparages Miranda. He is still infatuated with the girl he dreamed would be his. His language shifts from murderous to tender when he describes her:

> CALIBAN. And that most deeply to consider is
> The beauty of his daughter. He himself
> Calls her a nonpareil. I never saw a woman
> But only Sycorax, my dam, and she;
> But she as far surpasseth Sycorax
> As great'st does least. (*Tem.* 3.2.107-11)

In this play of isolation, reduction, and complex foils, Caliban and Miranda also mirror each other. Caliban says he has seen no woman but his mother and Miranda. Likewise, until she laid eyes on Ferdinand, Miranda says she has seen no man but her father and Caliban. Being the only eligible pairing on the island, it would be natural for Caliban and Miranda to couple. That having failed, in utter degradation at the hands of Prospero, Caliban - drunk from Stephano's bottle, and having lost Miranda who is poisoned by her father against him - holds her out as the superlative prize for his would-be new master, Stephano. Here, unexpectedly, in the midst of a booze-soaked, comedic scene of fools, appears some of Shakespeare's most stunningly beautiful verse, delivered by the so-called monster.

> CALIBAN. Be not afeard, the isle is full of noises,
> Sounds, and sweet airs, that give delight and hurt not.
> Sometimes a thousand twangling instruments
> Will hum about mine ears; and sometime voices,
> Will make me sleep again, and then in dreaming
> The clouds methought would open and show riches
> Ready to drop upon me, that when I waked
> I cried to dream again. (*Tem.* 3.2.148-56)

What are the riches Caliban dreams of? When Stephano and Trinculo fall for Prospero's "glistering apparel," which has been planted to bait them, Caliban says, "Let it alone, thou fool, it is but trash" (4.1.250), and "What do you mean / To dote thus on such luggage?" (4.1.267-8). He has no need for money or material wealth. Instead, he values the "qualities of the isle, / The fresh springs" and fertile places, and prior to his enslavement, he entrusted those precious things to Prospero and Miranda in exchange for their love. The wealth Caliban dreams of is Miranda. She remains the longed-for treasure ready to drop upon him in his dreams, but Prospero destroyed that dream.

Of all Shakespeare's lovers, Caliban is the most tragic. He loses his rights, freedom, family, property, dignity, and any dream of happiness or love. There is no clear indication that Caliban would attempt to harm or violate Miranda. Caliban is rather the victim of false accusation, usurpation, enslavement, torture, and theft at the hands of a patriarchal oppressor.

Based on the text alone and foregrounding what is back-grounded, I offer this plausible account of Caliban's life and plight—one that subverts the patriarchal narrative that is typically projected on the play by readers, directors, audiences, and even scholars:

A baby boy is born on an island that is devoid of human life, except for him and his mother, who has been banished from her Algerian homeland under the accusation of witchcraft. She has been dumped there by male sailors, pregnant, in the wild. The boy, Caliban, lives with his mother until she dies during his childhood. He survives her, entirely alone, for an undetermined length of time until a man with a three-year-old daughter washes ashore—about twelve years since the boy's mother washed ashore. The boy greets the newcomers, Prospero and Miranda, and offers them the island's most precious resources, fresh water and food. And so they all survive, living side-by-side. The man and girl look different from the boy; it is safe to assume that they, as Europeans, are fair-skinned, unlike Caliban, who is Algerian and most likely a moor. Since Caliban has grown up in isolation from other humans with only his mother's links to civilization, he behaves differently from them in terms of culture, religion, and other social factors. They do not understand his language, so he learns theirs. In their own tongue, they teach him their ways and treat him with physical affection, as they would a family member, or perhaps a pet. The newcomers survive with Caliban's assistance and knowledge, and they provide him with the human interaction he has missed since his mother's death. He loves them; they are his constant companions. The boy, Caliban, is at least nine years older than the girl, Miranda. When Miranda reaches puberty, the young people still play together as they always have, but the playing, no doubt, becomes charged with sexuality and flirting. The father, Prospero, is disturbed by the idea of his daughter coupling with any man, much less the native islander who is neither European nor white; he considers Caliban inferior to him and his daughter. When Prospero witnesses some romantic or sexually implicit behavior between Caliban and his daughter, he lashes out at Caliban, accusing him of sexual misbehavior. Prospero angrily separates them and convinces Miranda that Caliban's overtures have been violent, unnatural, and deserving of severe punishment. Miranda complies with her father for fear that he will disown her, or perhaps even harm her. On the accusation of attempted sexual violation, Prospero degrades, imprisons, enslaves, beats, and continually tortures Caliban. Where Caliban was once part of a family, he is now despised. In despair and disgrace, he loses everything: his freedom, his island, the people he loves, and any dream of building a family and life with Miranda.

Staging the Lovers

Spurred by my own burning questions about the text, in 2007 I wrote a play that reimagined *The Tempest* to show what its characters might look like outside the patriarchal gaze. That play, titled *Sycorax*, is a prequel to *The Tempest*, and in writing it I chose to follow certain rules of "canonicity" that riffed from the text, but remained consistent with ambiguous textual references in *The Tempest*. I sought to challenge the racism, misogyny, and ageism behind the characterization of Sycorax—and the many so-called witches and crones Sycorax echoes. I felt the need to do what feminists do when we feel frustrated with patriarchal texts that we also love: challenge and re-envision them; fulfill them by telling the deeper truth that lies buried in the original telling.

In challenging the representation of the silenced Sycorax, Caliban figured importantly into my project because as an extension of his mother, he is crushed by the same patriarchal values that sought to destroy her. From a racist, patriarchal perspective, Caliban is characterized in stereotypes based on his parentage—his class and race. According to that classist, racist perspective, he is considered undeserving of the basic pleasures of life, such as love, respect, comfort, and agency. I wanted my play to provide Caliban with a humanized heritage and backstory by dramatizing an alternative, plausible perspective that would exonerate him, along with the many dehumanized and oppressed men of color he surely represents.

Described in the playbill as "a take on Shakespeare's *The Tempest* that you've never seen – feminist theater at its most incendiary," a revised 2010 incarnation of *Sycorax* was produced and performed by the Weird Sisters Women's Theater Collective in Austin, Texas. The play was originally produced in 2007 by the Cohen New Works Festival and directed by Fadi Skeiker; it was also a Spring 2019 Season selection for Kansas University Department of Theater. In the original script of *Sycorax*, Caliban appeared only as an infant, but with the Weird Sisters production, I bookended the play with scenes that featured Sycorax's grown son, Caliban. In reverse chronology, the "Prologue" presented Caliban and Miranda as ex-lovers in the Act 1, scene 2 altercation, after Prospero's accusation and enslavement of Caliban, while the "Epilogue" presented them as an infatuated young couple before Prospero's accusation. The "Prologue" and "Epilogue" conveniently presented my interpretation of what lay beneath Prospero's accusation that Caliban sought to "violate the honor" of Miranda.

In the "Prologue," Miranda, now aligned with her father against Caliban, bristled and softened alternately, aware that her dalliance with Caliban was to blame for his enslavement. Caliban telegraphed resentment and incredulity. Ann Pleiss-Morris recalls, "Caliban was haggard and moved heavily. He often shook his shoulders after talking to Prospero as if trying to physically shake off the old man. The only real energy Caliban showed is when he interacted with Miranda" (128). When Caliban referred to their happy past, he delivered the lines directly to Miranda:

> CALIBAN. When thou cam'st first,
>   Thou strok'st me and made much of me; wouldst give me
>   Water with berries in 't, and teach me how
>   To name the bigger light and how the less,
>   That burn by day and night. (*Tem.* 1.2.397-401)

Miranda seemed to melt as Caliban pulled her into a tight embrace with:

> CALIBAN. And then I loved thee,
>   And showed thee all the qualities o' th' isle,
>   The fresh springs, brine pits, barren place and fertile— (1.2.401-5)

They nearly kissed, but of course the next line is, "Cursed be I that did so!" (1.2.406). Caliban broke the spell and shoved Miranda away from him. The remainder of the scene made for a juicy lovers' quarrel as Miranda venomously and condescendingly spat the famed lines that many editors have refused to assign to her, though clearly assigned in the Folio, and Caliban lost his cool and snapped back:

> MIRANDA. Abhorrèd slave,
>   Which any print of goodness wilt not take,
>   Being capable of all ill! I pitied thee,
>   Took pains to make thee speak, taught thee each hour
>   One thing or other. When thou didst not, savage,

> Know thine own meaning, but wouldst gabble like
> A thing most brutish, I endowed thy purposes
> With words that made them known. But thy vile race—
> Though thou didst learn—had that in't which good natures
> Could not abide to be with; therefore wast thou
> Deservedly confined into this rock,
> Who hadst deserved more than a prison.
> CALIBAN. You taught me language, and my profit on't
> Is I know how to curse. The red plague rid you
> For learning me your language! (*Tem.* 1.2.421-40)

Miranda's approach was to "protest too much," with an awareness that she was performing for Prospero, not Caliban, to prove her complete alliance with her father. Those rebellious editors who refused to assign the lines to Miranda were onto something, but in performance it was easy to see they had missed the crucial point: although Miranda is the speaker of the lines, the sentiment and expression are not her own; they are Prospero's; he controls her, and he controls her perspective and narrative. She parrots Prospero, which in the *Sycorax* "Prologue" made for a complex performance of the altercation. Throughout the lovers' contentious exchange, Prospero stood by smugly, knowing that his puppet-mastery over Miranda was successful.

At the end of *Sycorax*, the "Prologue" was complemented by the "Epilogue," a romantic and starkly contrasting prequel to the Act 1, scene 2 "Prologue," which our audience had only just watched at the top of the show. The lights dimmed, and the sound of gentle waves could be heard behind the exuberant voice of Caliban telling Miranda the legend of his ancestry. This take on the "Epilogue" appeared in an *Austinist* review:

> The play closes with an imagined scene between Caliban and Miranda, taking place before the time of *The Tempest*, an apparently mutually romantic moment, (perhaps meant to portray what Prospero implied was Caliban's attempted rape of the girl). The scene ties up Todd's story nicely, as Caliban tells the story of his mother and father, mirroring Sycorax's own fantastical self-penned origin story earlier in the play. (Young)

The same Miranda the audience had seen berating Caliban in the "Prologue" now cuddled with him. With his right hand, Caliban animated the story as though he were painting its images in the night sky above them while his left hand moved cautiously to her knee. She eagerly grabbed Caliban's hand, interlacing her light-skinned fingers in his dark ones, hanging on to every word he uttered. As Caliban's story ended, Prospero emerged upstage.

In her description of the play, Ann Pleiss Morris recalls, "Lurking in the shadows, [Prospero's] face fell. He seemed to recognize instantly the relationship transpiring between his daughter and [Caliban]" (138). In addition to the detailed observations of Ann Pleiss-Morris, who attended rehearsals and wrote extensively about the Weird Sisters and *Sycorax* in her doctoral dissertation, it is reassuring to read other critics' descriptions of the "Epilogue":

> The final scene shows Caliban, young and full of hope, recounting a lengthy mythic tale of his ancestors and himself to a worshipful Miranda. She huddles at his side in hypnotized adoration, eyes fastened upon him, hands brushing his side, her legs posed upon his. Caliban's attention is upward, toward the moon overhead. He reaches the moment of apotheosis in his tale just as Prospero materializes in the depth of the stage and stops to take in the scene. (Meigs)

As re-claimer of Sycorax's life and Caliban's backstory, I am a fortunate heir of four decades of postcolonial criticism of *The Tempest*, which instructs my interpretation and validates my revulsion at the pernicious racism, misogyny, and ageism implied in hate-filled references to a disabled, elderly, non-European female character who is convicted of trumped-up supernatural crimes, handed over to an all-male ship's crew, and dumped pregnant on an island where she gives birth and somehow keeps herself and her son alive. For me, the 2010 staging of Caliban and Miranda in the "Prologue" and "Epilogue" of *Sycorax* scratched an itch: it allowed me to explore what Caliban and Miranda might look like as lovers.

I believe the performance changed the way audiences will think about *The Tempest*. The play, as one critic put it, "fills in a gap in one of Shakespeare's universes" (Young). Theater practitioners and educators carry great social responsibility when we present Shakespeare's plays, complex and wrestling as those texts are with issues around equality and identity. Racism and classism may get reinforced, or at best ignored, every time Caliban enters the stage as a detestable creature that deserves his lot—and every time Prospero and Miranda appear virtuous and fair. Granted, there is risk in breaking with tradition: some critics will scoff, eyes will surely roll, and we may at times be relegated to parks and warehouses rather than playhouses. But post-colonial criticism has revealed what was, through the centuries, so blatantly there in *The Tempest* all along: a revenge play within a colonial microcosm, complete with "good" and "bad" slaves, swaggering imperialists, and a controlling patriarch. Shakespeare had the courage to expose the cruelty and hypocrisy in oppressive Europeans who were greedily staking their claim in the brave New World. We need to heed the immediacy of Shakespeare's words and examine the motives of the playwright himself, who living in England and learning about the exploitation and enslavement of people in far-off lands, chose to humanize Caliban, giving him exquisite verse and rational argument with which to state his case.

Works Cited

All textual citations refer to: Folger Shakespeare Library. *The Tempest,* from Folger Digital Texts. Ed. Barbara Mowat, Paul Werstine, Michael Poston, and Rebecca Niles. Folger Shakespeare Library, 11 April, 2017. www.folgerdigitaltexts.org.

Finkel, Donald L. *Teaching with Your Mouth Shut.* Boynton/Cook Publishers.2000.

Jerkins, Morgan. "Dear White Women, There Is Nothing Heroic About Not Having Sex With Nazis." *Allure Magazine,* 15 August 2017, www.allure.com/story/white-women-withholding-sex-from-nazis-is-not-heroic. Accessed 13 January 2018.

Meigs, Michael. Review of *Sycorax,* directed by Susan Gayle Todd and Christa French, AustinLive Theater, 23 June 2010.

Pleiss Morris, Ann Marie. "Possess His Books: Shakespeare, New Audiences, and Twenty-first Century Performances of *The Tempest.*" Dissertation, University of Iowa, 2011.

Shakespeare, William. *The Tempest.* Ed. Stephen Orgel. Oxford: Oxford UP, 2008. Print.

Todd, Susan Gayle. "Sycorax." 17–27 June 2010, Austin, Gemini Playhouse.

——— *Sycorax.* 2007. TS. Author's private collection.

Young, Georgia. Review of *Sycorax,* directed by Susan Gayle Todd and Christa French, *The Austinist,* 24 June 2010. *Austinist.com*

11. Behind Closed Doors: Sex, Lies and Servants

EDIT VILLARREAL

When thinking about villains and villainy in Shakespeare's plays, the great tragedies of *Romeo and Juliet, Othello, King Lear, Hamlet, Macbeth*, immediately come to mind. The sheer number of deaths in these plays can be exhilarating, stupefying and sobering. A close look at these tragedies reveals that the conduct of families is a crucial theme in the plays. Juliet's father is the play's main villain, demanding that his daughter acquiesce to a marriage she does not want. Desdemona, not much older than Juliet, has eloped with the older Othello, angering her father. Lear has two redoubtable daughters, Goneril and Regan, who conspire against him. The Macbeths are the poster couple for dysfunctional marriages.

In the families with children, we find a recurring trope of arrogant fathers dominating their vulnerable, young daughters. The father-daughter conflicts inevitably involve the family household, specifically servants or characters with lesser social status than the imperious fathers. Indeed, another familiar trope found in Shakespeare's dramatic strategy is the overt, covert, or accidental involvement of household servants in the villainous acts initiated by their masters. The villainy of an arrogant father in turn creates further villainy. In short, the world of the household reflects the world of the play, and, for Shakespeare's audiences, their own world thrown out of balance, out of propriety.

This essay proposes a recurrent dramatic strategy in four of Shakespeare's plays, in which he dramatizes the impact of villainous acts on the victims of villainy, who, in turn, commit lesser villainous acts of their own. Shakespeare often creates triangles of individuals – father-daughter-servant – as a dramaturgical device. I will explore these recurring triangle relationships in *Romeo and Juliet, Othello, Timon of Athens* and *Cymbeline*.

Romeo and Juliet: *Where are the adults?*

An avid reader of history, literature and mythology, Shakespeare found his young lovers in a long poem, *The Tragicall Historye of Romeus and Juliet*, first published 1562 by Arthur Brooke (possibly a translation from an Italian novel by Matteo Bandello). This early play of Shakespeare's is peppered with household servants. The play begins with two Capulet servants, Gregory and Sampson, armed with swords and bucklers, caught in a brawl mid-day on the streets of Verona. Quickly we meet Mercutio and Tybalt, two of several cocky young nobles looking for trouble. Other Capulet servants are used intermittently throughout the play for comic relief. One servant, however, Juliet's Nurse, is crucial to the tragedy that will unfold.

A course, ribald character, Shakespeare establishes the Nurse's strengths and weaknesses in short order. In her first scene, the Nurse feels an inordinate affinity for Juliet, since she lost a child of her own very close to Juliet's age. "Susan and she (God rest all Christian souls!) / Were of an age. Well, Susan is with God" (*R&J*, 1.3.20-21). But more significantly, in a rather graphic speech, the Nurse says she was Juliet's infant wet-nurse, more mother to Juliet than Lady Capulet, who was away in Mantua. All of these factors contribute to the Nurse acting as an improper parental surrogate to Juliet, encouraging Juliet's impulsive sexual fantasies. "Thou wilt fall backward when thou comest to age / Wilt thou not, Jule?" (1.3.61-62), and "Go girl, seek happy nights to happy days" (1.3.112), all the while living vicariously through Juliet's romance with Romeo.

Later in the play, after Juliet has consummated her secret marriage, the Nurse encourages Juliet to forget about Romeo, marry Paris, and thus commit bigamy. Her advice is vulgar but precise. "Go thy ways, wench. Serve God" (2.5. 46-47). The definition for "wench" is first "young woman", second "prostitute"; "to wench" meaning to fornicate. (https://en.oxforddicti onaries.com/definition/wench).

The Nurse reasons that Juliet is now damaged goods, and callously advises her to seek counsel from the pseudo-apothecary, Friar Laurence, who advises her to take a "distilling liquor" which will make her appear to be dead. When Juliet agrees to Friar Laurence's preposterous advice (why does she not just go to Mantua and join Romeo?) Shakespeare, in act four of the play, begins the final series of dire misunderstandings that leads to the deaths of Romeo and Juliet.

Completing the triangle of characters is Juliet's dotard father, Old Capulet. His first words in the play are full of bravado at the brawl, "Give me my long sword, ho!" (1.1.76). Preparing for the ball he appears old, rich and vain. His petulant bravado wells up again when he demands, at the ball, that Tybalt leave after discovering the presence of a Montague. "Am I the master here or you? Go to. "(1.5.87). With the wealthy Paris he is cordial, playing the indulgent parent, "My will to her consent is but a part" (1.2.17). He is an old man of many moods, primarily centered on himself. He disappears from the play until act three, when in a second scene with Paris, he impulsively decides to marry off his daughter. When he encounters resistance from Juliet, his anger rises. "But fettle your fine joints 'gainst Thursday next / To go with Paris to Saint Peter's Church /Or I will drag thee on a hurdle thither" (3.5.158-160). This burst of anger is quickly followed by the final blow between father and daughter:

> CAPULET. And you be mine I'll give you to my friend.
> And you be not, hang, beg, starve! die in the streets,
> For by my soul I'll ne'er acknowledge thee … (*R&J*, 3.5 203-05).

Juliet is 14 years old! The triangle of Father-Daughter-Servant is firmly established. Juliet seeks counsel from the pompous Friar Laurence, and by doing so she begins the bizarre series of events that will lead to her death and Romeo's.

The impact of Friar Laurence in the play is twofold because he is intimately intertwined with both Romeo and Juliet. He impulsively agrees to marry the lovers, foolishly believing that their clandestine marriage will somehow save the seething community of Verona from further violence. Not unlike the Nurse with Juliet, the Friar assumes more authority than his position warrants, a kind of hubris. Later when the desperate Juliet runs to him for counsel, he advises Juliet to take a "distilled liquor" which will make her appear, like death "stiff and stark and cold" (4.1.105), compromising his very authority as a cleric. With this advice, Friar Laurence becomes as amoral as the Nurse herself.

In the last two acts of the play, the young married lovers try as best they can to gain agency in a world that will inevitably deceive them. The obstacles to their agency and happiness are the adults, the villains in the play: an arrogant father whose promise of marriage to a rich man is of more weight than the happiness of his daughter; a garrulous female servant in the household; and a foolish priest in the community.

Othello: *Women and the men in their lives.*

The play begins in Venice. In the opening scenes, Shakespeare sets the overall tone of personal revenge, racial insults, lies, deception and political intrigue. Iago (Shakespeare's busiest and most eloquent villain) and Roderigo, seen first, have personal grievances. Iago was bypassed for second in command by Othello. Roderigo was refused by Brabantio, Desdemona's father, as a suitor. Iago convinces the younger man to disturb Brabantio in the middle of the night, informing him in vulgar and racist terms that his daughter has absconded from the family home with "the Moor."

Another Shakespeare father figure, Brabantio, impulsive and choleric, condemns his daughter, even after learning that Othello has married her. "O treason of the blood! / Fathers, from hence trust not your daughters' minds / By what you see them act." (*Othello*, 1.1.191-93). He tries to get Othello arrested, but fails. Venice is under possible attack by the Turks and Othello is needed for an emergency military mission off the coast of Cyprus. Publically rejected by her father, Othello orders Iago to accompany the homeless Desdemona to the island, mandating further that her nurse, Emilia accompany them as servant to Desdemona. Iago most likely wants to leave his wife in Venice, but his General has, yet again, gone against his wishes. Shakespeare sets in place this triangle of characters, Othello-Desdemona-Emilia, which will be crucial to the resolution of the play.

Iago's first villainous acts in Cyprus, an island fort, are child's play. Young Cassio, eager to please his General, welcomes Desdemona with pomp and circumstance. "You men of Cyprus, let her have your knees. / Hail to thee, lady" (2.1.94-95). A small moment, but it's possible that Desdemona exults in being treated like a Lady and not a child. The effusive Cassio then takes hold of her hand in parting. Seizing the moment, Iago makes his first move, casually informing the lovelorn Roderigo that Desdemona is "directly" in love with Cassio.

Shakespeare places Cassio as a central figure to the tragic action of the play. Like Friar Laurence's frequent intercessions with Romeo and Juliet, Cassio will interfere over and over again in the domestic life of the newly married couple. Iago's next act of deception, pitting the lovelorn Roderigo against Cassio, is also easily accomplished due to the naiveté of the young men. Iago, arguably Shakespeare's premiere villain, has an encompassing and eloquent ability to speak to anyone in a cordial language that serves his villainous purposes.

Iago's greatest challenge is the duping of Othello himself. In the magnificent "Temptation Scene" (Act 3, scene 3), Shakespeare reminds us that this is a soldiers' drama. The temptation of Othello begins in his private living quarters, behind closed doors. Iago plays with Othello's insecurities in the very place where his commander should feel most secure.

The Temptation Scene, one of the longest in the Shakespeare canon, is a long haul for Iago. Like a lion stalking his prey, he makes a move and then leans back into the grass to determine if the victim has been alerted to the pursuit. His options are few but fulsome. The scene is a dramatic delight with masterful linguistic twists and turns between the two men. But the most significant moments in the scene, furthering the tragic action of the play, are three.

Iago first plays on Othello's insecurities as an older man married to a younger woman, "Did Michael Cassio, when you wooed my lady, / Know of your love?" (3.3.105-6). Iago then implies that Othello's honor might also be in jeopardy:

> IAGO.　Who steals my purse steals trash. 'Tis something, nothing;
> 'Twas mine, 'tis his, and has been slave to thousands.
> But he that filches from me my good name
> Robs me of that which not enriches him
> And makes me poor indeed. (*Oth.* 3.3.184-190).

Othello now doubts his sexual manhood and his honor as a husband. He responds with the first sign of the tragic delirium that he will fall into later in the play, and, for the first time, speaks of Desdemona in the past. "She's gone" (3.3.308). He feels, already, that he has lost her. Within minutes, however, Othello finds the third source of insecurity, his honor as a soldier:

> OTHELLO. O, now, forever
> Farewell the tranquil mind! Farewell content!
> Farewell the plumed troops and the big wars
> That makes ambition virtue! O, farewell! (*Oth.* 3.3.399-402).

For Othello, honor as a man and honor as a soldier cannot be separated. With the psychological decline of Othello now established, Shakespeare returns to the second tragic action in the play: Desdemona's increasing plight, Emilia's response, and the trail of the infamous white handkerchief.

As Othello begins to doubt the virtue, and, specifically, the chastity of his young wife, Desdemona begins her own journey to wifehood. Like a child at play, she practices at being a wife, naively assuming greater authority over Othello than she will ever be able to have. Unlike Juliet, Desdemona has the opportunity to be an adult in the public square. Her rash decision to redeem

Cassio is reminiscent of Juliet's rash decision to marry Romeo and thereby claim adulthood.

Shakespeare intertwines the two actions of the play together through the infamous white handkerchief. Shaken by Desdemona's obsession with Cassio, Othello demands to see the handkerchief. When Desdemona cannot find it, the heirloom becomes beautiful, precious and virginal – everything that Othello now doubts her to be. As he turns against his wife, Desdemona, again like Juliet, turns to her servant for advice and comfort.

The quiet, suffering Emilia has heretofore stayed in the background. Some critics think she is reticent through fear of her husband. Other critics think that she is incapable of seeing her husband as the villain we know him to be. T.S. Eliot states that Emilia has "the human will to see things as they are not."[1] When Desdemona asks her how it was possible to lose the handkerchief, Emilia responds with the famous four words, "I know not, madam" (3.4.24). Shakespeare has chosen to keep Emilia in the background because she is not needed until Desdemona is in peril. In the last three acts, Emilia will join the triangle of characters (Othello-Desdemona-Emilia) and become crucial to the resolution of the play.

The Nurse and Emilia have much in common. They are, possibly, close in age. Both have been neglected by men in their lives. And they both give their wards brutal advice about the actions of men. Emilia, normally quiet, surprisingly admits a harsh truth to Desdemona:

EMILIA.   Tis not a year or two shows us a man.
            They are all but stomachs, and we all but food:
            They eat us hungrily, and when they are full
            They belch us out. (*Oth.* 3.4.120-23).

The turning point for Emilia, however, is not until act four, when she has her great reversal in the play. Some critics refer to the scene as one of the most feminist moments in Shakespeare. Both are rattled because Othello has commanded that Emilia be dismissed after she prepares Desdemona for bed. The scared Desdemona reverts to being a child again, "If I do die before thee, prithee, shroud me / In one of these same sheets" (4.3.25-26). In a motherly gesture, Emilia encourages the scared young girl to talk. One can imagine Emilia combing Desdemona's hair, as the scared girl sings a lullaby she remembers from her mother. Emilia gives her ward advice. The passage is so crucial to the action of the play that it must be rendered whole:

EMILIA.   But I do think that it is husband's faults
            If wives do fall. Say that they slack their duties,

And pour our treasures into foreign laps;
Or else break out in peevish jealousies,
Throwing restraint upon us. Or say they strike us,
Or scant our former having in despite.
Why, we have some galls, and though we have some grace,
Yet have we some revenge. Let husbands know
Their wives have sense like them. They see, and smell,
And have their palates both for sweet and sour,
As husbands have. What is it that they do
When they change us for others? Is it sport?
I think it is. And doth affection breed it?
I think it doth. Is't frailty that thus errs?
It is so too. And have we not affections,
Desires for sports, and frailty as men have?
Then let them use us well. Else let them know,
The ills we do, their ills instruct us so. (*Oth*. 4.3.97-115)

Emilia is speaking about herself. By the end of the speech she has freed herself from Iago's bondage. Determined to reveal Iago's deception, especially with the white handkerchief, she is now resolute, eager to be an active partner in the triangle of Othello-Desdemona/Emilia.

The die has been cast. The last act of the play moves quickly in a series of lurid encounters on the dark streets of Cyprus. Iago engineers a second brawl between Roderigo and Cassio, but things go wrong. In a matter of minutes, the lives of Emilia, Cassio and Iago (not to mention Othello and Desdemona) are turned upside down.

When the awful, final bedroom scene begins, we are prepared, if just a bit, for what is to come. Delirious, Othello is certain he is honoring Desdemona by stopping her wayward ways. "Yet she must die, else she'll betray more men" (5.2.6). Returning to the private quarters, Emilia sees the dying Desdemona and hears her last words. When Othello blames Iago for the murder ("Ask thy husband else ... / Thy husband knew it all." (5.2.166-70)), Emila having just seen him panicked in the street, will have none of it. "My husband? ... Help, help, ho, help! / The Moor hath killed my mistress" (5.2.178-203). As Iago enters the bedroom, with the Governor of Cyprus for protection, Emilia reveals all of his lies. He orders her to go home. She resists him, possibly for the first time in her life:

EMILIA.   Good gentlemen, let me have leave to speak.
           'Tis proper I obey him – but not now.
           Perchance, Iago, I will ne'er go home. (*Oth*. 5.2.233-4).

When Iago orders her home a second time, her words could have been plucked from her earlier reversal speech, "O murderous coxcomb, what should such a fool / Do with so good a wife?" (5.2.279-80). As she dies, her last words are gentle and free, "So come my soul to bliss, as I speak true. / So speaking as I think, alas, I die." (5.2.300-1).

For a moment, the male hierarchy in the play stands with both wives dead at the hands of their husbands. In his grief, and now knowing that he was cruelly deceived by Iago, Othello becomes a General again, the one arena in which he has always felt secure and honorable. Hardened by war, he prepares to kill himself as a warrior, "For nought I did in hate, but all in honor" (5.2.347). Remembering a battlefield from years earlier, he continues:

> OTHELLO.   And say besides that in Aleppo once,
> Where a malignant and turbaned Turk
> Beat a Venetian and traduced the state,
> I took by th' throat the circumcised dog
> And smote him thus. (*Oth.* 5.2.350-354)

With these words, he brings honor to himself by killing for a noble cause, the ultimate refrain of a soldier. Though many have argued about the virtues, or lack thereof, of Othello, his impulse, even at the end of his life, is to die for honor. His portion of nobility for those who will give it to him is irretrievably tied to his desperate need for nobility itself. Perhaps it was a soldier's play after all.

Cymbeline: *Another comedy of errors?*

Fifteen years and 23 plays separate *Romeo and Juliet* from *Cymbeline.* Nevertheless, Shakespeare wanted to dramatize yet another father-daughter story. Like Desdemona and Juliet, Imogen is secretly married, but her husband, Posthumus Leonatus, is not considered an acceptable mate because he is of lower status and an orphan. J. M. Nosworthy, editor for the 2nd Arden Shakespeare edition of *Cymbeline*, asserts that Shakespeare was "no longer concerned with historical drama or with comedy of intrigue but with the golden inconsequences of romance, ... existing in undefined dimensions of time and space ... and devoted to exclusion of more mundane affairs, to the adventures of princes and princesses, to the finding of lost children, to wizards and witches, and hermits dwelling in desert places, to the righting of old wrongs, and to the life that is happy ever after."[2]

As Nosworthy mentions, Shakespeare was not concerned with dramatic logic in *Cymbeline*. All of the characters react impulsively, not once but repeatedly. King Cymbeline, having raised the orphan Posthumus as a member of his royal household, nevertheless refuses him as husband for his daughter and banishes him from the court, the initiating incident for the play. Imogen and Posthumus are convinced that each has been unfaithful with remarkable celerity. The servant Pisanio is forced to change his allegiance from one master to another throughout the play, often with comic effect. Rounding out the bizarre antics in the play, we have an evil Queen, obsessed with poisonous potions; her blowhard son, Cloten, who literally loses his head; two long lost royal brothers of Imogen living in Arcadian innocence; prominent use of medieval objects of devoted love in the shape of rings and bracelets; nefarious use of mysterious boxes and trunks, made malignant by their contents; ghostly apparitions of Posthumus' dead parents; and finally a *deus ex machina* visit by the god Jupiter.

In this context, Shakespeare utilizes his dramatic strategy of triangles of relationships to tell his story. Perhaps, because he was wrangling with many different genres, he utilized not one but two sets of triangles of relationships. The primary triangle is Cymbeline, Imogen, and the servant Pisanio. This triangle will eventually, through a comedy of errors often caused by Pisanio, lead to the happy ending Shakespeare wanted for the play. The second triangle, Cymbeline-Queen-Cloten, is a triangle ripe for both fairy tales and deadly tragedy. The servant Pisanio becomes involved in the intrigues of both triangles.

The character of Posthumus is an interesting one. He *thinks* many evil thoughts, even going so far as deciding to kill Imogen. His impulsive thoughts, however, are never allowed to impact the play's action, primarily because of Pisanio. Posthumus is redeemed at the end of the play primarily by Imogen's constancy and love. Experimenting with a mix of tragedy and comedy, Shakespeare ends the play with Imogen and Posthumus reunited with the blessing of her father. In *Cymbeline*, then, Shakespeare, choosing plot over character, wrote a play that could have been a tragedy, but has a happy ending.

For example, Act Two includes the eerie voyeuristic scene behind closed doors, in which Iachimo emerges from a trunk in Imogen's bedroom. Imogen has set up a fairytale innocence with her bedtime prayer, "To your protection I commend me, gods. / From fairies and the tempters of the night / Guard me, beseech you" (*Cym.* 2.2.10-11). But the scene quickly goes to nightmare. Iachimo's behavior and speech are that of a voyeur. Yet Shakespeare reinforces the fairytale quality of the scene by introducing a medieval emblem of devotion and love when Iachimo removes a bracelet from Imogen's wrist without waking her. He then (creepily) opens her nightgown and sees a mole on her breast. Taking note of various objects in the room, he enters the truck once again. Though he has not violated her body, he has enough evidence to violate her good name with Posthumus when he returns to Rome.

The two triangles of relationships begin to collide when Cymbeline, like many father figures in Shakespeare, is angered by his daughter's behavior. He eventually promises the Queen's son, Cloten, that Imogen will marry him, despite her affection for Posthumus. Cloten does not mince words with Imogen about his rival, "The contract you pretend with that base wretch, / One bred of alms and fostered with cold dishes, / With scraps o' th' court - it is no contract, none;" (2.3.130-132).

Like Emilia in *Othello*, Pisanio now begins to grow in character (and in importance for the plot of the play). He will not follow his master's orders to kill the allegedly unfaithful Imogen. But at the same time, he cannot disregard the letter he has been entrusted with. Instead, he gives a false letter to Imogen, asking only that she come to Milford Haven. To his surprise, Imogen impulsively demands that Pisanio take her to Wales immediately, "How far is it / To this same blessed Milford. And by th' way / Tell me how Wales was made so happy as / T'inherit such a haven" (3.3.61-64).

The scene in Milford-Haven has some of the loveliest lines, as Imogen struggles to force Pisanio to do the bidding of his master Posthumus and kill her. The servant, desperately trying to come up with a solution that will allow Imogen to live, suggests a lie: "I'll give but notice you are dead, and send him / Some bloody sign of it" (3.4.142-43). It is Pisanio who then convinces Imogen to disguise herself as a boy, hide out in Wales, look for the Roman army camped nearby, and then go with the army and look for Posthumus.

Dramaturgically, Shakespeare uses this scene to serve yet another purpose in his plot. Bringing together the two triangles of relationships, Pisanio gives Imogen the box of (supposedly poisonous) medicinal herbs the Queen forced him to take for Posthumus, her son's rival.

A crazy plot indeed, but in Wales Imogen, like many of Shakespeare's heroines, discovers an idyllic Arcadian countryside, an innocent place without guile, a place far away from the vicious intrigues at court. In his early comedies, Shakespeare compares the Arcadian purity of the English countryside with the rigorous confines of the city or the royal state.

Shakespeare sets the Arcadian tone with the first words from old Belarius to his sons, Guiderius and Arviragus. "Stoop boys: this gate / Instructs you how t'adore the heavens and bows you / To a morning's holy office" (3.3.2-4). In this Arcadian innocence we encounter the two boys, both very close in age to Imogen, and raised not by a choleric King, but by a kind (and unknown to them, adoptive) father figure. Further embellishing the fairy tale aspects in the play, Shakespeare now introduces a meeting between Imogen, disguised as a boy, and (unbeknownst to her) her long lost brothers. Her response to both Wales and her brothers is eye opening. "These are kind creatures. God what lies / I have heard! / Our courtiers say all's savage but at court; / Experience, O, thou disprov'st report!" (4.2.39-41).

From this scene onward, with the advent of war between ancient Britain and Rome, Shakespeare begins a litany of patriotic refrains from King Cymbeline's court. Cloten, who usually talks only about himself, responds to the Roman threat with, "Britain's a world by itself, and we will nothing pay / for wearing our own noses" (3.1.14-15). In the same scene, his mother, the Queen, declares, "Caesar made here, but made not here his brag / Of 'Came, and saw, and overcame'" and that Britons still "strut with courage" (3.1. 26-36). Even Pisanio, the servant who has now sworn separate loyalties to Posthumus, the Queen, Imogen, Cloten, and finally Cymbeline, still thinks of his actions as patriotic. "Wherein I am false, I am honest; not true, to be true. / These present wars shall find I love my country" (4.3.50-51.)

As the country prepares for war, the fairy tale becomes more twisted. Cloten becomes more predatory, hatching his plot to dress in Postumous's clothes and encounter Imogen in Wales. But, as soon as he arrives in there, Guidarius chops off his head. Meanwhile Imogen, feeling sick, has taken the potion that Pisanio gave her in the evil Queen's box. Like Juliet, she falls into a death-like slumber. When Belarius finds her seemingly dead, he places her body next to the deceased Cloten, and prepares a proper funeral for them both. The "funeral" is filled with a fairy tale simplicity and some of Shakespeare's best verse: "Golden lads and girls all must, / As chimney-sweepers, come to dust" (4.2.335-36).

After her funeral, Imogen, like Juliet, awakens from her drugged state. Thinking that the headless Cloten is Posthumus, she decides that Pisanio has tricked her. "Damned Pisanio / Hath with forged letters - damned Pisanio - / From this most bravest vessel of the world / Struck the maintop" (4.2.390-93).

Found by Roman soldiers as she grieves, Imogen agrees to follow their leader back to Rome. With no husband, and the wrath of her father upon her, she is powerless to do otherwise. The only thing that might make things better is the return of Posthumus, which indeed happens. Disguised as a "Briton peasant" he fights the creepy Iachimo (who escapes for the moment). When Cymbeline himself is taken captive, who else in this fairy tale should come to his rescue but his missing royal sons?

For reasons left to our imagination (since he has been absent from the play for two acts), Posthumus has had a reversal of feeling and is now willing to devote himself entirely to Imogen, even to die for the wrongs he has committed on her. As Posthumus sleeps, we have the third scene in the play with sleeping characters: the first the infamous trunk scene in Imogen's bedroom; the second the Juliet-like scene in Wales with Cloten's dead body; and now, even more fairy-tale-like, as Posthumus is visited by the ghosts of his dead father and mother, and yes, *his* two dead siblings. As the parents pray to Jupiter ("thou king of gods"), asking that their son be forgiven for his impulsive acts against Imogen, they also pray for the return of a peaceful Britain.

Of course, the god himself appears as the *deus ex machina*, fulfilling the wishes of the dead ghosts, and cementing the reputations of Posthumus and Imogen with the health and the future of the nation. "From a stately cedar shall be lopp'd branches, which, being dead many years, shall after revive, be jointed to the old stock, and freshly grow, then shall Posthumus end his miseries, Britain be fortunate and flourish in peace and plenty" (5.4.143-146).

The rest of the play is a rapid series of confessions from almost everybody. The evil triangle of Cymbeline-Queen-Cloten is rendered nil with the report that the now dead Queen confessed her villainous intentions on her deathbed. Iachimo confesses his lies. Posthumus admits that once he wished Imogen dead. Doctor Cornelius, who gave the Queen poison designed to kill, confesses that he only gave her a sleeping potion. Pisanio confesses to all that he lied when he told Posthumus that Imogen was dead, and furthermore confesses to giving Cloten the suit of Posthumus to wear. Guiderius confesses that he killed Cloten, and finally Belarius confesses that he stole the two boys from the court years earlier and that they are in fact, of royal blood and Cymbeline's long lost sons (and Imogen's brothers). A handy Soothsayer promises Britain peace and plenty, and Imogen and Posthumus and vow eternal love for each other!

The play ends with Cymbeline projecting a strong and peaceful Britain, as his court, now restored, reflects the future promise of a nation centered on the enduring love of Imogen and Posthumus, fortified by the presence of the now noble sons, Guidarius and Arviragus, (men familiar with both the idyllic countryside and the royal court), and all embraced by Cymbeline and and his loyal servant, Belarius.

CYMBELINE. Publish we this peace
To all our subjects. Set we forward. Let
A Roman and a British ensign wave
Friendly together. So through Lud's Town march,

And in the temple of great Jupiter
Our peace we'll ratify, seal it with feasts.
Set on there. Never was a war did cease,
Ere bloody hands were washed, with such a peace. (*Cym.*
5.5.579-86)

Timon of Athens: *Freedom for the servant?*

Timon of Athens, co-written with Thomas Middleton, was never pro-
duced during Shakespeare's lifetime. Since its publication in 1623, critics
have attempted to determine which characters were written by the mature
Shakespeare and which characters were written by the younger Middleton.
Some critics claim that the character of Timon has resonances with Lear and
Coriolanus. In any event, between 1607 and 1610, Shakespeare was research-
ing or writing four plays: *Coriolanus, Timon of Athens, Pericles* and *Cymbeline*.
Three of the plays received productions, but with the death of Shakespeare in
1616, *Timon* remained unfinished, or at least not realized fully.

Like *Cymbeline, Timon* is a hybrid play. With *Timon*, however, Shakespeare
attempted to combine extremely broad political satire with tragedy. Unlike
Pericles or *Cymbeline* there is no concern for romantic comedy in the play.
Anthony P. Dawson and Gretchen E. Minton, editors of the 3rd Arden edition of the play,[3] describe it as combining tragedy with urban satire, adding
that the Athens in the play resembles Jacobean London more than it does the
city of Aristophanes or Plato.

Other critics contend that the play was intended to criticize the profli-
gate court of King James who assumed the throne in 1603. As Dawson and
Minton further state, the play bitterly and absolutely speaks to the changes
that were occurring during the early modern period. The economic world
was shifting inexorably from a feudal economy to a nascent competitive capitalist one. Timon, more reflective of the old feudal economy, can be seen as a
man whom the world has passed by. The play focuses on the evolving culture
of money and wealth from the point of view of the Senators of Athens, but
also from the point of view of the servants in Timon's home. When people
experience dire economic hardship or change, things get pretty rough. For
this reason, critic Giles Lytton Strachey aptly describes *Timon of Athens* as
"this whirlwind of furious ejaculation, this splendid storm of nastiness."[4]

Timon of Athens is singular for a number of reasons. Most importantly,
Shakespeare's Timon is a tragic man who, some contend, goes mad at the
end of the play. It is also Shakespeare's only play without family. We know
nothing about Timon's past, or his relations, or how he acquired his lands

and estate. The play begins in "mid-scene" with Timon already in debt, having borrowed heavily from his friends in order to maintain his magnanimous lifestyle.

The play also has a large number of servants, so many, in fact, that one of them, Flavius, is designated as Timon's 'Steward,' or primary housekeeper, whose job it is to maintain the household's books and monitor its expenditures. Flavius, acutely aware of the debt Timon is accruing, is knowledgeable of the emerging debt practices developing in the capitalist culture of Athens/London. The play is also noteworthy for the number of encounters between Timon's servants and wealthy Athenians. In *Timon of Athens* the servants do not die (as does Emilia) but lose their livelihood, except for, perhaps, the steward Flavius.

Though events in the play move forward at Shakespeare's usual fast clip, attention to character development in this unfinished play is uneven. Some critics contend that this is because Shakespeare and Middleton divided up the characters they would write. Critics agree that Shakespeare wrote the lines for Timon, whose dialogue throughout, but especially in Act 5, rings with a poetic fury and loss equal to that of Lear. Likewise, the laconic barbs between Timon and Apmantus, his only friend, indicate a strong poetic command of imagery and wit.

Some critics think that the more droll and satiric Middleton was given the job of writing the dialogue for the characters in the play who represent the emerging capitalist society, including Flavius and the embittered Athenian captain, Alcibiades. But even in this divided and unfinished play, Shakespeare's dramatic strategy of using a triangle of relationships can be discerned. In this case the triangle being Timon-Alcibiades-Flavius. Like Emilia in *Othello*, Alcibiades drops out of the play for two acts, but then returns as an integral part of the resolution of the play on his way back from the wars. Though Flavius consistently raises concerns about Timon's descent into poverty and even madness, his curious appearances in the last act have elicited different interpretations from critics, directors and actors playing the role.

The play begins with a lavish banquet in Timon's residence, attended by all the main characters in the play. Shakespeare establishes Timon's attitude about his wealth early in the play, "We are born to do benefits. And what better or properer can we call our own than the riches of our friends?" (*Tim.* 1.2.104-6). In short order the sycophantic Senators, Alcibiades and Apemantus, a Cynic philosopher, arrive. Alcibiades is quick to pay homage to Timon because of his support of the army in the field. "My heart is ever at your service, my lord" (1.2. 77). Only Apemantus stands apart, refusing to participate in the excessive festivities.

Flavius's first speech in the play establishes that he, like Apemantus, is concerned with Timon's excessive entertaining. He is well aware of Timon's indebtedness, and is already anticipating that when Timon runs out of money his debtors will not respond kindly. In a scene between master and servant that is noteworthy for its intimacy and directness, Timon petulantly complains that Flavius has kept him in the dark. "You make me marvel wherefore ere this time / Had you not fully laid out my state before me" (2.2.138-40). Flavius responds with startling directness, "At many times I brought in my accounts / Laid them before you. You would throw them off" (2.2.150-51). Flavius is well aware of the fiscal dangers looming. Knowing that Timon has run out of cash and mortgaged his lands, Flavius declares bluntly,

> FLAVIUS. Though you hear now too late, yet now's a time.
> The greatest of your having lacks a half
> To pay your present debts. (*Tim.* 2.2.160-63)

This frank and intimate exchange between servant and master could readily occur between husband and wife behind closed doors. Though Flavius tries valiantly throughout the play to change the behavior of his master, it is his own attitude and behavior that will need to change.

Act Two begins in a sharply different tone. An Athenian Senator demands payment of Timon's debt to him. The Senator, like many wealthy Athenians, is practicing usury within a capitalist framework of contracts and due dates. Timon's affection for a feudal economy, in which wealth and value are bartered through social means, begins to shatter. He is besieged by his creditors who use language of the new mercantile London ("speedy payment', "'twas due on forfeiture" "six weeks and past"), a far cry from the long-term understanding among landowners in the pastoral countryside.

Once again, Flavius beseeches Timon to understand his dire financial condition. Clinging to his bucolic dream, Timon insists that his friends will be as generous to him as he has been to them. "Why dost thou weep? Canst thou the conscious lack / To think I shall lack friends? Secure thy heart ... / I am wealthy in my friends" (2.2.197-207).

After this exchange, a series of darkly comedic encounters occurs between Timon's servants and the rich Senators, in which social custom is inverted. Servants demand generosity from their superiors. As the servants are rudely dismissed, their anger rises. With no masters present, the servants express their true feelings, preparing us for Timon's rage later in the play.

In this same act, however, Alcibiades, out of the blue, suddenly returns to Athens accused of killing another soldier in the field. Though Alcibiades's character development in this unfinished play is minimal at this point, the fortunes of both Timon and Alcibiades begin to converge. Like Timon, Alcibiades is betrayed by the Senators, who banish him from Athens. Like Timon, he is outraged by the betrayal of his benefactors. "I have kept back their foes / While they have told their money and let out / Their coin upon large interest, I myself / Rich only in large hurts. All those, for this?" (3.5. 114-17). The banished Alcibiades swears revenge against Athens in language that could very well come from Timon himself. "Is this the balsam that the usurping Senate / Pours into captains' wounds? Banishment. / It comes not ill. I hate to be banished. / It is a cause worthy my spleen and fury, / That I may strike at Athens" (3.5.118-22).

At the same moment in time, Timon is planning his own revenge. Inviting his so-called friends to another banquet, he serves them bowls of lukewarm water:

> TIMON.   This is Timon's last,
>   Who, stuck and spangled with your flatteries,
>   Washes it off and sprinkles in your faces
>   Your reeking villainy. (*Tim.* 3.6.93-96).

In some productions, Timon washes his face in his own bowl of water and then hurls the dirty water at his guests. As the Senators flee, he hurls other objects after them, exclaiming, like Alcibiades, "Burn, house! Sink, Athens! henceforth hated be / Of Timon man and all humanity!" (3.6.109-10). With these contiguous scenes, Shakespeare establishes the triangle of relationships that we will follow for the rest of the play: Timon-Alcibiades-Flavius.

Act four begins with Timon's magnificent speech as he prepares to go into exile in the woods nearby ("Let me look back upon thee" (4.1.1)). In this damning speech, Timon divests himself of his fine robes and strips himself, perhaps naked:

> TIMON.   Matrons, turn incontinent! ...
>   Bankrupts, hold fast! ... Bound servants, steal!
>   ... Degrees, observances, customs, and laws,
>   Decline to your confounding contraries
>   And let confusion live! ... Breath infect breath,
>   That (Athenian) society, as their friendship, may
>   Be merely poison! Nothing I'll bear from thee
>   But nakedness, thou detestable town! ...
>   Timon will to the woods ...
>   And grant, as Timon grows, his hate may grow
>   To the whole race of mankind, high and low!
>   Amen. (*Tim.* 4.1.8-42).

Unlike the bucolic Wales in *Cybeline*, or the pleasant countryside of pastoral England in Shakespeare's comedies, Timon's return to nature is a brutal one. He is alone, perhaps naked, perhaps mad, in a cave near the sea. His vituperative diatribe against mankind is followed by a plaintive scene between Timon's servants. Alone in the house (how often do we see Shakespeare's servants on stage without their masters present?) they despair of their new condition. "We are fellows still, / Serving alike in sorrow. Leaked is our bark, / And we, poor mates stand on the dying deck, / Hearing the surges threat. We must all part / Into this sea of air" (4.2.21-25). The imagery is reminiscent of Pisanio's lovely line in *Cybeline*, "Fortune brings in some boats that are not steered" (4.3.54).

It is noteworthy that, in this scene, Flavius assumes the role of master, distributing what is left of the household monies to the other servants. Flavius then delivers a speech that has given numerous critics, directors and actors pause. Deciding to go search for Timon, he states:

FLAVIUS.   Alas, kind lord!
             He's flung in rage from this ingrateful seat
             Of monstrous friends,
             Nor has he with him to supply his life,
             Or that which can command it.
             I'll follow and inquire him out.
             I'll ever serve his mind with my best will.
             Whilst I have gold, I'll be his steward still. (*Tim.* 4.2.49-56)

It is unclear how much gold Flavius offered to his fellow servants, and it is equally unclear how much Flavius took for himself. With Timon now sequestered in the woods, two extremely ironic events occur. The bankrupt Timon finds a large cache of gold while digging for roots to eat. Suddenly he is rich again, and just as suddenly all of the main characters in the play, hearing of his newfound wealth, visit him in his squalor. What follows is a bitter parody of the first banquet scene. In quick order he is visited by Alcibiades, accompanied by two prostitutes; Apemantus, his fellow misanthrope; a gang of thieves; his servant Flavius; the Poet and Painter who sought his patronage in act one; and finally, Flavius again, accompanied by several Senators.

Timon is as generous with his gold with the prostitutes and thieves as he was with his friends. Profligacy is still his personality, but now it is redirected against mankind instead of toward it. Perhaps he has gone mad, as some actors have played the scenes. Some actors have played Timon starving to death and having hallucinations. Perhaps like Lear in the heath, his belief in the kindness of mankind is unalterably broken, "There's nothing level in our cursed natures / But direct villainy" (4.3.20-21).

Timon is now a resolute misanthrope. But how should we interpret the sequence of visitors that come to him in his wretched cave? Various productions have taken the liberty of rearranging the sequence of visits, attempting to bring more clarity to the play as a whole. Following the sequence of scenes in the Arden edition of the play, Alcibiades arrives first, inexplicably accompanied by two prostitutes. Timon rebuffs him immediately. When Alcibiades attempts to befriend him, Timon refuses. When Alcibiades offers Timon gold, Timon refuses it. "Keep it. I cannot eat it" (4.3.112). When Alcibiades confesses that he is planning to attack Athens for the wrongs committed against him, Timon urges him on, giving Alcibiades and the girls some of his gold. The visit from Apemantus is quite long (198 lines). He first advises Timon to become like the rest of venal Athens, but Timon is wiser now than his glib, fellow misanthrope, declaring his reasons:

> TIMON.   The mouths, the tongues, the eyes and hearts of men ...
> That numberless upon me stuck as leaves
> Do on the oak, have with one winter's brush
> Fell from their boughs and left me open, bare
> For every storm that blows – I to bear this,
> That never knew but better, is some burden. (*Tim.* 4.3.295–302).

When the thieves visit, unlike Alcibiades and Apemantus, they have come specifically to steal Timon's gold. To their surprise, Timon congratulates them and showers them with gold, and retreats to his cave.

The visit from Flavius is relatively short (only 77 lines) but full of nuance. This scene, more than any of the others, supports the theory that Timon has gone mad. Flavius asks repeatedly if Timon recognizes him. At first Timon is touched by the loyalty of Flavius who confesses he still has some monies from the household. "Had I a steward / So true, so just and now so comfortable?" (4.3.550-51).

Note that the word "comfortable" is meant as "pleasing, comforting", unlike the modern meaning, but Timon's spirit has been permanently broken. He rejects Flavius. In this short scene, master and servant have one last dialogue on the subject of money and debt:

> FLAVIUS.   No, my most worthy master, in whose breast
> Doubt and suspect, alas, are placed too late.
> You should have feared false times when you did feast.
> Suspect still comes where an estate is least. (*Tim.* 4.3.571--509).

Ready to remove himself from his new found gold, Timon gives Flavius the rest of it,, "Go, live rich and happy" (4.3. 586). He further orders Flavius to "Stay not. Fly whist thou art blessed and free. / Ne'er see thou man, and let me ne'er see thee" (4.3. 600-01).

The scene is full of ambiguities. Flavius does not give the household monies to Timon. Instead, he is offered, and takes, the rest of Timon's gold, which we hear later was a large sum. Dawson and Minton, in their introduction to the play, suggest that if Middleton wrote the character of Flavius he deftly laid bare the contradictions between a gift and cash economy.

Timon gives the gold as a gift, but we already know that Flavius is well aware of how a cash economy operates. Flavius will advance himself in the new capitalist world. He is now a rich man. One could argue that Flavius, with assets of his own, is also a free man. The servant will not only outlive his master, but he will also learn from his master's plight and gain power. And, indeed, the next time we see Flavius he is accompanying the Senators to Timon's cave.

Some critics assert that Flavius, in spite of his attempts to protect Timon, ultimately profits from Timon's financial ruin, arguing that the play has no moral center if Flavius willingly takes all of Timon's wealth, before and after his decline.

Returning to the sequence of visits to Timon's cave, some questions arise. Why does it take Flavius so long to arrive at the cave? Why is his short visit placed between the visits of the thieves and the rapacious Senators? Visually, the message is clear. Flavius knows the mercenary ways of the world like the thieves, and he is now in the company of the rich Senators. However, there is one more resolution to the triangle of relationships of Timon-Alcibiades-Flavius in the play.

Alcibiades returns to attack Athens. "Sound to this coward and lascivious town / Our terrible approach" (5.4.1-2). But in a surprising reversal, Alcibiades instead negotiates with the Senators and the attack is postponed.

> ALCIBIADES. Then there's my glove.
> Descend and open your uncharged ports.
> Those enemies of Timon's and mine own
> Who you yourselves shall set out for reproof
> Fall, and no more. (*Tim.* 5.4. 64-68)

Simultaneous with Alcibiades's pact with the Senators, word comes that Timon has died, "Entombed upon the very hem o'the sea" (5.4.77-78). Though Alcibiades was negotiating for both of them, it is too late to save Timon. Though Timon is ruined and dies due to the villainy of the venal

Senators, Alcibiades and Flavius are both transformed by Timon's suffering. They will be more successful citizens.

Because *Timon of Athens* is an unfinished play, the last act of the play has remained obscure, with many questions left unanswered. If Middleton did write the dialogue for Flavius, is Flavius a representative of the feudal servant becoming independent and able to join the society of capitalistic Athens? What purpose does Alcibiades serve in the play? Is he the braggart soldier from *commedia dell arte,* or does he have a more nuanced purpose in the play? Is *Timon of Athens* a morality play? Why do the Senators, Poet and Painter have no names?

Whatever the answers to these questions, the character of Timon is a delight for actors to perform. Like Lear, he runs the gamut of human emotions. And though the play remains unfinished, it combines Middleton's mordant satire with Shakespeare's poetic pathos. The play continues to influence more modern plays, including Caryl Churchill's *Serious Money* (1987), the critical and ribald plays of Joe Orton, and even Beckett's *Waiting for Godot.*

In conclusion, an analysis of the role of Shakespeare's servants in *Romeo and Juliet, Othello, Cymbeline,* and *Timon of Athens* reveals that, for Shakespeare, villainy and the actions of villains inevitably involve a wider circle of characters within the families or households in which Shakespeare sets many of his plays. While one can say, philosophically, that villainy corrupts everyone in its vicinity, Shakespeare's plays vividly dramatize why and how this happens. The world of his plays is, for better or worse, our world.

Notes

1 T.S. Eliot, *Shakespeare and the Stoicism of Seneca.* Folcroft Library Editions, 1973.
2 Shakespeare, William. *Cymbeline.* Ed. J.M. Nosworthy. The Arden Shakespeare, 2nd Edition (paperback), 1969.
3 Shakespeare, William. *Timon of Athens.* Ed. Anthony Dawson; Gretchen Minton. The Arden Shakespeare, 3rd Edition, 2008.
4 Strachey, Lytton. Books and Characters French and English. University of Adelaide. 1922. ebooks@Adelaide. 2014. ebooks.adelaide.edu.au/s/strachey/lytton/books_and_characters/chapter3.html

Works Cited

All textual citations refer to: *Shakespeare's Plays,* from Folger Digital Texts. Ed. Barbara Mowat, Paul Werstine, Michael Poston, and Rebecca Niles. Folger Shakespeare Library, 12 January, 2019. www.folgerdigitaltexts.org.

12. *"Very fine people …"*

Louis Fantasia

Empires collapse. Gang leaders
Are strutting about like statesmen. The peoples
Can no longer be seen under all those armaments.
So the future lies in darkness and the forces of right
Are weak. All this was plain to you
When you destroyed a torturable body.

"On the Suicide of the Refugee W.B" - Bertolt Brecht[1]

Let's assume for the moment that President Donald J. Trump was right when he said, in 2017, that there were "some very fine people" on both sides of a white nationalist "Unite the Right" rally held in Charlottesville. A young woman was killed and dozens injured at this rally by some "very fine people."[2]

Let's assume, too, that there were very fine people at the Nuremburg rallies, Cambodian killing fields, and Klan lynchings. Let's also assume that there were very fine people on both sides in Kosovo, Myanmar and Rwanda. And let's assume that there is no such thing as evil, and that there are only fine people on both sides, doing what they think is right and good.

Let's assume that the fine people on both sides send their kids to school, pay taxes, vote, and go to church. Let's assume, too, that because they are good and very fine, these people love more than they hate. They love their country, their race, their family, tribe and clan. They love their God, who usually is an angry God, and they love their neighbor, as long as their neighbor is like them. They love all this more than they hate the enemy – the other – whomever or whatever that "other" might be. As the President said in his 2018 speech from the Oval Office, people "don't build walls because they hate the people on the outside but because they love the people on the inside" (https://www.nytimes.com/2019/01/08/us/politics/trump-speech-transcript.html).

Next, let's assume that someone named Iago lives among these very good, fine people, as do Richard Gloucester, Mrs. Macbeth, and the Lear sisters, whom we shall visit in a moment. I know that it is always dangerous to mistake literary constructs for real persons, but in the theater our job, or at least part of our job, is to bring these two-dimensional literary figures to three-dimensional life. So let us assume that this Iago lives amongst the very fine people of both sides.

Notice that the President did not say that these people were very "nice," even though he often says there are very "bad" people everywhere. Very fine, good people often have to do things that are not nice, like exterminate Jews or hang Negroes, or torture leftists, or fly planes into tall buildings, or lock migrant children up in cages. It's not nice, but good people sometimes have to do these things because, as stated above, they love their God or their country or their family or their clan more than they hate their enemy. While there may be very good people on both sides of the border, we have to build a wall to keep the rapists, murderers and "dirty people" out because we love our country.[3]

I suppose at this point, other than explaining the concept of irony, I should, in the context of current literary and educational theory, post "trigger" warnings about the content to be discussed. But since there are no warnings for the knock on the door at midnight, or the suppression of your vote or a woman's right to choose, or the car that runs you over at a rally,[4] or the beating you get on a barbed wire fence, just get over it.

Iago is very fine, but not nice, which is an important distinction. I once saw a production of *Othello* by a major theater company in a nice Northwestern American city, where Iago was nice, and Othello was nice, and Desdemona was nice and they all tried to be nice to one another but stuff just happened. When I asked the artistic director about his choices (I was a guest at the theater, so I, too, was being nice), I was told that he didn't want to show racism on stage.

Then why do the play?! Good grief! There are at least 36 other plays by Shakespeare, and I can think of at least a few of them (*Hamlet, King Lear, As You Like It*, perhaps? *Julius Caesar*?) that don't have anything to do with racism. But *Othello*? Lest I seem unkind to my colleague, it should be noted that outside this theater, or more precisely, out beside one of the parking lots near this theater, was a billboard advertising a unisex perfume called "Unbreakable" by Kloé Kardashian and her then husband, the basketball star Lamar Odom.[5] Ms. Kardashian is white. Mr. Odom is Black. The ad seemed to suggest that they were (mostly) naked, happy and, apparently, sexually and romantically intimate. That their perfume's brand name was ironic, to say the least, given the subsequent state of their relationship, is beside the point here.

In the billboard they were very fine people, of two different races, who were being nice to each other. Their relationship and marriage went bad. That's sad. That's life. But it is not *Othello*. But the image the ad for their perfume was trying to project was one that I think this director was trying to stage inside: we are all nice people, we can all get along. We can accept our differences, can't we?

No, we cannot. We are not nice. We are fine. We are good. And very fine, good people, have to do what's right. Prior to the 1960s, that is, well within my lifetime, such mixed race coupling would have been illegal in many states, if not just immoral. For those of you not familiar with the crime of miscegenation in our post-modern, multi-cultural, multi-racial society, I refer you to the 2016 film *Loving* about the inter-racial marriage of Richard & Mildred Loving, and their trials, personal and legal, in the American south (https://www.imdb.com/title/tt4669986/).

Still, even in the Twenty-first century, some very good, fine people consider such an "amalgamation" of races as against God's will. For example, this from the *Faith & Heritage* website, a webzine presenting "the views of Occidental Christians who are determined to preserve both Western Civilization and Western Peoples," on mixed race relationships:

> " [T]hen it follows that God intentionally made the different races of mankind, and moreover, that He intentionally made the exact number of races of mankind. God created racial diversity for a good purpose (*Acts* 17:26-27), and did not intend for the diversity He created to be undone through amalgamation. Interestingly, this was the specific reasoning of Leon Bazile, the judge whose 1959 anti-miscegenation decision was overturned in the Loving v. Virginia case of 1967:
>
> 'Almighty God created the races white, black, yellow, malay and red, and he placed them on separate continents. And but for the interference with his arrangement there would be no cause for such marriages. The fact that he separated the races shows that he did not intend for the races to mix.'
>
> This is important: the premise of racial realism immediately points us to the conclusion that racial amalgamation is wrong. If God has created us with a specific racial identity, which we ought to love and cherish, then how could we think it permissible (in ordinary circumstances, at least) to cut off our identity? We ought to preserve our own people, and therefore we ought not to interracially marry. We should, when confronted with God's creation, perceive all the boundaries He has embedded in His created order, and honor them by maintaining their distinctions. Interracial marriage, consequently, has very strong moral weight placed against it. It is unnatural, and it can run against the purposes and teleology of the Lord in creating the races. It is not hatred of other races, but love of our God, to maintain the diversity with which He has imbued His creation."[6]

As I was saying, very fine people. On both sides. Let's assume Iago is a good Christian and a good defender of Western Civilization and Culture. After all, he does go out to sea with Othello to battle the infidel Turks. Othello's inter-racial love with Desdemona might have landed him in jail (as it did Richard Loving), were it not for the fact that the Duke has summoned Othello to defend the Venetian state. Othello is dispatched against the Ottomans with Iago by his side. The tragedy begins when Desdemona begs to be sent to the Cypriot front with her husband. Fortune is smiling on Iago. Desdemona is clearly a woman who doesn't know her place!

II

Iago is 28. He has "looked upon the world for four times seven years" (1.3.352). Othello is an "old black ram" (1.1.97), offending Iago's youth and virility as much as his race. Michael Cassio, whom Iago feels has unjustly been given his promotion, is an effete arithmetician, an arty, intellectual Florentine (not even a real Venetian!), and a man who cannot hold his liquor. In other words, not a real man. Roderigo, whom Iago gulls for money and murder, is a simpleton. Bianca is a camp-following whore. Iago suspects his wife Emelia is not much better, having, in his mind at least, slept with Othello and possibly Cassio. Desdemona is the worst, a race traitor who bandies dirty jokes with Iago as soon as she sets foot on the sultry Cypriot shore (2.1.115- 95). When her black husband arrives, they shamelessly kiss in public in front of his troops. It's the end of civilization as we know it, despite Ms. Kardashian's and Mr. Odom's best efforts.

Very fine people need to put a stop to this. I *know* that there are reasons given in the text for Iago's hatred, such as his jealousy, his stifled promotion, his wanton villainy. I have read the play a few times and directed it more than once since the late 1970s! But, as I said above, let's assume for the moment that not only is there no evil, but that Iago is a patriot and defender of the faith. Today Iago is a "Proud Boy", an incel (involuntary celibate), a member of the Fraternal Order of the Alt-Knights, an Oath Keeper and a Three Percenter, and so on. I know you will say these are "hate groups" (the U.S. Federal Government has actually designated some of them as such), but is that how they see themselves? Perhaps (although I doubt he thinks this deeply) Iago is a "paleoconservative," someone who, according to the international relations scholar Michael Foley, presses for

> " . . . restrictions on immigration, a rollback of multicultural programs, the decentralization of federal policy, the restoration of controls upon free trade, a greater emphasis upon economic nationalism . . . and (has) a generally revanchist outlook

upon a social order in need of recovering old lines of distinction and in particular the assignment of roles in accordance with traditional categories of gender,
ethnicity, and race" (Foley, 318).[7]

More likely, Iago belongs to a young man's group, like the Atomwaffen
Division, who go about God's work as (as one member reportedly put it),
"a one man gay Jew wrecking crew." (https://www.propublica.org/article/
atomwaffen-division-inside-white-hate-group). Now, this is nothing new, at
least in America, going back to the Know Nothing Party, the KKK, the
John Birch Society, and the Council of Conservative Citizens, among others. Europe had its Nazis and Fascists, Russia its Stalinists, and there are
plenty of "national front" parties today on all continents. In Shakespeare's
day Catholics and Protestants burnt each other's heretics with relish, all the
while claiming God was on their side. Iago is not evil. Everyone else is. Just
ask Steve Bannon.[8]

Shakespeare populates his plays with a surprisingly large number of young,
male losers. As I wrote in my essay in the first volume of this series, "we tend
to think of Shakespeare's lovers as "successful," in that they get the girl, even
if they, too, wind up dead at the end of a tragedy ... But Shakespeare's plays
are littered with "surplus men" ... (who) have no function outside of battle
... Male energy has descended into (online) debates about cosmic order."[9]

Who knows what websites this construct named Iago subscribes to, but
I am certain they reinforce, rather than challenge, his world view, providing
him safety in numbers, and more important, the reassuring comfort that
there are "some very fine people" just like him out there and they are not
afraid to act. Just ask Dylan Roof, Robert Bowers, or James Alex Fields, Jr.
For those of you who don't remember, Roof killed nine African-Americans
in a Charleston, S.C., church on June 17, 2015. Bowers murdered eleven
Jews at a Pittsburgh Synagogue on October 27, 2018. Fields drove his car
into the crowd at Charlottesville during at "Unite the Right" rally, killing
32-year old Heather Heyer. The American Psychological Association has
recently declared this toxic form of "traditional masculinity" as "harmful" –
an understatement if there ever was one.[10] Very fine people indeed.

III

As in many fairy tales, the king has three daughters. Invariably one is pretty,
and the other two not so much. They may be step-sisters, with a wicked witch
or step-mother lurking around somewhere, but there are very few mothers
in Shakespeare's plays. Sometimes the good daughter gets lost going into
the woods or racing back from the ball. Ultimately, though, her goodness

shines through in an evil world and the Prince finds her, she evades the wolf, or escapes the clutches of the aforementioned wicked step-mother or witch.

Not in Shakespeare, however. He is too much of a realist. Cordelia and Lear die, victims of a cruel world that doesn't care about goodness, or even love. They are very fine people – sensitive, intelligent, articulate (Cordelia is incapable of speaking only in front of her father), if somewhat rash and stubborn. But there are very fine people on both sides – like her sisters and their husbands, and her sisters' shared lover, Edmund.

Regan and Goneril got bad raps for centuries. Had they mustaches, they would have twirled them. Edmund, who seduces both of them, was Gloucester's bastard son, and his illegitimacy was all one needed to know for his motivation. Goneril, the ruthless eldest daughter, is married to Albany, a man so unlike her father as to invite immediate Freudian analysis. Regan, the middle child who never seems to be quite enough for anyone, has married Cornwall, who is a cardboard cut-out version of the worst parts of her dad. Again, Freud might have helped. Yet these are all very fine people. They dress well and speak well. They have sense enough not to go out in raging storms. They band together to fight off the invading French army, led (from their point of view) by their traitorous baby sister. Right from the beginning, when Lear asks his daughters to tell him how much each of them loves him in order to gain their portion of the kingdom, we understand that the (significantly) older sisters have a point:

> GONERIL. Sir,
>> I love you more than word can wield the matter,
>> Dearer than eyesight, space, and liberty,
>> Beyond what can be valued, rich or rare,
>> No less than life, with grace, health, beauty, honor;
>> As much as child e'er loved, or father found;
>> A love that makes breath poor, and speech unable.
>> Beyond all manner of so much I love you. (*Lear*, 1.1.60-67)

And then:

> REGAN. I am made of that self mettle as my sister
>> And prize me at her worth. In my true heart
>> I find she names my very deed of love;
>> Only she comes too short, that I profess
>> Myself an enemy to all other joys
>> Which the most precious square of sense possesses,
>> And find I am alone felicitate
>> In your dear Highness' love. (*Lear*, 1.1.76-84)

The fact that little sister will not or cannot play along and says "nothing" repeatedly, provoking the old man's fury, is not their problem. The sisters, like all very fine people, are completely rational. Why does Lear, who has given the kingdom to them, need a hundred knights, or even one? The two daughters, as any adult child with a senile parent knows, put up with Lear's abuses:

GONERIL. By day and night he wrongs me. Every hour
           He flashes into one gross crime or other
           That sets us all at odds. I'll not endure it. (*Lear*, 1.3.4-6)

But they do. There's too much at stake not too, despite being called "marble-hearted fiends," "detested kites" (crows) and the like. Even by the end of Act II, when Lear rails against both daughters ("Reason not the need"), we still, in a successful production I believe, see Lear's reaction as being out of proportion to his two daughters' actions:

LEAR.   No, you unnatural hags,
           I will have such revenges on you both
           That all the world shall—I will do such things—
           What they are yet I know not, but they shall be
           The terrors of the Earth! You think I'll weep.
           No, I'll not weep.
           I have full cause of weeping, but this heart
           Shall break into a hundred thousand flaws
           Or ere I'll weep. O Fool, I shall go mad!
           Storm and tempest. Lear, Kent, and Fool exit. (*Lear*, 2.4.219-29)

They have done nothing wrong, and are perfectly rational in their justifications:

REGAN.   This house is little. The old man and 's people
           Cannot be well bestowed.
GONERIL. Tis his own blame hath put himself from rest,
           And must needs taste his folly.
REGAN.   For his particular, I'll receive him gladly,
           But not one follower.
GONERIL. So am I purposed. (*Lear*, 2.4.229-35)

They are very fine people. And if the old man would just be "nice" everything would be all right. But Lear will not be nice. He feels abused and violated by his daughters' treatment (when in fact it is his own guilt over his treatment of Cordelia that lashes him). He behaves rashly, impulsively;

tragically. But he is not a "very fine" person now. Very fine people do not go naked in storms or shelter in hovels with fools and madmen. Very fine people do not speak up for the homeless, weak, and oppressed, as Lear does:

> LEAR. Poor naked wretches, wheresoe'er you are,
>   That bide the pelting of this pitiless storm,
>   How shall your houseless heads and unfed sides,
>   Your looped and windowed raggedness defend you
>   From seasons such as these? O, I have ta'en
>   Too little care of this. Take physic, pomp.
>   Expose thyself to feel what wretches feel,
>   That thou may'st shake the superflux to them
>   And show the heavens more just. (*Lear,* 3.4.31-41)

Lear is irrelevant here.[11] He has taken himself out of the society of very fine people, and we must return to his daughters. But we will find them missing. As the Act III storm rages, they do not appear until scene 7, the last scene of the act, where they encourage Cornwall to either hang Gloucester or pluck out his eyes, because, thanks to Edmund's betrayal, they have discovered he has helped Lear escape. Very fine people. They decide to pluck out his eyes.

This cruelty and lack of empathy is not new in the world. "Critics as different as George Steiner and Terry Eagleton pointed out that some of those in charge of the Nazi concentration camps had been cultivated men who listened to Mozart and read Goethe."[12] So what have Goneril and Regan been reading and listening to since last we met? Fox News?

Goneril rides off with Edmund to try and capture Lear. Regan and Cornwall pin Gloucester down and blind him, forcing out the "vile jelly" of his eyes. A Servant, one of the poor naked wretches of the world, has the guts to stand up to Cornwall and stabs him. Cornwall will bleed to death offstage. His wife will immediately demand her sister's lover be her next husband. What happened to these women?!

At this point in the play (and from this point forward to the end of the play) it is no longer possible to give these very fine people the benefit of the doubt. The car has been driven into the rally. The shooter is in the synagogue. The cross has been set afire. There is no going back. The director Peter Brook calls this the "shifting point,"[13] where we not only, as an audience, re-evaluate a character but also our own relationship to that character. We were willing to give Regan and Goneril the benefit of the doubt (and Edmund, too – how many people cheer his "gods, stand up for bastards" speech ?(1.2.21)). And then we realize that we've been had. These "very fine people," to whom we listened, and nodded, and understood their points of view, now want to pluck out the eyes of the man who helped the king. What were we thinking? How could we have been so naïve? Maybe earlier productions were right to cast the sisters as evil and Edmund as a villain, but perhaps that was because that time had clearer (if often wrong-headed) ideas of good and evil, right and wrong. For a hundred and fifty years, *Lear* was performed in Nahum Tate's version, where Lear and Cordelia are rescued, in the end, by Edgar, whom she marries. Lear then retires, leaving the peaceful kingdom safely in the next generation's hands.

No one will buy that happy ending today. We had our Camelot moment and it ended on a grassy knoll and was followed by Viet Nam, the deaths of Bobby Kennedy and Martin Luther King, Watergate and the rest. For two generations we have given very fine people the benefit of the doubt, as we launched wars on drugs, terror, aliens and anything that could be perceived as "other."

Regan and Goneril go into battle in the fourth act to defend the homeland. Cordelia leads an invading army of French mercenaries, and she and her father are defeated. Why aren't we cheering? Because we know now, now that it is too late, that these are "tigers, not daughters" (4.2.49) as Albany says. Despite his moral core, he is as guilty as anyone else in letting things get to this point. Among the very fine people he is perhaps the worst: the good, weak person who will close his window's shutters and turn away.

Some of Shakespeare's best female characters play what used to be called "breeches parts," where they dress as men: Rosaline, Imogen, Viola and so forth. Regan and Goneril are the perversions of these parts. They do what "traditional" men do – ride into battle, plot, scheme, murder, cheat, and fight over the same lover, who has no problem, figuratively or literally, screwing them both. Goneril goes so far as to write Edmund a letter (intercepted!) urging him to kill her husband. She wants Edmund to free her from husband's bed, "the loathed warmth whereof deliver me and supply the place for your labor" (4.7.295-99).

Is it that Goneril and Regan always lacked empathy or compassion? Certainly, in the modern sense, they have suffered the slings and arrows of their father's abuse. Having been given half the kingdom each, was it greed that made them want more? Married to inadequate men, was it Edmund's male sexual energy, his lupine hunger and restlessness, that stirred long-dead emotions? Make them as sympathetic as you want, they have still gone too far.

This is the progression of evil I spoke about in my introduction. It begins with what the Catholics used to call "the near occasions of sin": a white lie to make Dad happy, a flirtatious look at the new boy at court, an inflexibility with your father's servants, a stickler for which days he resides with you.

"Reason not the need!" (2.4.304). The friend of my enemy is my enemy. We have too much at stake. The border must be protected, and so on and so on. Suddenly anything is permissible, all is allowed, and no one may judge. By the fifth act the sisters are squabbling over Edmund as if were sexual booty from a battlefield, right in front of Goneril's husband:

> REGAN.   He led our powers,
>   Bore the commission of my place and person,
>   The which immediacy may well stand up
>   And call itself your brother.
> GONERIL. Not so hot.
>   In his own grace he doth exalt himself
>   More than in your addition.
> REGAN.   In my rights,
>   By me invested, he compeers the best.
> GONERIL. That were the most if he should husband you.
> REGAN.   Jesters do oft prove prophets.
> GONERIL. Holla, holla!
>   That eye that told you so looked but asquint.
> REGAN.   Lady, I am not well, else I should answer
>   From a full-flowing stomach. *To Edmund.*
>   General,
>   Take thou my soldiers, prisoners, patrimony.
>   Dispose of them, of me; the walls is thine.
>   Witness the world that I create thee here
>   My lord and master.
> GONERIL. Mean you to enjoy him?
> ALBANY.   The let-alone lies not in your goodwill. (*Lear*, 5.3.73-94)

Finally, Albany has had enough and shows some spine, some sense of shame, but the sisters have none, or if they did, are beyond it now. As I have argued elsewhere,[14] while we have been right in the last half of the Twentieth century to eliminate the toxic result of shaming in our lives, we live in a society where celebrities, and indeed our highest public officials, have no shame. What ultimately saves Lear and Cordelia, or rather saves their humanity since they die in the play, is that they are ashamed of the way they have treated each other, and have the love, the power of love, to forgive one another.

Shame goes back to the Garden of Eden, when Adam and Eve realized they had done wrong and knew they were naked in front of one another. I have always advocated going for the forbidden fruit, exploring what was around the corner or down the road, intellectually, spiritually, sexually, creatively. But perhaps, in my old age, my point of view has shifted, and looking back, wonder if it was worth it. Goneril and Regan and Edmund should have been stopped before intermission. But we are very fine people, and we try and understand and see things their way. But now, in the final act, we see them for what they are and what they have done and what they have wrought: chaos and destruction. Regan dies by her own hand, after poisoning her sister. Edmund is slain in a duel. As he is carried off, he has his most pathetic line, "Yet Edmund was beloved" (5.3.287), as if that justified everything.

And what is left? The fine, clever, smart people were given the kingdom and ruined it. That doesn't make Lear or Cordelia right, only human. Unlike in *Hamlet,* most of the dead bodies are off stage for the final scene, except for the inverted pieta of Cordelia, dead in her father's arms, with Kent, Edgar and Albany grouped behind them. All very fine people, with nowhere to go:

> ALBANY. The weight of this sad time we must obey,
> Speak what we feel, not what we ought to say.
> The oldest hath borne most; we that are young
> Shall never see so much nor live so long. (*Lear,* 5.3.391-95)

The comedy is over. The Iagos, Edmunds, Regans and Gonerils have met their just desserts, but there is no happy ending. The curtain will rise again tomorrow. The very fine people will get another chance.

Notes

1 Brecht, Bertolt. *Poems 1913–1956*, Edited by John Willett and Ralph Manheim, with the cooperation of Erich Fried. Eyre Metheun, 1976. p. 363

2 Gray, Rosie. "Trump Defends White-Nationalist Protestors." *The Atlantic*. www.theatlantic.com/politics/archive/2017/08/trump-defends-white-nationalist-protesters-some-very-fine-people-on-both-sides/537012/

3 Wemple, Eric. "Tucker Carlson said immigration make America 'dirtier'. So an advertiser took action." *Washington Post.* www.washingtonpost.com/opinions/2018/12/15/tucker-carlson-said-immigration-makes-america-dirtier-so-an-advertiser-took-action/?noredirect=on&utm_term=.8b4a48c60b5a.

4 On November 22, 2021 jurors found the main organizers of the deadly far-right rally in Charlottesville, Va., in 2017 liable under state law, awarding more than $25 million in damages, but deadlocked on federal conspiracy charges. (See: Farquhar, Neil: "Jury Finds Organizers Responsible for Charlottesville Violence." *New York Times,* Nov. 23, 2021. https://www.nytimes.com/2021/11/23/us/charlottesville-rally-verdict.html)

5 "Unbreakable" ad: www.youtube.com/watch?v=Wk9Ap4nBiOM

6 Nil Desperandum (pseud.) "On Interracial Marriage: The Moral Status of Miscegenation." www.faithandheritage.com/2011/05/the-moral-status-of-miscegenation/.

7   Foley, Michael. *American Credo: The Place of Ideas in US Politics.* Oxford University Press, 2007. p. 318

8   Storey, Kate and Friedman, Megan. "Who is Steve Bannon? 19 Things about Donald Trump's Former Chief Strategist." *Cosmopolitan.* www.cosmopolitan.com/politics/a8288455/who-is-steve-bannon-trump-chief-strategist/.

9   Fantasia, Louis. "Speak Low – Shakespeare's Language of Love." *Playing Shakespeare's Lovers.* Peter Lang Publishers, 2019.

10 Berry, Susan: "Psychologists Declare Traditional Masculinity 'Harmful.'" *Breitbart.com.* www.breitbart.com/politics/2019/01/09/psychologists-declare-traditional-masculinity-harmful/. (The commentary on the right-wing *Breitbart News* site is as interesting as is its reporting.)

11 Fantasia, Louis. "King Lear or Survivor." *Tragedy in the Age of Oprah: Essays on Five Great Plays*; Scarecrow Press, 2012

12 Ellis, David. *Memoirs of a Leavisite: The Decline and Fall of Cambridge English.* Liverpool University Press, 2013. p. 119

13 Brook, Peter. *The Shifting Point: Theater, Film, Opera 1946–1987*; TCG. Reprint Edition, 1994

14 Fantasia, "Introduction." *Tragedy in the Age of Oprah.*

Works Cited

All textual citations refer to: Folger Shakespeare Library. *Shakespeare's Plays,* from Folger Digital Texts. Ed. Barbara Mowat, Paul Werstine, Michael Poston, and Rebecca Niles. Folger Shakespeare Library, 12 January, 2019. www.folgerdigitaltexts.org.